HENRY WADSWORTH LONGFELLOW

LITERARY FRIENDS

AND

ACQUAINTANCE

A PERSONAL RETROSPECT OF
AMERICAN AUTHORSHIP

By W. D. HOWELLS

ILLUSTRATED

HARPER & BROTHERS PUBLISHERS

NEW YORK AND LONDON

1901

NOTE

It seems to me that if one is to write such a book as this at all, one cannot profitably do so without a frankness concerning one's self as well as others which might be misunderstood. But I wish to make of my own personality merely a background which divers important figures are projected against, and I am willing to sacrifice myself a little in giving them relief. I will try to show them as they seemed to me, and I shall not blame any one who says that they are not truly represented; I shall only claim that I have truly represented their appearance, and I shall not claim that I could fully conceive of them in their reality.

CONTENTS

v

ILLUSTRATIONS

ILLUSTRATIONS

ILLUSTRATIONS

LITERARY
FRIENDS AND ACQUAINTANCE

Part First

MY FIRST VISIT TO NEW ENGLAND

I

IF there was any one in the world who had his being more wholly in literature than I had in 1860, I am sure I should not have known where to find him, and I doubt if he could have been found nearer the centres of literary activity than I then was, or among those more purely devoted to literature than myself. I had been for three years a writer of news paragraphs, book notices, and political leaders on a daily paper in an inland city, and I do not know that my life differed outwardly from that of any other young journalist, who had begun as I had in a country printing-office, and might be supposed to be looking forward to advancement in his profession or in public affairs. But inwardly it was altogether different with me. Inwardly I was a poet, with no wish to be anything else, unless in a moment of careless affluence I might so far forget myself as to be a novelist. I was, with my friend J. J. Piatt, the half-author of a little volume of very

A   1

unknown verse, and Mr. Lowell had lately accepted and
had begun to print in the *Atlantic Monthly* five or six
poems of mine. Besides this I had written poems, and
sketches, and criticisms for the *Saturday Press* of New
York, a long-forgotten but once very lively expression
of literary intention in an extinct bohemia of that city;
and I was always writing poems, and sketches, and
criticisms in our own paper. These, as well as my feats
in the renowned periodicals of the East, met with kindness, if not honor, in my own city which ought to have
given me grave doubts whether I was any real prophet.
But it only intensified my literary ambition, already
so strong that my veins might well have run ink rather
than blood, and gave me a higher opinion of my
fellow-citizens, if such a thing could be. They were
indeed very charming people, and such of them as
I mostly saw were readers and lovers of books. Society in Columbus at that day had a pleasant refinement which I think I do not exaggerate in the fond
retrospect. It had the finality which it seems to have
had nowhere since the war; it had certain fixed ideals,
which were none the less graceful and becoming because they were the simple old American ideals, now
vanished, or fast vanishing, before the knowledge of
good and evil as they have it in Europe, and as it has
imparted itself to American travel and sojourn. There
was a mixture of many strains in the capital of Ohio,
as there was throughout the State. Virginia, Ken-
tucky, Pennsylvania, New York, and New England
all joined to characterize the manners and customs.
I suppose it was the South which gave the social tone;
the intellectual taste among the elders was the Southern taste for the classic and the standard in literature;
but we who were younger preferred the modern authors: we read Thackeray, and George Eliot, and Haw-

2

BAYARD TAYLOR IN ARAB COSTUME

thorne, and Charles Reade, and De Quincey, and Tennyson, and Browning, and Emerson, and Longfellow; and I—I read Heine, and evermore Heine, when there was not some new thing from the others. Now and then an immediate French book penetrated to us: we read Michelet and About, I remember. We looked to England and the East largely for our literary opinions; we accepted the *Saturday Review* as law if we could not quite receive it as gospel. One of us took the *Cornhill Magazine,* because Thackeray was the editor; the *Atlantic Monthly* counted many readers among us; and a visiting young lady from New England, who screamed at sight of the periodical in one of our houses, " Why, have you got the *Atlantic Monthly out here?*" could be answered, with cold superiority, " There are several *contributors* to the *Atlantic* in Columbus." There were in fact two: my room-mate, who wrote Browning for it, while I wrote Heine and Longfellow. But I suppose two are as rightfully several as twenty are.

II

That was the heyday of lecturing, and now and then a literary light from the East swam into our skies. I heard and saw Emerson, and I once met Bayard Taylor socially, at the hospitable house where he was a guest after his lecture. Heaven knows how I got through the evening. I do not think I opened my mouth to address him a word; it was as much as I could do to sit and look at him, while he tranquilly smoked, and chatted with our host, and quaffed the beer which we had very good in the West. All the while I did him homage as the first author by calling whom I had met. I longed to tell him how much I liked his poems, which we used to get by heart in those

3

days, and I longed (how much more I longed!) to have him know that—

"Auch ich war in Arkadien geboren,"

that I had printed poems in the *Atlantic Monthly* and the *Saturday Press,* and was the potential author of things destined to eclipse all literature hitherto attempted. But I could not tell him; and there was no one else who thought to tell him. Perhaps it was as well so; I might have perished of his recognition, for my modesty was equal to my merit.

In fact I think we were all rather modest young fellows, we who formed the group wont to spend some part of every evening at that house, where there was always music, or whist, or gay talk, or all three. We had our opinions of literary matters, but (perhaps because we had mostly accepted them from England or New England, as I have said) we were not vain of them; and we would by no means have urged them before a living literary man like that. I believe none of us ventured to speak, except the poet, my roommate, who said, He believed so and so was the original of so and so; and was promptly told, He had no right to say such a thing. Naturally, we came away rather critical of our host's guest, whom I afterwards knew as the kindliest heart in the world. But we had not shone in his presence, and that galled us; and we chose to think that he had not shone in ours.

III

At that time he was filling a large space in the thoughts of the young people who had any thoughts about literature. He had come to his full repute as an agreeable and intelligent traveller, and he still

MR. HOWELLS AND BAYARD TAYLOR, 1860

wore the halo of his early adventures afoot in foreign lands when they were yet really foreign. He had not written his novels of American life, once so welcomed, and now so forgotten; it was very long before he had achieved that incomparable translation of Faust which must always remain the finest and best, and which would keep his name alive with Goethe's, if he had done nothing else worthy of remembrance. But what then most commended him to the regard of us star-eyed youth (now blinking sadly toward our seventies) was the poetry which he printed in the magazines from time to time: in the first *Putnam's* (where there was a dashing picture of him in an Arab burnoose and a turban), and in *Harper's,* and in the *Atlantic*. It was often very lovely poetry, I thought, and I still think so; and it was rightfully his, though it paid the inevitable allegiance to the manner of the great masters of the day. It was graced for us by the pathetic romance of his early love, which some of its sweetest and saddest numbers confessed, for the young girl he married almost in her death hour; and we who were hoping to have our hearts broken, or already had them so, would have been glad of something more of the obvious poet in the popular lecturer we had seen refreshing himself after his hour on the platform.

He remained for nearly a year the only author I had seen, and I met him once again before I saw any other. Our second meeting was far from Columbus, as far as remote Quebec, when I was on my way to New England by way of Niagara and the Canadian rivers and cities. I stopped in Toronto, and realized myself abroad without any signal adventures; but at Montreal something very pretty happened to me. I came into the hotel office, the evening of a first day's lonely sight-seeing, and vainly explored the register for the name of some acquaintance; as I turned from it two smartly dressed young fellows embraced it, and I heard one of them say, to my great amaze and happiness, " Hello, here's Howells!"

" Oh," I broke out upon him, " I was just looking for some one *I* knew. I hope you are some one who knows *me!*"

" Only through your contributions to the *Saturday Press*," said the young fellow, and with these golden words, the precious first personal recognition of my authorship I had ever received from a stranger, and the rich reward of all my literary endeavor, he introduced himself and his friend. I do not know what became of this friend, or where or how he eliminated himself; but we two others were inseparable from that moment. He was a young lawyer from New York, and when I came back from Italy, four or five years later, I used to see his sign in Wall Street, with a never-fulfilled intention of going in to see him. In whatever world he happens now to be, I should like to send him my greetings, and confess to him that my art has never since brought me so sweet a recompense, and nothing a thousandth part so much like Fame, as that outcry of his over the hotel register in Montreal. We were comrades for four or five rich days, and shared our pleasures and expenses in viewing the monuments of those ancient Canadian capitals, which I think we valued at all their picturesque worth. We made jokes to mask our emotions; we giggled and made giggle, in the right way; we fell in and out of love with all the pretty faces and dresses we saw; and we talked evermore about literature and literary people. He had more acquaintance with the one, and more passion for the other, but he could tell me of Pfaff's lager-beer cellar on Broadway, where the

Saturday Press fellows and the other bohemians met; and this, for the time, was enough: I resolved to visit it as soon as I reached New York, in spite of the tobacco and beer (which I was given to understand were *de rigueur*), though they both, so far as I had known them, were apt to make me sick.

I was very desolate after I parted from this good fellow, who returned to Montreal on his way to New York, while I remained in Quebec to continue later on mine to New England. When I came in from seeing him off in a calash for the boat, I discovered Bayard Taylor in the reading-room, where he sat sunken in what seemed a somewhat weary muse. He did not know me, or even notice me, though I made several errands in and out of the reading-room in the vain hope that he might do so: doubly vain, for I am aware now that I was still flown with the pride of that pretty experience in Montreal, and trusted in a repetition of something like it. At last, as no chance volunteered to help me, I mustered courage to go up to him and name myself, and say I had once had the pleasure of meeting him at Doctor ——'s in Columbus. The poet gave no sign of consciousness at the sound of a name which I had fondly begun to think might not be so all unknown. He looked up with an unkindling eye, and asked, Ah, how was the Doctor? and when I had reported favorably of the Doctor, our conversation ended.

He was probably as tired as he looked, and he must have classed me with that multitude all over the country who had shared the pleasure I professed in meeting him before; it was surely my fault that I did not speak my name loud enough to be recognized, if I spoke it at all; but the courage I had mustered did not quite suffice for that. In after years he assured me, first by letter and then by word, of his grief for an incident which I can only recall now as the untoward beginning of a cordial friendship. It was often my privilege, in those days, as reviewer and editor, to testify my sense of the beautiful things he did in so many kinds of literature, but I never liked any of them better than I liked him. He had a fervent devotion to his art, and he was always going to do the greatest things in it, with an expectation of effect that never failed him. The things he actually did were none of them mean, or wanting in quality, and some of them are of a lasting charm that any one may feel who will turn to his poems; but no doubt many of them fell short of his hopes of them with the reader. It was fine to meet him when he was full of a new scheme; he talked of it with a single-hearted joy, and tried to make you see it of the same colors and proportions it wore to his eyes. He spared no toil to make it the perfect thing he dreamed it, and he was not discouraged by any disappointment he suffered with the critic or the public.

He was a tireless worker, and at last his health failed under his labors at the newspaper desk, beneath the midnight gas, when he should long have rested from such labors. I believe he was obliged to do them through one of those business fortuities which deform and embitter all our lives; but he was not the man to spare himself in any case. He was always attempting new things, and he never ceased endeavoring to make his scholarship reparation for the want of earlier opportunity and training. I remember that I met him once in a Cambridge street with a book in his hand which he let me take in mine. It was a Greek author, and he said he was just beginnnig to read the language at fifty: a patriarchal age to me of the early thirties!

8

THE HOUSE IN WHICH LONGFELLOW WAS BORN

I suppose I intimated the surprise I felt at his taking it up so late in the day, for he said, with charming seriousness, " Oh, but you know, I expect to use it in the other world." Yes, that made it worth while, I consented; but was he sure of the other world? " As sure as I am of this," he said; and I have always kept the impression of the young faith which spoke in his voice and was more than his words.

I saw him last in the hour of those tremendous adieux which were paid him in New York before he sailed to be minister in Germany. It was one of the most graceful things done by President Hayes, who, most of all our Presidents after Lincoln, honored himself in honoring literature by his appointments, to give that place to Bayard Taylor. There was no one more fit for it, and it was peculiarly fit that he should be so distinguished to a people who knew and valued his scholarship and the service he had done German letters. He was as happy in it, apparently, as a man could be in anything here below, and he enjoyed to the last drop the many cups of kindness pressed to his lips in parting; though I believe these farewells, at a time when he was already fagged with work and excitement, were notably harmful to him, and helped to hasten his end. Some of us who were near of friendship went down to see him off when he sailed, as the dismal and futile wont of friends is; and I recall the kind, great fellow standing in the cabin, amid those sad flowers that heaped the tables, saying good-by to one after another, and smiling fondly, smiling wearily, upon all. There was champagne, of course, and an odious hilarity, without meaning and without remission, till the warning bell chased us ashore, and our brave poet escaped with what was left of his life.

9

IV

I have followed him far from the moment of our first meeting; but even on my way to venerate those New England luminaries, which chiefly drew my eyes, I could not pay a less devoir to an author who, if Curtis was not, was chief of the New York group of authors in that day. I distinguished between the New-Englanders and the New-Yorkers, and I suppose there is no question but our literary centre was then in Boston, wherever it is, or is not, at present. But I thought Taylor then, and I think him now, one of the first in our whole American province of the republic of letters, in a day when it was in a recognizably flourishing state, whether we regard quantity or quality in the names that gave it lustre. Lowell was then in perfect command of those varied forces which will long, if not lastingly, keep him in memory as first among our literary men, and master in more kinds than any other American. Longfellow was in the fulness of his world-wide fame, and in the ripeness of the beautiful genius which was not to know decay while life endured. Emerson had emerged from the popular darkness which had so long held him a hopeless mystic, and was shining a lambent star of poesy and prophecy at the zenith. Hawthorne, the exquisite artist, the unrivalled dreamer, whom we still always liken this one and that one to, whenever this one or that one promises greatly to please us, and still leave without a rival, without a companion, had lately returned from his long sojourn abroad, and had given us the last of the incomparable romances which the world was to have perfect from his hand. Doctor Holmes had surpassed all expectations in those who

10

most admired his brilliant humor and charming poetry by the invention of a new attitude if not a new sort in literature. The turn that civic affairs had taken was favorable to the widest recognition of Whittier's splendid lyrical gift; and that heart of fire, doubly snow-bound by Quaker tradition and Puritan environment, was penetrating every generous breast with its flamy impulses, and fusing all wills in its noble purpose. Mrs. Stowe, who far outfamed the rest as the author of the most renowned novel ever written, was proving it no accident or miracle by the fiction she was still writing.

This great New England group might be enlarged perhaps without loss of quality by the inclusion of Thoreau, who came somewhat before his time, and whose drastic criticism of our expediential and mainly futile civilization would find more intelligent acceptance now than it did then, when all resentment of its defects was specialized in enmity to Southern slavery. Doctor Edward Everett Hale belonged in this group too, by virtue of that humor, the most inventive and the most fantastic, the sanest, the sweetest, the truest, which had begun to find expression in the *Atlantic Monthly;* and there a wonderful young girl had written a series of vivid sketches and taken the heart of youth everywhere with amaze and joy, so that I thought it would be no less an event to meet Harriet Prescott than to meet any of those I have named.

I expected somehow to meet them all, and I imagined them all easily accessible in the office of the *Atlantic Monthly,* which had lately adventured in the fine air of high literature where so many other periodicals had gasped and died before it. The best of these, hitherto, and better even than the *Atlantic* for some reasons, the lamented *Putnam's Magazine,* had perished of inanition at New York, and the claim of the commercial capital to the literary primacy had passed with that brilliant venture. New York had nothing distinctive to show for American literature but the decrepit and doting *Knickerbocker Magazine. Harper's New Monthly,* though Curtis had already come to it from the wreck of *Putnam's,* and it had long ceased to be eclectic in material, and had begun to stand for native work in the allied arts which it has since so magnificently advanced, was not distinctively literary, and the *Weekly* had just begun to make itself known. The *Century, Scribner's,* the *Cosmopolitan, McClure's,* and I know not what others, were still unimagined by five, and ten, and twenty years, and the *Galaxy* was to flash and fade before any of them should kindle its more effectual fires. The *Nation,* which was destined to chastise rather than nurture our young literature, had still six years of dreamless potentiality before it; and the *Nation* was always more Bostonian than New-Yorkish by nature, whatever it was by nativity.

Philadelphia had long counted for nothing in the literary field. *Graham's Magazine* at one time showed a certain critical force, but it seemed to perish of this expression of vitality; and there remained *Godey's Lady's Book* and *Peterson's Magazine,* publications really incredible in their insipidity. In the South there was nothing but a mistaken social ideal, with the moral principles all standing on their heads in defence of slavery; and in the West there was a feeble and foolish notion that Western talent was repressed by Eastern jealousy. At Boston chiefly, if not at Boston alone, was there a vigorous intellectual life among such authors as I have named. Every young writer was ambitious to join his name with theirs in the

12

THE LONGFELLOW MANSION AT PORTLAND

Atlantic Monthly, and in the lists of Ticknor &
Fields, who were literary publishers in a sense such
as the business world has known nowhere else before
or since. Their imprint was a warrant of quality to
the reader and of immortality to the author, so that
if I could have had a book issued by them at that
day I should now be in the full enjoyment of an undying fame.

V

Such was the literary situation as the passionate
pilgrim from the West approached his holy land at
Boston, by way of the Grand Trunk Railway from
Quebec to Portland. I have no recollection of a sleep-
ing-car, and I suppose I waked and watched during the
whole of that long, rough journey; but I should hardly
have slept if there had been a car for the purpose. I
was too eager to see what New England was like, and
too anxious not to lose the least glimpse of it, to close
my eyes after I crossed the border at Island Pond.
I found that in the elm-dotted levels of Maine it was
very like the Western Reserve in northern Ohio, which
is, indeed, a portion of New England transferred with
all its characteristic features, and flattened out along
the lake shore. It was not till I began to run south-
ward into the older regions of the country that it lost
this look, and became gratefully strange to me. It
never had the effect of hoary antiquity which I had expected of a country settled more than two centuries;
with its wood-built farms and villages it looked newer
than the coal-smoked brick of southern Ohio. I had
prefigured the New England landscape bare of forests,
relieved here and there with the trees of orchards or
plantations; but I found apparently as much woodland
as at home.

13

At Portland I first saw the ocean, and this was a sort of disappointment. Tides and salt water I had already had at Quebec, so that I was no longer on the alert for them; but the color and the vastness of the sea I was still to try upon my vision. When I stood on the Promenade at Portland with the kind young Unitarian minister whom I had brought a letter to, and who led me there for a most impressive first view of the ocean, I could not make more of it than there was of Lake Erie; and I have never thought the color of the sea comparable to the tender blue of the lake. I did not hint my disappointment to my friend; I had too much regard for the feelings of an Eastern man to decry his ocean to his face, and I felt besides that it would be vulgar and provincial to make comparisons. I am glad now that I held my tongue, for that kind soul is no longer in this world, and I should not like to think he knew how far short of my expectations the sea he was so proud of had fallen. I went up with him into a tower or belvedere there was at hand; and when he pointed to the eastern horizon and said, Now there was nothing but sea between us and Africa, I pretended to expand with the thought, and began to sound myself for the emotions which I ought to have felt at such a sight. But in my heart I was empty, and heaven knows whether I saw the steamer which the ancient mariner in charge of that tower invited me to look at through his telescope. I never could see anything but a vitreous glare through a telescope, which has a vicious habit of dodging about through space, and failing to bring down anything of less than planetary magnitude.

But there was something at Portland vastly more to me than seas or continents, and that was the house where Longfellow was born. I believe, now, I did not

14

PORTLAND HARBOR, FROM MUNJOY HILL

get the right house, but only the house he went to live
in later; but it served, and I rejoiced in it with a rapture that could not have been more genuine if it had
been the real birthplace of the poet. I got my friend
to show me

> "—the breezy dome of groves,
> The shadows of Deering's woods,"

because they were in one of Longfellow's loveliest and
tenderest poems; and I made an errand to the docks,
for the sake of the

> "—black wharves and the slips,
> And the sea-tides tossing free,
> And Spanish sailors with bearded lips,
> And the beauty and mystery of the ships,
> And the magic of the sea,"

mainly for the reason that these were colors and shapes
of the fond vision of the poet's past. I am in doubt
whether it was at this time or a later time that I went
to revere

> "—the dead captains as they lay
> In their graves o'erlooking the tranquil bay,
> Where they in battle died,"

but I am quite sure it was now that I wandered under

> "—the trees which shadow each well-known street,
> As they balance up and down,"

for when I was next in Portland the great fire had
swept the city avenues bare of most of those beautiful
elms, whose Gothic arches and traceries I well remember.

The fact is that in those days I was bursting with
the most romantic expectations of life in every way,
and I looked at the whole world as material that might
be turned into literature, or that might be associated

with it somehow. I do not know how I managed to keep these preposterous hopes within me, but perhaps the trick of satirizing them, which I had early learnt, helped me to do it. I was at that particular moment resolved above all things to see things as Heinrich Heine saw them, or at least to report them as he did, no matter how I saw them; and I went about framing phrases to this end, and trying to match the objects of interest to them whenever there was the least chance of getting them together.

VI

I do not know how I first arrived in Boston, or whether it was before or after I had passed a day or two in Salem. As Salem is on the way from Portland, I will suppose that I stopped there first, and explored the quaint old town (quainter then than now, but still quaint enough) for the memorials of Hawthorne and of the witches which united to form the Salem I cared for. I went and looked up the House of Seven Gables, and suffered an unreasonable disappointment that it had not a great many more of them; but there was no loss in the death-warrant of Bridget Bishop, with the sheriff's return of execution upon it, which I found at the Court-house; if anything, the pathos of that witness of one of the cruelest delusions in the world was rather in excess of my needs; I could have got on with less. I saw the pins which the witches were sworn to have thrust into the afflicted children, and I saw Gallows Hill, where the hapless victims of the perjury were hanged. But that death-warrant remained the most vivid color of my experience of the tragedy; I had no need to invite myself to a sense of it, and it is still like a stain of red in my memory.

16

The kind old ship's captain whose guest I was, and who was transfigured to poetry in my sense by the fact that he used to voyage to the African coast for palm-oil in former days, led me all about the town, and showed me the Custom-house, which I desired to see because it was in the preface to the *Scarlet Letter*. But I perceived that he did not share my enthusiasm for the author, and I became more and more sensible that in Salem air there was a cool undercurrent of feeling about him. No doubt the place was not altogether grateful for the celebrity his romance had given it, and would have valued more the uninterrupted quiet of its own flattering thoughts of itself; but when it came to hearing a young lady say she knew a girl who said she would like to poison Hawthorne, it seemed to the devout young pilgrim from the West that something more of love for the great romancer would not have been too much for him. Hawthorne had already had his say, however, and he had not used his native town with any great tenderness. Indeed, the advantages to any place of having a great genius born and reared in its midst are so doubtful that it might be well for localities designing to become the birthplaces of distinguished authors to think twice about it. Perhaps only the largest capitals, like London and Paris, and New York and Chicago, ought to risk it. But the authors have an unaccountable perversity, and will seldom come into the world in the large cities, which are alone without the sense of neighborhood, and the personal susceptibilities so unfavorable to the practice of the literary art.

I dare say that it was owing to the local indifference to her greatest name, or her reluctance from it, that I got a clearer impression of Salem in some other respects than I should have had if I had been invited there to

B 17.

devote myself solely to the associations of Hawthorne. For the first time I saw an old New England town, I do not know but the most characteristic, and took into my young Western consciousness the fact of a more complex civilization than I had yet known. My whole life had been passed in a region where men were just beginning ancestors, and the conception of family was very imperfect. Literature of course was full of it, and it was not for a devotee of Thackeray to be theoretically ignorant of its manifestations; but I had hitherto carelessly supposed that family was nowhere regarded seriously in America except in Virginia, where it furnished a joke for the rest of the nation. But now I found myself confronted with it in its ancient houses, and heard its names pronounced with a certain consideration, which I dare say was as much their due in Salem as it could be anywhere. The names were all strange, and all indifferent to me, but those fine square wooden mansions, of a tasteful architecture, and a pale buff-color, withdrawing themselves in quiet reserve from the quiet street, gave me an impression of family as an actuality and a force which I had never had before, but which no Westerner can yet understand the East without taking into account. I do not suppose that I conceived of family as a fact of vital import then; I think I rather regarded it as a color to be used in any æsthetic study of the local conditions. I am not sure that I valued it more even for literary purposes, than the steeple which the captain pointed out as the first and last thing he saw when he came and went on his long voyages, or than the great palm-oil casks, which he showed me, and which I related to the tree that stood

"Auf brennender Felsenwand."

Whether that was the kind of palm that gives the oil, or was a sort only suitable to be the dream of a lonely fir-tree in the North on a cold height, I am in doubt to this day.

I heard, not without concern, that the neighboring industry of Lynn was penetrating Salem, and that the ancient haunt of the witches and the birthplace of our subtlest and somberest wizard was becoming a great shoe-town; but my concern was less for its memories and sensibilities than for an odious duty which I owed that industry, together with all the others in New England. Before I left home I had promised my earliest publisher that I would undertake to edit, or compile, or do something literary to, a work on the operation of the more distinctive mechanical inventions of our country, which he had conceived the notion of publishing by subscription. He had furnished me, the most immechanical of humankind, with a letter addressed generally to the great mills and factories of the East, entreating their managers to unfold their mysteries to me for the purposes of this volume. His letter had the effect of shutting up some of them like clams, and others it put upon their guard against my researches, lest I should seize the secret of their special inventions and publish it to the world. I could not tell the managers that I was both morally and mentally incapable of this; that they might have explained and demonstrated the properties and functions of their most recondite machinery, and upon examination afterwards found me guiltless of having anything but a few verses of Heine or Tennyson or Longfellow in my head. So I had to suffer in several places from their unjust anxieties, and from my own weariness of their ingenious engines, or else endure the pangs of a bad conscience from ignoring them. As long as

19

I was in Canada I was happy, for there was no industry in Canada that I saw, except that of the peasant
girls, in their Evangeline hats and kirtles, tossing
the hay in the way-side fields; but when I reached
Portland my troubles began. I went with that young
minister of whom I have spoken to a large foundry,
where they were casting some sort of ironmongery,
and inspected the process from a distance beyond any
chance spurt of the molten metal, and came away sadly
uncertain of putting the rather fine spectacle to any
practical use. A manufactory where they did something with coal-oil (which I now heard for the first
time called kerosene) refused itself to me, and I said
to myself that probably all the other industries of Portland were as reserved, and I would not seek to explore
them; but when I got to Salem, my conscience stirred
again. If I knew that there were shoe-shops in Salem,
ought not I to go and inspect their processes? This
was a question which would not answer itself to my
satisfaction, and I had no peace till I learned that I
could see shoemaking much better at Lynn, and that
Lynn was such a little way from Boston that I could
readily run up there, if I did not wish to examine the
shoe machinery at once. I promised myself that I
would run up from Boston, but in order to do this I
must first go to Boston.

VII

I am supposing still that I saw Salem before I saw
Boston, but however the fact may be, I am sure that I
decided it would be better to see shoemaking in Lynn,
where I really did see it, thirty years later. For the
purposes of the present visit, I contented myself with
looking at a machine in Haverhill, which chewed a

20

RETURN WARRANT OF SHERIFF GEORGE COR-
WIN FOR HANGING BRIDGET BISHOP

shoe sole full of pegs, and dropped it out of its iron jaws with an indifference as great as my own, and probably as little sense of how it had done its work. I may be unjust to that machine; heaven knows I would not wrong it; and I must confess that my head had no room in it for the conception of any machinery but the mythological, which, also I despised, in my revulsion from the eighteenth-century poets to those of my own day.

I cannot quite make out after the lapse of so many years just how or when I got to Haverhill, or whether it was before or after I had been in Salem. There is an apparitional quality in my presences, at this point or that, in the dim past; but I hope that, for the credit of their order, ghosts are not commonly taken with such trivial things as I was. For instance, in Haverhill I was much interested by the sight of a young man, coming gayly down the steps of the hotel where I lodged, in peg-top trousers so much more peg-top than my own that I seemed to be wearing mere spring-bottoms in comparison; and in a day when every one who respected himself had a necktie as narrow as he could get, this youth had one no wider than a shoestring, and red at that, while mine measured almost an inch, and was black. To be sure, he was one of a band of negro minstrels, who were to give a concert that night, and he had a right to excel in fashion.

I will suppose, for convenience' sake, that I visited Haverhill, too, before I reached Boston: somehow that shoe-pegging machine must come in, and it may as well come in here. When I actually found myself in Boston, there were perhaps industries which it would have been well for me to celebrate, but I either made believe there were none, or else I honestly forgot all about them. In either case I released myself altogether to the literary and historical associations of the place. I need not say that I gave myself first to the first, and it rather surprised me to find that the literary associations of Boston referred so largely to Cambridge. I did not know much about Cambridge, except that it was the seat of the university where Lowell was, and Longfellow had been, professor; and somehow I had not realized it as the home of these poets. That was rather stupid of me, but it is best to own the truth, and afterward I came to know the place so well that I may safely confess my earlier ignorance.

I had stopped in Boston at the Tremont House, which was still one of the first hostelries of the country, and I must have inquired my way to Cambridge there; but I was sceptical of the direction the Cambridge horse-car took when I found it, and I hinted to the driver my anxieties as to why he should be starting east when I had been told that Cambridge was west of Boston. He reassured me in the laconic and sarcastic manner of his kind, and we really reached Cambridge by the route he had taken.

The beautiful elms that shaded great part of the way massed themselves in the " groves of academe " at the Square, and showed pleasant glimpses of " Old Harvard's scholar factories red," then far fewer than now. It must have been in vacation, for I met no one as I wandered through the college yard, trying to make up my mind as to how I should learn where Lowell lived; for it was he whom I had come to find. He had not only taken the poems I sent him, but he had printed two of them in a single number of the *Atlantic,* and had even written me a little note about them, which I wore next my heart in my breast pocket till I almost wore it out; and so I thought I might fitly report myself to him. But I have always been helpless in finding my way, and I was still depressed by my failure to con-

A TYPICAL STREET IN OLD SALEM

vince the horse-car driver that he had taken the wrong road. I let several people go by without questioning them, and those I did ask abashed me farther by not knowing what I wanted to know. When I had remitted my search for the moment, an ancient man, with an open mouth and an inquiring eye, whom I never afterwards made out in Cambridge, addressed me with a hospitable offer to show me the Washington Elm. I thought this would give me time to embolden myself for the meeting with the editor of the *Atlantic* if I should ever find him, and I went with that kind old man, who when he had shown me the tree, and the spot where Washington stood when he took command of the Continental forces, said that he had a branch of it, and that if I would come to his house with him he would give me a piece. In the end, I meant merely to flatter him into telling me where I could find Lowell, but I dissembled my purpose and pretended a passion for a piece of the historic elm, and the old man led me not only to his house but his wood-house, where he sawed me off a block so generous that I could not get it into my pocket. I feigned the gratitude which I could see that he expected, and then I took courage to put my question to him. Perhaps that patriarch lived only in the past, and cared for history and not literature. He confessed that he could not tell me where to find Lowell; but he did not forsake me; he set forth with me upon the street again, and let no man pass without asking him. In the end we met one who was able to say where Mr. Lowell was, and I found him at last in a little study at the rear of a pleasant, old-fashioned house near the Delta.

Lowell was not then at the height of his fame; he had just reached this thirty years after, when he died; but I doubt if he was ever after a greater power in his own country, or more completely embodied the literary aspiration which would not and could not part itself from the love of freedom and the hope of justice. For the sake of these he had been willing to suffer the reproach which followed their friends in the earlier days of the anti-slavery struggle. He had outlived the reproach long before; but the fear of his strength remained with those who had felt it, and he had not made himself more generally loved by the *Fable for Critics* than by the *Biglow Papers,* probably. But in the *Vision of Sir Launfal* and the *Legend of Brittany* he had won a liking if not a listening far wider than his humor and his wit had got him; and in his lectures on the English poets, given not many years before he came to the charge of the *Atlantic,* he had proved himself easily the wisest and finest critic in our language. He was already, more than any American poet,

> " Dowered with the hate of hate, the scorn of scorn,
>   The love of love,"

and he held a place in the public sense which no other author among us has held. I had myself never been a great reader of his poetry, when I met him, though when I was a boy of ten years I had heard my father repeat passages from the *Biglow Papers* against war and slavery and the war for slavery upon Mexico, and later I had read those criticisms of English poetry, and I knew Sir Launfal must be Lowell in some sort; but my love for him as a poet was chiefly centred in my love for his tender rhyme, *Auf Wiedersehen,* which I cannot yet read without something of the young pathos it first stirred in me. I knew and felt his greatness somehow apart from the literary proofs of it; he ruled my fancy and held my allegiance as a character, as a man; and I am neither sorry nor ashamed that I was abashed

24

when I first came into his presence; and that in spite
of his words of welcome I sat inwardly quaking before
him. He was then forty-one years old, and nineteen
my senior, and if there had been nothing else to awe
me, I might well have been quelled by the disparity of
our ages. But I have always been willing and even
eager to do homage to men who have done something,
and notably to men who have done something in the
sort I wished to do something in, myself. I could
never recognize any other sort of superiority; but that
I am proud to recognize; and I had before Lowell some
such feeling as an obscure subaltern might have before
his general. He was by nature a bit of a disciplinarian,
and the effect was from him as well as in me; I dare
say he let me feel whatever difference there was, as
helplessly as I felt it. At the first encounter with
people he always was apt to have a certain frosty shyness, a smiling cold, as from the long, high-sunned winters of his Puritan race; he was not quite himself till
he had made you aware of his quality: then no one
could be sweeter, tenderer, warmer than he; then he
made you free of his whole heart; but you must be his
captive before he could do that. His whole personality
had now an instant charm for me; I could not keep
my eyes from those beautiful eyes of his, which had a
certain starry serenity, and looked out so purely from
under his white forehead, shadowed with auburn hair
untouched by age; or from the smile that shaped the
auburn beard, and gave the face in its form and color
the Christ-look which Page's portrait has flattered in it.

His voice had as great a fascination for me as his
face. The vibrant tenderness and the crisp clearness of
the tones, the perfect modulation, the clear enunciation,
the exquisite accent, the elect diction—I did not know
enough then to know that these were the gifts, these

were the graces, of one from whose tongue our rough English came music such as I should never hear from any other. In this speech there was nothing of our slipshod American slovenliness, but a truly Italian conscience and an artistic sense of beauty in the instrument.

I saw, before he sat down across his writing-table from me, that he was not far from the medium height; but his erect carriage made the most of his five feet and odd inches. He had been smoking the pipe he loved, and he put it back in his mouth, presently, as if he found himself at greater ease with it, when he began to chat, or rather to let me show what manner of young man I was by giving me the first word. I told him of the trouble I had in finding him, and I could not help dragging in something about Heine's search for Börne, when he went to see him in Frankfort; but I felt at once this was a false start, for Lowell was such an impassioned lover of Cambridge, which was truly his *patria,* in the Italian sense, that it must have hurt him to be unknown to any one in it; he said, a little dryly, that he should not have thought I would have so much difficulty; but he added, forgivingly, that this was not his own house, which he was out of for the time. Then he spoke to me of Heine, and when I showed my ardor for him, he sought to temper it with some judicious criticisms, and told me that he had kept the first poem I sent him, for the long time it had been unacknowledged, to make sure that it was not a translation. He asked me about myself, and my name, and its Welsh origin, and seemed to find the vanity I had in this harmless enough. When I said I had tried hard to believe that I was at least the literary descendant of Sir James Howels, he corrected me gently with " James Howel," and took down a volume of the *Familiar Let-*

"GIRLS IN EVANGELINE HATS AND KIRTLES TOSSING HAY"

ters from the shelves behind him to prove me wrong.
This was always his habit, as I found afterwards:
when he quoted anything from a book he liked to get
it and read the passage over, as if he tasted a kind of
hoarded sweetness in the words.   It visibly vexed him
if they showed him in the least mistaken; but

"The love he bore to learning was at fault"

for this foible, and that other of setting people right if
he thought them wrong.   I could not assert myself
against his version of Howel's name, for my edition of
his letters was far away in ·Ohio, and I was obliged to
own that the name was spelt in several different ways
in it.   He perceived, no doubt, why I had chosen the
form likest my own, with the title which the pleasant
old turncoat ought to have had from the many masters
he served according to their many minds, but never
had except from that erring edition.   He did not af-
flict me for it, though; probably it amused him too
much; he asked me about the West, and when he found
that I was as proud of the West as I was of Wales, he
seemed even better pleased, and said he had always
fancied that human nature was laid out on rather a
larger scale there than in the East, but he had seen very
little of the West.   In my heart I did not think this then,
and I do not think it now; human nature has had more
ground to spread over in the West; that is all; but " it
was not for me to bandy words with my sovereign."
He said he liked to hear of the differences between the
different sections, for what we had most to fear in our
country was a wearisome sameness of type.

He did not say now, or at any other time during the
many years I knew him, any of those slighting things
of the West which I had so often to suffer from Eastern
people, but suffered me to praise it all I would.   He

27

asked me what way I had taken in coming to New Eng·
land, and when I told him, and began to rave of the
beauty and quaintness of French Canada, and to pour
out my joy in Quebec, he said, with a smile that had
now lost all its frost, Yes, Quebec was a bit of the
seventeenth century; it was in many ways more French
than France, and its people spoke the language of Voltaire, with the accent of Voltaire's time.

I do not remember what else he talked of, though
once I remembered it with what I believed an inef-
faceable distinctness. I set nothing of it down at the
time; I was too busy with the letters I was writing for
a Cincinnati paper; and I was severely bent upon keeping all personalities out of them. This was very well,
but I could wish now that I had transgressed at least
so far as to report some of the things that Lowell said;
for the paper did not print my letters, and it would
have been perfectly safe, and very useful for the present
purpose. But perhaps he did not say anything very
memorable; to do that you must have something positive in your listener; and I was the mere response, the
hollow echo, that youth must be in like circumstances.
I was all the time afraid of wearing my welcome out,
and I hurried to go when I would so gladly have staid.
I do not remember where I meant to go, or why he
should have undertaken to show me the way across-lots,
but this was what he did; and when we came to a fence,
which I clambered gracelessly over, he put his hands
on the top, and tried to take it at a bound. He tried
twice, and then laughed at his failure, but not with
any great pleasure, and he was not content till a
third trial carried him across. Then he said, " I
commonly do that the first time," as if it were a
frequent habit with him, while I remained discreetly
silent, and for that moment at least felt myself the

GROVES OF ACADEME, HARVARD

elder of the man who had so much of the boy in him. He had, indeed, much of the boy in him to the last, and he parted with each hour of his youth reluctantly, pathetically.

VIII

We walked across what must have been Jarvis Field to what must have been North Avenue, and there he left me. But before he let me go he held my hand while he could say that he wished me to dine with him; only, he was not in his own house, and he would ask me to dine with him at the Parker House in Boston, and would send me word of the time later.

I suppose I may have spent part of the intervening time in viewing the wonders of Boston, and visiting the historic scenes and places in it and about it. I certainly went over to Charlestown, and ascended Bunker Hill Monument, and explored the navy-yard, where the immemorial man-of-war begun in Jackson's time was then silently stretching itself under its long shed in a poetic arrest, as if the failure of the appropriation for its completion had been some kind of enchantment. In Boston, I early presented my letter of credit to the publisher it was drawn upon, not that I needed money at the moment, but from a young eagerness to see if it would be honored; and a literary attaché of the house kindly went about with me, and showed me the life of the city. A great city it seemed to me then, and a seething vortex of business as well as a whirl of gayety, as I saw it in Washington Street, and in a promenade concert at Copeland's restaurant in Tremont Row. Probably I brought some idealizing force to bear upon it, for I was not all so strange to the world as I must seem; perhaps I accounted for quality as well as quantity in my impressions of the New England metropolis, and aggrandized it in the ratio of its literary importance. It seemed to me old, even after Quebec, and very likely I credited the actual town with all the dead and gone Bostonians in my sentimental census. If I did not, it was no fault of my cicerone, who thought even more of the city he showed me than I did. I do not know now who he was, and I never saw him after I came to live there, with any certainty that it was he, though I was often tormented with the vision of a spectacled face like his, but not like enough to warrant me in addressing him.

He became part of that ghostly Boston of my first visit, which would sometimes return and possess again the city I came to know so familiarly in later years, and to be so passionately interested in. Some color of my prime impressions has tinged the fictitious experiences of people in my books, but I find very little of it in my memory. This is like a web of frayed old lace, which I have to take carefully into my hold for fear of its fragility, and make out as best I can the figure once so distinct in it. There are the narrow streets, stretching saltwards to the docks, which I haunted for their quaintness, and there is Faneuil Hall, which I cared to see so much more because Wendell Phillips had spoken in it than because Otis and Adams had. There is the old Colonial House, and there is the State House, which I dare say I explored, with the Common sloping before it. There is Beacon Street, with the Hancock House where it is incredibly no more, and there are the beginnings of Commonwealth Avenue, and the other streets of the Back Bay, laid out with their basements left hollowed in the made land, which the gravel trains were yet making out of the westward hills. There is the Public Garden, newly planned and planted, but without the massive bridge destined to make so ungrate-

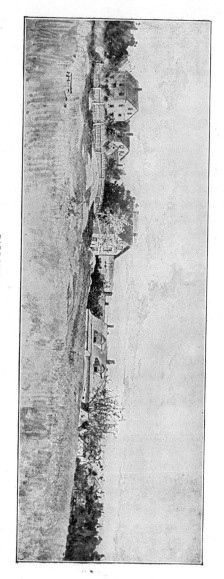

GALLOWS HILL, SALEM

fully little of the lake that occasioned it. But it is all very vague, and I could easily believe now that it was some one else who saw it then in my place.

I think that I did not try to see Cambridge the same day that I saw Lowell, but wisely came back to my hotel in Boston, and tried to realize the fact. I went out another day, with an acquaintance from Ohio, whom I ran upon in the street. We went to Mount Auburn together, and I viewed its monuments with a reverence which I dare say their artistic quality did not merit. But I am not sorry for this, for perhaps they are not quite so bad as some people pretend. The Gothic chapel of the cemetery, unstoried as it was, gave me, with its half-dozen statues standing or sitting about, an emotion such as I am afraid I could not receive now from the Acropolis, Westminster Abbey, and Santa Croce in one. I tried hard for some æsthetic sense of it, and I made believe that I thought this thing and that thing in the place moved me with its fitness or beauty; but the truth is that I had no taste in anything but literature, and did not feel the effect I would so willingly have experienced.

I did genuinely love the elmy quiet of the dear old Cambridge streets, though, and I had a real and instant pleasure in the yellow colonial houses, with their white corners and casements and their green blinds, that lurked behind the shrubbery of the avenue I passed through to Mount Auburn. The most beautiful among them was the most interesting for me, for it was the house of Longfellow; my companion, who had seen it before, pointed it out to me with an air of custom, and I would not let him see that I valued the first sight of it as I did. I had hoped that somehow I might be so favored as to see Longfellow himself, but when I asked about him of those who knew, they said, "Oh, he is at

Nahant," and I thought that Nahant must be a great way off, and at any rate I did not feel authorized to go to him there. Neither did I go to see the author of *The Amber Gods,* who lived at Newburyport, I was told, as if I should know where Newburyport was; I did not know, and I hated to ask. Besides, it did not seem so simple as it had seemed in Ohio, to go and see a young lady simply because I was infatuated with her literature; even as the envoy of all the infatuated young people of Columbus, I could not quite do this; and when I got home, I had to account for my failure as best I could. Another failure of mine was the sight of Whittier, which I then very much longed to have. They said, " Oh, Whittier lives at Amesbury," but that put him at an indefinite distance, and without the introduction I never would ask for, I found it impossible to set out in quest of him. In the end, I saw no one in New England whom I was not presented to in the regular way, except Lowell, whom I thought I had a right to call upon in my quality of contributor, and from the acquaintance I had with him by letter. I neither praise nor blame myself for this; it was my shyness that withheld me rather than my merit. There is really no harm in seeking the presence of a famous man, and I doubt if the famous man resents the wish of people to look upon him without some measure, great or little, of affectation. There are bores everywhere, but he is likelier to find them in the wonted figures of society than in those young people, or old people, who come to him in the love of what he has done. I am well aware how furiously Tennyson sometimes met his worshippers, and how insolently Carlyle, but I think these facts are little specks in their sincerity. Our own gentler and honester celebrities did not forbid approach, and I have known some of them caress adorers who seemed hardly worthy

32

of their kindness; but that was better than to have hurt any sensitive spirit who had ventured too far, by the rules that govern us with common men.

IX

My business relations were with the house that so promptly honored my letter of credit. This house had published in the East the campaign life of Lincoln which I had lately written, and I dare say would have published the volume of poems I had written earlier with my friend Piatt, if there had been any public for it; at least, I saw large numbers of the book on the counters. But all my literary affiliations were with Ticknor & Fields, and it was the Old Corner Book-Store on Washington Street that drew my heart as soon as I had replenished my pocket in Cornhill. After verifying the editor of the *Atlantic Monthly* I wished to verify its publishers, and it very fitly happened that when I was shown into Mr. Fields's little room at the back of the store, with its window looking upon School Street, and its scholarly keeping in books and prints, he had just got the magazine sheets of a poem of mine from the Cambridge printers. He was then lately from abroad, and he had the zest for American things which a foreign sojourn is apt to renew in us, though I did not know this then, and could not account for it in the kindness he expressed for my poem. He introduced me to Mr. Ticknor, who I fancied had not read my poem; but he seemed to know what it was from the junior partner, and he asked me whether I had been paid for it. I confessed that I had not, and then he got out a chamois-leather bag, and took from it five half-eagles in gold and laid them on the green cloth top of the desk, in much the shape and of much

c 33

the size of the Great Bear. I have never since felt myself paid so lavishly for any literary work, though I have had more for a single piece than the twenty-five dollars that dazzled me in this constellation. The publisher seemed aware of the poetic character of the transaction; he let the pieces lie a moment, before he gathered them up and put them into my hand, and said, " I always think it is pleasant to have it in gold."

But a terrible experience with the poem awaited me, and quenched for the moment all my pleasure and pride. It was *The Pilot's Story,* which I suppose has had as much acceptance as anything of mine in verse (I do not boast of a vast acceptance for it), and I had attempted to treat in it a phase of the national tragedy of slavery, as I had imagined it on a Mississippi steamboat. A young planter has gambled away the slave-girl who is the mother of his child, and when he tells her, she breaks out upon him with the demand:

" What will you say to our boy when he cries for me, there in Saint Louis?"

I had thought this very well, and natural and simple, but a fatal proof-reader had not thought it well enough, or simple and natural enough, and he had made the line read:

" What will you say to our boy when he cries for ' *Ma,*' there in Saint Louis?"

He had even had the inspiration to quote the word he preferred to the one I had written, so that there was no merciful possibility of mistaking it for a misprint, and my blood froze in my veins at sight of it. Mr. Fields had given me the sheets to read while he looked over some letters, and he either felt the chill of my horror, or I made some sign or sound of dismay that caught his notice, for he looked round at me. I could

34

only show him the passage with a gasp. I dare say he might have liked to laugh, for it was cruelly funny, but he did not; he was concerned for the magazine as well as for me. He declared that when he first read the line he had thought I could not have written it so, and he agreed with me that it would kill the poem if it came out in that shape. He instantly set about repairing the mischief, so far as could be. He found that the whole edition of that sheet had been printed, and the air blackened round me again, lighted up here and there with baleful flashes of the newspaper wit at my cost, which I previsioned in my misery; I knew what I should have said of such a thing myself, if it had been another's. But the publisher at once decided that the sheet must be reprinted, and I went away weak as if in the escape from some deadly peril. Afterwards it appeared that the line had passed the first proof-reader as I wrote it, but that the final reader had entered so sympathetically into the realistic intention of my poem as to contribute the modification which had nearly been my end.

X

As it fell out, I lived without farther difficulty to the day and hour of the dinner Lowell made for me; and I really think, looking at myself impersonally, and remembering the sort of young fellow I was, that it would have been a great pity if I had not. The dinner was at the old-fashioned Boston hour of two, and the table was laid for four people in some little upper room at Parker's, which I was never afterwards able to make sure of. Lowell was already there when I came, and he presented me, to my inexpressible delight and surprise, to Dr. Holmes, who was there with him.

Holmes was in the most brilliant hour of that wonderful second youth which his fame flowered into long after the world thought he had completed the cycle of his literary life. He had already received full recognition as a poet of delicate wit, nimble humor, airy imagination, and exquisite grace, when the Autocrat papers advanced his name indefinitely beyond the bounds which most immortals would have found range enough. The marvel of his invention was still fresh in the minds of men, and time had not dulled in any measure the sense of its novelty. His readers all fondly identified him with his work; and I fully expected to find myself in the Autocrat's presence when I met Dr. Holmes. But the fascination was none the less for that reason; and the winning smile, the wise and humorous glance, the whole genial manner was as important to me as if I had foreboded something altogether different. I found him physically of the Napoleonic height which spiritually overtops the Alps, and I could look into his face without that unpleasant effort which giants of inferior mind so often cost the man of five feet four.

A little while after, Fields came in, and then our number and my pleasure were complete.

Nothing else so richly satisfactory, indeed, as the whole affair could have happened to a like youth at such a point in his career; and when I sat down with Doctor Holmes and Mr. Fields, on Lowell's right, I felt through and through the dramatic perfection of the event. The kindly Autocrat recognized some such quality of it in terms which were not the less precious and gracious for their humorous excess. I have no reason to think that he had yet read any of my poor verses, or had me otherwise than wholly on trust from Lowell; but he leaned over towards his host, and said,

with a laughing look at me, " Well, James, this is something like the apostolic succession; this is the laying on of hands." I took his sweet and caressing irony as he meant it; but the charm of it went to my head long before any drop of wine, together with the charm of hearing him and Lowell calling each other James and Wendell, and of finding them still cordially boys together.

I would gladly have glimmered before those great lights in the talk that followed, if I could have thought of anything brilliant to say, but I could not, and so I let them shine without a ray of reflected splendor from me. It was such talk as I had, of course, never heard before, and it is not saying enough to say that I have never heard such talk since except from these two men. It was as light and kind as it was deep and true, and it ranged over a hundred things, with a perpetual sparkle of Doctor Holmes's wit, and the constant glow of Lowell's incandescent sense. From time to time Fields came in with one of his delightful stories (sketches of character they were, which he sometimes did not mind caricaturing), or with some criticism of the literary situation from his stand-point of both lover and publisher of books. I heard fames that I had accepted as proofs of power treated as factitious, and witnessed a frankness concerning authorship, far and near, that I had not dreamed of authors using. When Doctor Holmes understood that I wrote for the *Saturday Press,* which was running amuck among some Bostonian immortalities of the day, he seemed willing that I should know they were not thought so very undying in Boston, and that I should not take the notion of a Mutual Admiration Society too seriously, or accept the New York bohemian view of Boston as true. For the most part the talk did not address itself to me, but became an exchange of thoughts and fancies between himself and Lowell. They touched, I remember, on certain matters of technique, and the doctor confessed that he had a prejudice against some words that he could not overcome; for instance, he said, nothing could induce him to use *'neath* for *beneath,* no exigency of versification or stress of rhyme. Lowell contended that he would use any word that carried his meaning; and I think he did this to the hurt of some of his earlier things. He was then probably in the revolt against too much literature in literature, which every one is destined sooner or later to share; there was a certain roughness, very like crudeness, which he indulged before his thought and phrase mellowed to one music in his later work. I tacitly agreed rather with the doctor, though I did not swerve from my allegiance to Lowell, and if I had spoken I should have sided with him: I would have given that or any other proof of my devotion. Fields casually mentioned that he thought " The Dandelion " was the most popularly liked of Lowell's briefer poems, and I made haste to say that I thought so too, though I did not really think anything about it; and then I was sorry, for I could see that the poet did not like it, quite; and I felt that I was duly punished for my dishonesty.

Hawthorne was named among other authors, probably by Fields, whose house had just published his " Marble Faun," and who had recently come home on the same steamer with him. Doctor Holmes asked if I had met Hawthorne yet, and when I confessed that I had hardly yet even hoped for such a thing, he smiled his winning smile, and said: " Ah, well! I don't know that you will ever feel you have really met him. He is like a dim room with a little taper of personality burning on the corner of the mantel."

They all spoke of Hawthorne, and with the same

affection, but the same sense of something mystical and remote in him; and every word was priceless to me. But these masters of the craft I was 'prentice to probably could not have said anything that I should not have found wise and well, and I am sure now I should have been the loser if the talk had shunned any of the phases of human nature which it touched. It is best to find that all men are of the same make, and that there are certain universal things which interest them as much as the supernal things, and amuse them even more. There was a saying of Lowell's which he was fond of repeating at the menace of any form of the transcendental, and he liked to warn himself and others with his homely, "Remember the dinner-bell." What I recall of the whole effect of a time so happy for me is that in all that was said, however high, however fine, we were never out of hearing of the dinner-bell; and perhaps this is the best effect I can leave with the reader. It was the first dinner served in courses that I had sat down to, and I felt that this service gave it a romantic importance which the older fashion of the West still wanted. Even at Governor Chase's table in Columbus the Governor carved; I knew of the dinner *à la Russe,* as it was then called, only from books; and it was a sort of literary flavor that I tasted in the successive dishes. When it came to the black coffee, and then to the *petits verres* of cognac, with lumps of sugar set fire to atop, it was something that so far transcended my home-kept experience that it began to seem altogether visionary.

Neither Fields nor Doctor Holmes smoked, and I had to confess that I did not; but Lowell smoked enough for all three, and the spark of his cigar began to show in the waning light before we rose from the table. The time that never had, nor can ever have, its fellow for me, had to come to an end, as all times must, and when I shook hands with Lowell in parting, he overwhelmed me by saying that if I thought of going to Concord he would send me a letter to Hawthorne. I was not to see Lowell again during my stay in Boston; but Doctor Holmes asked me to tea for the next evening, and Fields said I must come to breakfast with him in the morning.

XI

I recall with the affection due to his friendly nature, and to the kindness afterwards to pass between us for many years, the whole aspect of the publisher when I first saw him. His abundant hair, and his full " beard as broad as ony spade," that flowed from his throat in Homeric curls, were touched with the first frost. He had a fine color, and his eyes, as keen as they were kind, twinkled restlessly above the wholesome russet-red of his cheeks. His portly frame was clad in those Scotch tweeds which had not yet displaced the traditional broadcloth with us in the West, though I had sent to New York for a rough suit, and so felt myself not quite unworthy to meet a man fresh from the hands of the London tailor.

Otherwise I stood as much in awe of him as his jovial soul would let me; and if I might I should like to suggest to the literary youth of this day some notion of the importance of his name to the literary youth of my day. He gave æsthetic character to the house of Ticknor & Fields, but he was by no means a silent partner on the economic side. No one can forecast the fortune of a new book, but he knew as well as any publisher can know not only whether a book was good, but whether the reader would think so; and I suppose that his house made as few bad guesses, along with their good ones, as any

40

house that ever tried the uncertain temper of the public
with its ventures. In the minds of all who loved the
plain brown cloth and tasteful print of its issues he was
more or less intimately associated with their literature;
and those who were not mistaken in thinking De Quincey one of the delightfulest authors in the world, were
especially grateful to the man who first edited his writings in book form, and proud that this edition was the
effect of American sympathy with them. At that day,
I believed authorship the noblest calling in the world,
and I should still be at a loss to name any nobler. The
great authors I had met were to me the sum of greatness, and if I could not rank their publisher with them
by virtue of equal achievement, I handsomely brevetted
him worthy of their friendship, and honored him in the
visible measure of it.

In his house beside the Charles, and in the close
neighborhood of Doctor Holmes, I found an odor and
an air of books such as I fancied might belong to the
famous literary houses of London. It is still there, that
friendly home of lettered refinement, and the gracious
spirit which knew how to welcome me, and make the
least of my shyness and strangeness, and the most of
the little else there was in me, illumines it still, though
my host of that rapturous moment has many years been
of those who are only with us unseen and unheard. I
remember his burlesque pretence that morning of an inextinguishable grief when I owned that I had never
eaten blueberry cake before, and how he kept returning
to the pathos of the fact that there should be a region
of the earth where blueberry cake was unknown. We
breakfasted in the pretty room whose windows look out
through leaves and flowers upon the river's coming and
going tides, and whose walls were covered with the faces
and the autographs of all the contemporary poets and

novelists. The Fieldses had spent some days with Tennyson in their recent English sojourn, and Mrs. Fields had much to tell of him, h .; he looked, how he smoked, how he read aloud, and how he said, when he asked her to go with him to the tower of his house, " Come up and see the sad English sunset!" which had an instant value to me such as some rich verse of his might have had. I was very new to it all, how new I could not very well say, but I flattered myself that I breathed in that atmosphere as if in the return from life-long exile. Still I patriotically bragged of the West a little, and I told them proudly that in Columbus no book since *Uncle Tom's Cabin* had sold so well as *The Marble Faun*. This made the effect that I wished, but whether it was true or not, heaven knows; I only know that I heard it from our leading bookseller, and I made no question of it myself.

After breakfast, Fields went away to the office, and I lingered, while Mrs. Fields showed me from shelf to shelf in the library, and dazzled me with the sight of authors' copies, and volumes invaluable with the autographs and the pencilled notes of the men whose names were dear to me from my love of their work. Everywhere was some souvenir of the living celebrities my hosts had met; and whom had they not met in that English sojourn in days before England embittered herself to us during our civil war? Not Tennyson only, but Thackeray, but Dickens, but Charles Reade, but Carlyle, but many a minor fame was in my ears from converse so recent with them that it was as if I heard their voices in their echoed words.

I do not remember how long I stayed; I remember I was afraid of staying too long, and so I am sure I did not stay as long as I should have liked. But I have not the least notion how I got away, and I am not cer-

JAMES T. FIELDS

(About 1870)

tain where I spent the rest of a day that began in the clouds, but had to be ended on the common earth. I suppose I gave it mostly to wandering about the city, and partly to recording my impressions of it for that newspaper which never published them. The summer weather in Boston, with its sunny heat struck through and through with the coolness of the sea, and its clear air untainted with a breath of smoke, I have always loved, but it had then a zest unknown before; and I should have thought it enough simply to be alive in it. But everywhere I came upon something that fed my famine for the old, the quaint, the picturesque, and however the day passed it was a banquet, a festival. I can only recall my breathless first sight of the Public Library and of the Athenæum Gallery: great sights then, which the Vatican and the Pitti hardly afterwards eclipsed for mere emotion. In fact I did not see these elder treasuries of literature and art between breakfasting with the Autocrat's publisher in the morning, and taking tea with the Autocrat himself in the evening, and that made a whole world's difference.

XII

The tea of that simpler time is wholly inconceivable to this generation, which knows the thing only as a mild form of afternoon reception; but I suppose that in 1860 very few dined late in our whole pastoral republic. Tea was the meal people asked people to when they wished to sit at long leisure and large ease; it came at the end of the day, at six o'clock, or seven; and one went to it in morning dress. It had an unceremonied domesticity in the abundance of its light dishes, and I fancy these did not vary much from East to West, except that we had a Southern touch in our fried chicken and corn bread; but at the Autocrat's tea table the cheering cup had a flavor unknown to me before that day. He asked me if I knew it, and I said it was English breakfast tea; for I had drunk it at the publisher's in the morning, and was willing not to seem strange to it. "Ah, yes," he said; "but this is the flower of the souchong; it is the blossom, the poetry of tea," and then he told me how it had been given him by a friend, a merchant in the China trade, which used to flourish in Boston, and was the poetry of commerce, as this delicate beverage was of tea. That commerce is long past, and I fancy that the plant ceased to bloom when the traffic fell into decay.

The Autocrat's windows had the same outlook upon the Charles as the publisher's, and after tea we went up into a back parlor of the same orientation, and saw the sunset die over the water, and the westering flats and hills. Nowhere else in the world has the day a lovelier close, and our talk took something of the mystic coloring that the heavens gave those mantling expanses. It was chiefly his talk, but I have always found the best talkers are willing that you should talk if you like, and a quick sympathy and a subtle sense met all that I had to say from him and from the unbroken circle of kindred intelligences about him. I saw him then in the midst of his family, and perhaps never afterwards to better advantage, or in a finer mood. We spoke of the things that people perhaps once liked to deal with more than they do now; of the intimations of immortality, of the experiences of morbid youth, and of all those messages from the tremulous nerves which we take for prophecies. I was not ashamed, before his tolerant wisdom, to acknowledge the effects that had lingered so long with me in fancy and even in conduct,

44

from a time of broken health and troubled spirit; and I remember the exquisite tact in him which recognized them as things common to all, however peculiar in each, which left them mine for whatever obscure vanity I might have in them, and yet gave me the companionship of the whole race in their experience. We spoke of forebodings and presentiments; we approached the mystic confines of the world from which no traveller has yet returned with a passport *en règle* and properly *visé;* and he held his light course through these filmy impalpabilities with a charming sincerity, with the scientific conscience that refuses either to deny the substance of things unseen, or to affirm it. In the gathering dusk, so weird did my fortune of being there and listening to him seem, that I might well have been a blessed ghost, for all the reality I felt in myself.

I tried to tell him how much I had read him from my boyhood, and with what joy and gain; and he was patient of these futilities, and I have no doubt imagined the love that inspired them, and accepted that instead of the poor praise. When the sunset passed, and the lamps were lighted, and we all came back to our dear little firm-set earth, he began to question me about my native region of it. From many forgotten inquiries I recall his asking me what was the fashionable religion in Columbus, or the Church that socially corresponded to the Unitarian Church in Boston. He had first to clarify my intelligence as to what Unitarianism was; we had Universalists but not Unitarians; but when I understood, I answered from such vantage as my own wholly outside Swedenborgianism gave me, that I thought most of the most respectable people with us were of the Presbyterian Church; some were certainly Episcopalians, but upon the whole the largest number were Presbyterians. He found that very strange indeed; and said

45

that he did not believe there was a Presbyterian Church in Boston; that the New England Calvinists were all of the Orthodox Church. He had to explain Oxthodoxy to me, and then I could confess to one Congregational Church in Columbus.

Probably I failed to give the Autocrat any very clear image of our social frame in the West, but the fault was altogether mine, if I did. Such lecturing tours as he had made had not taken him among us, as those of Emerson and other New-Englanders had, and my report was positive rather than comparative. I was full of pride in journalism at that day, and I dare say that I vaunted the brilliancy and power of our newspapers more than they merited; I should not have been likely to wrong them otherwise. It is strange that in all the talk I had with him and Lowell, or rather heard from them, I can recall nothing said of political affairs, though Lincoln had then been nominated by the Republicans, and the Civil War had practically begun. But we did not imagine such a thing in the North; we rested secure in the belief that if Lincoln were elected the South would eat all its fiery words, perhaps from the mere love and inveterate habit of fire-eating.

I rent myself away from the Autocrat's presence as early as I could, and as my evening had been too full of happiness to sleep upon at once, I spent the rest of the night till two in the morning wandering about the streets and in the Common with a Harvard Senior whom I had met. He was a youth of like literary passions with myself, but of such different traditions in every possible way that his deeply schooled and definitely regulated life seemed as anomalous to me as my own desultory and self-found way must have seemed to him. We passed the time in the delight of trying to make ourselves known to each other, and in a promise to continue by letter the effort, which duly lapsed into silent patience with the necessarily insoluble problem.

XIII

I must have lingered in Boston for the introduction to Hawthorne which Lowell had offered me, for when it came, with a little note of kindness and counsel for myself such as only Lowell had the gift of writing, it was already so near Sunday that I stayed over till Monday before I started. I do not recall what I did with the time, except keep myself from making it a burden to the people I knew, and wandering about the city alone. Nothing of it remains to me except the fortune that favored me that Sunday night with a view of the old Granary Burying-ground on Tremont Street. I found the gates open, and I explored every path in the place, wreaking myself in such meagre emotion as I could get from the tomb of the Franklin family, and rejoicing with the whole soul of my Western modernity in the evidence of a remote antiquity which so many of the dim inscriptions afforded. I do not think that I have ever known anything practically older than these monuments, though I have since supped so full of classic and mediæval ruin. I am sure that I was more deeply touched by the epitaph of a poor little Puritan maiden who died at sixteen in the early sixteen-thirties than afterwards by the tomb of Cæcilia Metella, and that the heartache which I tried to put into verse when I got back to my room in the hotel was none the less genuine because it would not lend itself to my literary purpose, and remains nothing but pathos to this day.

I am not able to say how I reached the town of Lowell, where I went before going to Concord, that

I might ease the unhappy conscience I had about those factories which I hated so much to see, and have it clean for the pleasure of meeting the fabricator of visions whom I was authorized to molest in any air-castle where I might find him. I only know that I went to Lowell, and visited one of the great mills, which with their whirring spools, the ceaseless flight of their shuttles, and the bewildering sight and sound of all their mechanism have since seemed to me the death of the joy that ought to come from work, if not the captivity of those who tended them. But then I thought it right and well for me to be standing by,

"With sick and scornful looks averse,"

while these others toiled; I did not see the tragedy in it, and I got my pitiful literary antipathy away as soon as I could, no wiser for the sight of the ingenious contrivances I inspected, and I am sorry to say no sadder. In the cool of the evening I sat at the door of my hotel, and watched the long files of the work-worn factory-girls stream by, with no concern for them but to see which was pretty and which was plain, and with no dream of a truer order than that which gave them ten hours' work a day in those hideous mills and lodged them in the barracks where they rested from their toil.

XIV

I wonder if there is a stage that still runs between Lowell and Concord, past meadow walls, and under the caressing boughs of way-side elms, and through the bird-haunted gloom of woodland roads, in the freshness of the summer morning? By a blessed chance I found that there was such a stage in 1860, and I took it from my hotel, instead of going back to

Boston and up to Concord as I must have had to do by train. The journey gave me the intimacy of the New England country as I could have had it in no other fashion, and for the first time I saw it in all the summer sweetness which I have often steeped my soul in since. The meadows were newly mown, and the air was fragrant with the grass, stretching in long winrows among the brown bowlders, or capped with canvas in the little haycocks it had been gathered into the day before. I was fresh from the affluent farms of the Western Reserve, and this care of the grass touched me with a rude pity, which I also bestowed on the meagre fields of corn and wheat; but still the land was lovelier than any I had ever seen, with its old farmhouses, and brambled gray stone walls, its stony hillsides, its staggering orchards, its wooded tops, and its thick-brackened valleys. From West to East the difference was as great as I afterwards found it from America to Europe, and my impression of something quaint and strange was no keener when I saw Old England the next year than when I saw New England now. I had imagined the landscape bare of trees, and I was astonished to find it almost as full of them as at home, though they all looked very little, as they well might to eyes used to the primeval forests of Ohio. The road ran through them from time to time, and took their coolness on its smooth hard reaches, and then issued again in the glisten of the open fields.

I made phrases to myself about the scenery as we drove along; and yes, I suppose I made phrases about the young girl who was one of the inside passengers, and who, when the common strangeness had somewhat worn off, began to sing, and sang most of the way to Concord. Perhaps she was not very sage, and I am sure she was not of the caste of Vere de Vere, but she

was pretty enough, and she had a voice of a birdlike
tunableness, so that I would not have her out of the
memory of that pleasant journey if I could. She was
long ago an elderly woman, if she lives, and I suppose
she would not now point out her fellow-passenger if
he strolled in the evening by the house where she had
dismounted, upon her arrival in Concord, and laugh
and pull another girl away from the window, in the
high excitement of the prodigious adventure.

XV

Her fellow-passenger was in far other excitement;
he was to see Hawthorne, and in a manner to meet Pris-
cilla and Zenobia, and Hester Prynne and little Pearl,
and Miriam and Hilda, and Hollingsworth and Cover-
dale, and Chillingworth and Dimmesdale, and Dona-
tello and Kenyon; and he had no heart for any such
poor little reality as that, who could not have been
got into any story that one could respect, and must
have been difficult even in a Heinesque poem.

I wasted that whole evening and the next morning
in fond delaying, and it was not until after the indifferent dinner I got at the tavern where I stopped, that
I found courage to go and present Lowell's letter to
Hawthorne. I would almost have foregone meeting
the weird genius only to have kept that letter, for it
said certain infinitely precious things of me with such
a sweetness, such a grace as Lowell alone could give
his praise. Years afterwards, when Hawthorne was
dead, I met Mrs. Hawthorne, and told her of the pang
I had in parting with it, and she sent it me, doubly enriched by Hawthorne's keeping. But now if I were
to see him at all I must give up my letter, and I carried
it in my hand to the door of the cottage he called The

Wayside. It was never otherwise than a very modest place, but the modesty was greater then than to-day, and there was already some preliminary carpentry at one end of the cottage, which I saw was to result in an addition to it. I recall pleasant fields across the road before it; behind rose a hill wooded with low pines, such as is made in *Septimius Felton* the scene of the involuntary duel between Septimius and the young British officer. I have a sense of the woods coming quite down to the house, but if this was so I do not know what to do with a grassy slope which seems to have stretched part way up the hill. As I approached, I looked for the tower which the author was fabled to climb into at sight of the coming guest, and pull the ladder up after him; and I wondered whether he would fly before me in that sort, or imagine some easier means of escaping me.

The door was opened to my ring by a tall handsome boy whom I suppose to have been Mr. Julian Hawthorne; and the next moment I found myself in the presence of the romancer, who entered from some room beyond. He advanced carrying his head with a heavy forward droop, and with a pace for which I decided that the word would be *pondering*. It was the pace of a bulky man of fifty, and his head was that beautiful head we all know from the many pictures of it. But Hawthorne's *look* was different from that of any picture of him that I have seen. It was sombre and brooding, as the look of such a poet should have been; it was the look of a man who had dealt faithfully and therefore sorrowfully with that problem of evil which forever attracted, forever evaded Hawthorne. It was by no means troubled; it was full of a dark repose. Others who knew him better and saw him oftener were familiar with other aspects, and I remember that one night at Longfellow's table, when one of the guests happened to speak of the photograph of Hawthorne which hung in a corner of the room, Lowell said, after a glance at it, " Yes, it's good; but it hasn't his fine *accipitral* look."

In the face that confronted me, however, there was nothing of keen alertness; but only a sort of quiet, patient intelligence, for which I seek the right word in vain. It was a very regular face, with beautiful eyes; the mustache, still entirely dark, was dense over the fine mouth. Hawthorne was dressed in black, and he had a certain effect which I remember, of seeming to have on a black cravat with no visible collar. He was such a man that if I had ignorantly met him anywhere I should have instantly felt him to be a personage.

I must have given him the letter myself, for I have no recollection of parting with it before, but I only remember his offering me his hand, and making me shyly and tentatively welcome. After a few moments of the demoralization which followed his hospitable attempts in me, he asked if I would not like to go up on his hill with him and sit there, where he smoked in the afternoon. He offered me a cigar, and when I said that I did not smoke, he lighted it for himself, and we climbed the hill together. At the top, where there was an outlook in the pines over the Concord meadows, we found a log, and he invited me to a place on it beside him, and at intervals of a minute or so he talked while he smoked. Heaven preserved me from the folly of trying to tell him how much his books had been to me, and though we got on rapidly at no time, I think we got on better for this interposition. He asked me about Lowell, I dare say, for I told him of my joy in meeting him and Doctor Holmes, and this

seemed greatly to interest him. Perhaps because
he was so lately from Europe, where our great men
are always seen through the wrong end of the telescope, he appeared surprised at my devotion, and asked me whether I cared as much for meeting them as
I should care for meeting the famous English authors.
I professed that I cared much more, though whether
this was true, I now have my doubts, and I think Hawthorne doubted it at the time. But he said nothing
in comment, and went on to speak generally of Europe
and America. He was curious about the West, which
he seemed to fancy much more purely American, and
said he would like to see some part of the country on
which the shadow (or, if I must be precise, the damned
shadow) of Europe had not fallen. I told him I
thought the West must finally be characterized by the
Germans, whom we had in great numbers, and, purely
from my zeal for German poetry, I tried to allege some
proofs of their present influence, though I could think
of none outside of politics, which I thought they affected wholesomely. I knew Hawthorne was a Democrat, and I felt it well to touch politics lightly, but
he had no more to say about the fateful election then
pending than Holmes or Lowell had.

With the abrupt transition of his talk throughout,
he began somehow to speak of women, and said he
had never seen a woman whom he thought quite beautiful. In the same way he spoke of the New England
temperament, and suggested that the apparent coldness
in it was also real, and that the suppression of emotion
for generations would extinguish it at last. Then he
questioned me as to my knowledge of Concord, and
whether I had seen any of the notable people. I answered that I had met no one but himself, as yet, but
I very much wished to see Emerson and Thoreau. I

did not think it needful to say that I wished to see
Thoreau quite as much because he had suffered in the
cause of John Brown as because he had written the
books which had taken me; and when he said that
Thoreau prided himself on coming nearer the heart
of a pine-tree than any other human being, I could say
honestly enough that I would rather come near the
heart of a man. This visibly pleased him, and I saw
that it did not displease him, when he asked whether I
was not going to see his next neighbor Mr. Alcott,
and I confessed that I had never heard of him. That
surprised as well as pleased him; he remarked, with
whatever intention, that there was nothing like recognition to make a man modest; and he entered into some
account of the philosopher, whom I suppose I need not
be much ashamed of not knowing then, since his influence was of the immediate sort that makes a man
important to his townsmen while he is still strange
to his countrymen.

Hawthorne descanted a little upon the landscape,
and said certain of the pleasant fields below us belonged to him; but he preferred his hill-top, and if he
could have his way those arable fields should be grown
up to pines too. He smoked fitfully, and slowly, and
in the hour that we spent together, his whiffs were of
the desultory and unfinal character of his words.
When we went down, he asked me into his house again,
and would have me stay to tea, for which we found
the table laid. But there was a great deal of silence in
it all, and at times, in spite of his shadowy kindness, I
felt my spirits sink. After tea, he showed me a book-
case, where there were a few books toppling about on
the half-filled shelves, and said, coldly, " This is my
library." I knew that men were his books, and though
I myself cared for books so much, I found it fit and

54

LARCH WALK, WAYSIDE

Trees planted by Hawthorne between Alcott's House and Wayside

fine that he should care so little, or seem to care so little. Some of his own romances were among the volumes on these shelves, and when I put my finger on the *Blithedale Romance* and said that I preferred that to the others, his face lighted up, and he said that he believed the Germans liked that best too.

Upon the whole we parted such good friends that when I offered to take leave he asked me how long I was to be in Concord, and not only bade me come to see him again, but said he would give me a card to Emerson, if I liked. I answered, of course, that I should like it beyond all things; and he wrote on the back of his card something which I found, when I got away, to be, " I find this young man worthy." The quaintness, the little stiffness of it, if one pleases to call it so, was amusing to one who was not without his sense of humor, but the kindness filled me to the throat with joy. In fact, I entirely liked Hawthorne. He had been as cordial as so shy a man could show himself; and I perceived, with the repose that nothing else can give, the entire sincerity of his soul.

Nothing could have been further from the behavior of this very great man than any sort of posing, apparently, or a wish to affect me with a sense of his greatness. I saw that he was as much abashed by our encounter as I was; he was visibly shy to the point of discomfort, but in no ignoble sense was he conscious, and as nearly as he could with one so much his younger he made an absolute equality between us. My memory of him is without alloy one of the finest pleasures of my life. In my heart I paid him the same glad homage that I paid Lowell and Holmes, and he did nothing to make me think that I had overpaid him. This seems perhaps very little to say in his praise, but to my mind it is saying everything, for I have known but few great men, especially of those I met in early life, when I wished to lavish my admiration upon them, whom I have not the impression of having left in my debt. Then, a defect of the Puritan quality, which I have found in many New-Englanders, is that, wittingly or unwittingly, they propose themselves to you as an example, or if not quite this, that they surround themselves with a subtle ether of potential disapprobation, in which, at the first sign of unworthiness in you, they helplessly suffer you to gasp and perish; they have good hearts, and they would probably come to your succor out of humanity, if they knew how, but they do not know how. Hawthorne had nothing of this about him; he was no more tacitly than he was explicitly didactic. I thought him as thoroughly in keeping with his romances as Doctor Holmes had seemed with his essays and poems, and I met him as I had met the Autocrat in the upreme hour of his fame. He had just given the world the last of those incomparable works which it was to have finished from his hand; the *Marble Faun* had worthily followed, at a somewhat longer interval than usual, the *Blithedale Romance,* and the *House of Seven Gables,* and the *Scarlet Letter,* and had perhaps carried his name higher than all the rest, and certainly farther. Everybody was reading it, and more or less bewailing its indefinite close, but yielding him that full honor and praise which a writer can hope for but once in his life. Nobody dreamed that thereafter only precious fragments, sketches more or less faltering, though all with the divine touch in them, were further to enrich a legacy which in its kind is the finest the race has received from any mind. As I have said, we are always finding new Hawthorne's, but the illusion soon wears away, and then we perceive that they were not Hawthornes at all; that he had some peculiar difference from them, which, by-

56

NATHANIEL HAWTHORNE

and-by, we shall no doubt consent must be his difference from all men evermore.

I am painfully aware that I have not summoned before the reader the image of the man as it has always stood in my memory, and I feel a sort of shame for my failure. He was so altogether simple that it seems as if it would be easy to do so; but perhaps a spirit from the other world would be simple too, and yet would no more stand at parle, or consent to be sketched, than Hawthorne. In fact, he was always more or less merging into the shadow, which was in a few years wholly to close over him; there was nothing uncanny in his presence, there was nothing even unwilling, but he had that apparitional quality of some great minds which kept Shakespeare largely unknown to those who thought themselves his intimates, and has at last left him a sort of doubt. There was nothing teasing or wilfully elusive in Hawthorne's impalpability, such as I afterwards felt in Thoreau; if he was not there to your touch, it was no fault of his; it was because your touch was dull, and wanted the use of contact with such natures. The hand passes through the veridical phantom without a sense of its presence, but the phantom is none the less veridical for all that.

XVI

I kept the evening of the day I met Hawthorne wholly for the thoughts of him, or rather for that reverberation which continues in the young sensibilities after some important encounter. It must have been the next morning that I went to find Thoreau, and I am dimly aware of making one or two failures to find him, if I ever really found him at all.

He is an author who has fallen into that abeyance, awaiting all authors, great or small, at some time or another; but I think that with him, at least in regard to his most important book, it can be only transitory. I have not read the story of his hermitage beside Walden Pond since the year 1858, but I have a fancy that if I should take it up now, I should think it a wiser and truer conception of the world than I thought it then. It is no solution of the problem; men are not going to answer the riddle of the painful earth by building themselves shanties and living upon beans and watching ant-fights; but I do not believe Tolstoy himself has more clearly shown the hollowness, the hopelessness, the unworthiness of the life of the world than Thoreau did in that book. If it were newly written it could not fail of a far vaster acceptance than it had then, when to those who thought and felt seriously it seemed that if slavery could only be controlled, all things else would come right of themselves with us. Slavery has not only been controlled, but it has been destroyed, and yet things have not begun to come right with us; but it was in the order of Providence that chattel slavery should cease before industrial slavery, and the infinitely crueler and stupider vanity and luxury bred of it, should be attacked. If there was then any prevision of the struggle now at hand, the seers averted their eyes, and strove only to cope with the less evil. Thoreau himself, who had so clear a vision of the falsity and folly of society as we still have it, threw himself into the tide that was already, in Kansas and Virginia, reddened with war; he aided and abetted the John Brown raid, I do not recall how much or in what sort; and he had suffered in prison for his opinions and actions. It was this inevitable heroism of his that, more than his literature even, made me wish to see him and revere him; and I do not believe that I should have

58

HENRY DAVID THOREAU

found the veneration difficult, when at last I met him in his insufficient person, if he had otherwise been present to my glowing expectation. He came into the room a quaint, stump figure of a man, whose effect of long trunk and short limbs was heightened by his fashionless trousers being let down too low. He had a noble face, with tossed hair, a distraught eye, and a fine aquilinity of profile, which made me think at once of Don Quixote and of Cervantes; but his nose failed to add that foot to his stature which Lamb says a nose of that shape will always give a man. He tried to place me geographically after he had given me a chair not quite so far off as Ohio, though still across the whole room, for he sat against one wall, and I against the other; but apparently he failed to pull himself out of his revery by the effort, for he remained in a dreamy muse, which all my attempts to say something fit about John Brown and Walden Pond seemed only to deepen upon him. I have not the least doubt that I was needless and valueless about both, and that what I said could not well have prompted an important response; but I did my poor best, and I was terribly disappointed in the result. The truth is that in those days I was a helplessly concrete young person, and all forms of the abstract, the air-drawn, afflicted me like physical discomforts. I do not remember that Thoreau spoke of his books or of himself at all, and when he began to speak of John Brown, it was not the warm, palpable, loving, fearful old man of my conception, but a sort of John Brown type, a John Brown ideal, a John Brown principle, which we were somehow (with long pauses between the vague, orphic phrases) to cherish, and to nourish ourselves upon.

It was not merely a defeat of my hopes, it was a rout, and I felt myself so scattered over the field of thought

59

that I could hardly bring my forces together for retreat. I must have made some effort, vain and foolish enough, to rematerialize my old demigod, but when I came away it was with the feeling that there was very little more left of John Brown than there was of me. His body was not mouldering in the grave, neither was his soul marching on; his ideal, his type, his principle alone existed, and I did not know what to do with it. I am not blaming Thoreau; his words were addressed to a far other understanding than mine, and it was my misfortune if I could not profit by them. I think, or I venture to hope, that I could profit better by them now; but in this record I am trying honestly to report their effect with the sort of youth I was then.

XVII

Such as I was, I rather wonder that I had the courage, after this experiment of Thoreau, to present the card Hawthorne had given me to Emerson. I must have gone to him at once, however, for I cannot make out any interval of time between my visit to the disciple and my visit to the master. I think it was Emerson himself who opened his door to me, for I have a vision of the fine old man standing tall on his threshold, with the card in his hand, and looking from it to me with a vague serenity, while I waited a moment on the door-step below him. He must then have been about sixty, but I remember nothing of age in his aspect, though I have called him an old man. His hair, I am sure, was still entirely dark, and his face had a kind of marble youthfulness, chiselled to a delicate intelligence by the highest and noblest thinking that any man has done. There was a strange charm in Emerson's eyes, which I felt then and

RALPH WALDO EMERSON

always, something like that I saw in Lincoln's, but shyer, but sweeter and less sad. His smile was the very sweetest I have ever beheld, and the contour of the mask and the line of the profile were in keeping with this incomparable sweetness of the mouth, at once grave and quaint, though quaint is not quite the word for it either, but subtly, not unkindly arch, which again is not the word.

It was his great fortune to have been mostly misunderstood, and to have reached the dense intelligence of his fellow-men after a whole lifetime of perfectly simple and lucid appeal, and his countenance expressed the patience and forbearance of a wise man content to bide his time. It would be hard to persuade people now that Emerson once represented to the popular mind all that was most hopelessly impossible, and that in a certain sort he was a national joke, the type of the incomprehensible, the byword of the poor paragrapher. He had perhaps disabused the community somewhat by presenting himself here and there as a lecturer, and talking face to face with men in terms which they could not refuse to find as clear as they were wise; he was more and more read, by certain persons, here and there; but we are still so far behind him in the reach of his far-thinking that it need not be matter of wonder that twenty years before his death he was the most misunderstood man in America. Yet in that twilight where he dwelt he loomed large upon the imagination; the minds that could not conceive him were still aware of his greatness. I myself had not read much of him, but I knew the essays he was printing in the *Atlantic,* and I knew certain of his poems, though by no means many; yet I had this sense of him, that he was somehow, beyond and above my ken, a presence of force and beauty and wisdom, uncompanioned in our literature. He had lately stooped from his ethereal heights to take part in the battle of humanity, and I suppose that if the truth were told he was more to my young fervor because he had said that John Brown had made the gallows glorious like the cross, than because he had uttered all those truer and wiser things which will still a hundred years hence be leading the thought of the world.

I do not know in just what sort he made me welcome, but I am aware of sitting with him in his study or library, and of his presently speaking of Hawthorne, whom I probably celebrated as I best could, and whom he praised for his personal excellence, and for his fine qualities as a neighbor. " But his last book," he added, reflectively, " is a mere mush," and I perceived that this great man was no better equipped to judge an artistic fiction than the groundlings who were then crying out upon the indefinite close of the *Marble Faun*. Apparently he had read it, as they had, for the story, but it seems to me now, if it did not seem to me then, that as far as the problem of evil was involved, the book must leave it where it found it. That is forever insoluble, and it was rather with that than with his more or less shadowy people that the romancer was concerned. Emerson had, in fact, a defective sense as to specific pieces of literature; he praised extravagantly, and in the wrong place, especially among the new things, and he failed to see the worth of much that was fine and precious beside the line of his fancy.

He began to ask me about the West, and about some unknown man in Michigan, who had been sending him poems, and whom he seemed to think very promising, though he has not apparently kept his word to do great things. I did not find what Emerson had to say of my section very accurate or important, though it was kindly enough, and just enough as to what the West ought to

EMERSON'S HOUSE AT CONCORD

do in literature. He thought it a pity that a literary periodical which had lately been started in Cincinnati should be appealing to the East for contributions, instead of relying upon the writers nearer home; and he listened with what patience he could to my modest opinion that we had not the writers nearer home. I never was of those Westerners who believed that the West was kept out of literature by the jealousy of the East, and I tried to explain why we had not the men to write that magazine full in Ohio. He alleged the man in Michigan as one who alone could do much to fill it worthily, and again I had to say that I had never heard of him.

I felt rather guilty in my ignorance, and I had a notion that it did not commend me, but happily at this moment Mr. Emerson was called to dinner, and he asked me to come with him. After dinner we walked about in his " pleached garden " a little, and then we came again into his library, where I meant to linger only till I could fitly get away. He questioned me about what I had seen of Concord, and whom besides Hawthorne I had met, and when I told him only Thoreau, he asked me if I knew the poems of Mr. William Henry Channing. I have known them since, and felt their quality, which I have gladly owned a genuine and original poetry; but I answered then truly that I knew them only from Poe's criticisms: cruel and spiteful things which I should be ashamed of enjoying as I once did.

" Whose criticisms ?" asked Emerson.

" Poe's," I said again.

" Oh," he cried out, after a moment, as if he had returned from a far search for my meaning, " *you mean the jingle-man!*"

I do not know why this should have put me to such confusion, but if I had written the criticisms myself I do not think I could have been more abashed. Perhaps I felt an edge of reproof, of admonition, in a characterization of Poe which the world will hardly agree with; though I do not agree with the world about him, myself, in its admiration. At any rate, it made an end of me for the time, and I remained as if already absent, while Emerson questioned me as to what I had written in the *Atlantic Monthly*. He had evidently read none of my contributions, for he looked at them, in the bound volume of the magazine which he got down, with the effect of being wholly strange to them, and then gravely affixed my initials to each. He followed me to the door, still speaking of poetry, and as he took a kindly enough leave of me, he said one might very well give a pleasant hour to it now and then.

A pleasant hour to poetry! I was meaning to give all time and all eternity to poetry, and I should by no means have wished to find pleasure in it; I should have thought that a proof of inferior quality in the work; I should have preferred anxiety, anguish even, to pleasure. But if Emerson thought from the glance he gave my verses that I had better not lavish myself upon that kind of thing, unless there was a great deal more of me than I could have made apparent in our meeting, no doubt he was right. I was only too painfully aware of my shortcoming, but I felt that it was shorter-coming than it need have been. I had somehow not prospered in my visit to Emerson as I had with Hawthorne, and I came away wondering in what sort I had gone wrong. I was not a forth-putting youth, and I could not blame myself for anything in my approaches that merited withholding; indeed, I made no approaches; but as I must needs blame myself for something, I fell upon the fact that in my confused retreat from Emerson's presence I had failed in a certain slight point of ceremony,

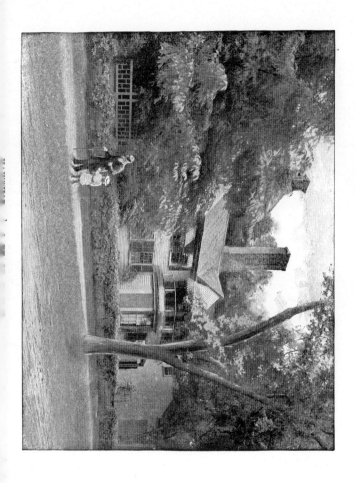

and I magnified this into an offence of capital importance. I went home to my hotel, and passed the afternoon in pure misery. I had moments of wild question when I debated whether it would be better to go back and own my error, or whether it would be better to write him a note, and try to set myself right in that way. But in the end I did neither, and I have since survived my mortal shame some forty years or more. But at the time it did not seem possible that I should live through the day with it, and I thought that I ought at least to go and confess it to Hawthorne, and let him disown the wretch who had so poorly repaid the kindness of his introduction by such misbehavior. I did indeed walk down by the Wayside, in the cool of the evening, and there I saw Hawthorne for the last time. He was sitting on one of the timbers beside his cottage, and smoking with an air of friendly calm. I had got on very well with him, and I longed to go in, and tell him how ill I had got on with Emerson; I believed that though he cast me off, he would understand me, and would perhaps see some hope for me in another world, though there could be none in this.

But I had not the courage to speak of the affair to any one but Fields, to whom I unpacked my heart when I got back to Boston, and he asked me about my adventures in Concord. By this time I could see it in a humorous light, and I did not much mind his lying back in his chair and laughing and laughing, till I thought he would roll out of it. He perfectly conceived the situation, and got an amusement from it that I could get only through sympathy with him. But I thought it a favorable moment to propose myself as the assistant editor of the *Atlantic Monthly*, which I had the belief I could very well become, with advantage to myself if not to the magazine. He seemed to think so too; he said that if the place had not just been filled, I should certainly have had it; and it was to his recollection of this prompt ambition of mine that I suppose I may have owed my succession to a like vacancy some four years later. He was charmingly kind; he entered with the sweetest interest into the story of my economic life, which had been full of changes and chances already. But when I said very seriously that now I was tired of these fortuities, and would like to be settled in something, he asked, with dancing eyes,

"Why, how old are you?"

"I am twenty-three," I answered, and then the laughing fit took him again.

"Well," he said, "you begin young, out there!"

In my heart I did not think that twenty-three was so very young, but perhaps it was; and if any one were to say that I had been portraying here a youth whose aims were certainly beyond his achievements, who was morbidly sensitive, and if not conceited was intolerably conscious, who had met with incredible kindness, and had suffered no more than was good for him, though he might not have merited his pain any more than his joy, I do not know that I should gainsay him, for I am not at all sure that I was not just that kind of youth when I paid my first visit to New England.

Part Second

FIRST IMPRESSIONS OF LITERARY NEW YORK

IT was by boat that I arrived from Boston, on an August morning of 1860, which was probably of the same quality as an August morning of 1900. I used not to mind the weather much in those days; it was hot or it was cold, it was wet or it was dry, but it was not my affair; and I suppose that I sweltered about the strange city, with no sense of anything very personal in the temperature, until nightfall. What I remember is being high up in a hotel long since laid low, listening in the summer dark, after the long day was done, to the Niagara roar of the omnibuses whose tide then swept Broadway from curb to curb, for all the miles of its length. At that hour the other city noises were stilled, or lost in this vaster volume of sound, which seemed to fill the whole night. It had a solemnity which the modern comer to New York will hardly imagine, for that tide of omnibuses has long since ebbed away, and has left the air to the strident discords of the elevated trains and the irregular alarum of the grip-car gongs, which blend to no such harmonious thunder as rose from the procession of those ponderous and innumerable vans. There was a sort of inner quiet in the sound, and when I chose I slept off to it, and woke to it in the morning refreshed and strengthened to explore the literary situation in the metropolis.

I

Not that I think I left this to the second day. Very probably I lost no time in going to the office of the *Saturday Press,* as soon as I had my breakfast after arriving, and I have a dim impression of anticipating the earliest of the Bohemians, whose gay theory of life obliged them to a good many hardships in lying down early in the morning, and rising up late in the day. If it was the office-boy who bore me company during the first hour of my visit, by-and-by the editors and contributors actually began to come in. I would not be very specific about them if I could, for since that Bohemia has faded from the map of the republic of letters, it has grown more and more difficult to trace its citizenship to any certain writer. There are some living who knew the Bohemians and even loved them, but there are increasingly few who were of them, even in the fond retrospect of youthful follies and errors. It was in fact but a sickly colony, transplanted from the mother asphalt of Paris, and never really striking root in the pavements of New York; it was a colony of ideas, of theories, which had perhaps never had any deep root anywhere. What these ideas, these theories, were in art and in life, it would not be very easy to say; but in the *Saturday Press* they came to violent expression, not to say explosion, against all existing forms of respectability. If respectability was your *bête noire,* then you were a Bohemian; and if you were in the habit of rendering yourself in prose, then you necessarily shredded your prose into very fine paragraphs of a sentence each, or of a very few words, or even of one word. I believe this fashion prevailed till very lately with some of the dramatic critics, who

CHARLES F. BROWNE ("ARTEMUS WARD")

thought that it gave a quality of epigram to the style; and I suppose it was borrowed from the more spasmodic moments of Victor Hugo by the editor of the *Press*. He brought it back with him when he came home from one of those sojourns in Paris which possess one of the French accent rather than the French language; I long desired to write in that fashion myself, but I had not the courage.

This editor was a man of such open and avowed cynicism that he may have been, for all I know, a kindly optimist at heart; some say, however, that he had really talked himself into being what he seemed. I only know that his talk, the first day I saw him, was of such a sort that if he was half as bad, he would have been too bad to be. He walked up and down his room saying what lurid things he would directly do if any one accused him of respectability, so that he might disabuse the minds of all witnesses. There were four or five of his assistants and contributors listening to the dreadful threats, which did not deceive even so great innocence as mine, but I do not know whether they found it the sorry farce that I did. They probably felt the fascination for him which I could not disown, in spite of my inner disgust; and were watchful at the same time for the effect of his words with one who was confessedly fresh from Boston, and was full of delight in the people he had seen there. It appeared, with him, to be proof of the inferiority of Boston that if you passed down Washington Street, half a dozen men in the crowd would know you were Holmes, or Lowell, or Longfellow, or Wendell Phillips; but in Broadway no one would know who you were, or care to the measure of his smallest blasphemy. I have since heard this more than once urged as a signal advantage of New York for the æsthetic inhabitant, but I am not sure, yet, that it is so. The unrecognized celebrity probably has his mind quite as much upon himself as if some one pointed him out, and otherwise I cannot think that the sense of neighborhood is such a bad thing for the artist in any sort. It involves the sense of responsibility, which cannot be too constant or too keen. If it narrows, it deepens; and this may be the secret of Boston.

II

It would not be easy to say just why the Bohemian group represented New York literature to my imagination, for I certainly associated other names with its best work, but perhaps it was because I had written for the *Saturday Press* myself, and had my pride in it, and perhaps it was because that paper really embodied the new literary life of the city. It was clever, and full of the wit that tries its teeth upon everything. It attacked all literary shams but its own, and it made itself felt and feared. The young writers throughout the country were ambitious to be seen in it, and they gave their best to it; they gave literally, for the *Saturday Press* never paid in anything but hopes of paying, vaguer even than promises. It is not too much to say that it was very nearly as well for one to be accepted by the *Press* as to be accepted by the *Atlantic,* and for the time there was no other literary comparison. To be in it was to be in the company of Fitz James O'Brien, Fitzhugh Ludlow, Mr. Aldrich, Mr. Stedman, and whoever else was liveliest in prose or loveliest in verse at that day in New York. It was a power, and although it is true that, as Henry Giles said of it, " Man cannot live by snapping-turtle alone," the *Press* was very good snapping-turtle. Or, it seemed so then; I should be almost afraid to test it now, for I do not

EDMUND CLARENCE STEDMAN

like snapping-turtle so much as I once did, and I have grown nicer in my taste, and want my snapping-turtle of the very best. What is certain is that I went to the office of the *Saturday Press* in New York with much the same sort of feeling I had in going to the office of the *Atlantic Monthly* in Boston, but I came away with a very different feeling. I had found there a bitterness against Boston as great as the bitterness against respectability, and as Boston was then rapidly becoming my second country, I could not join in the scorn thought of her and said of her by the Bohemians. I fancied a conspiracy among them to shock the literary pilgrim, and to minify the precious emotions he had experienced in visiting other shrines; but I found no harm in that, for I knew just how much to be shocked, and I thought I knew better how to value certain things of the soul than they. Yet when their chief asked me how I got on with Hawthorne, and I began to say that he was very shy and I was rather shy, and the king of Bohemia took his pipe out to break in upon me with "Oh, a couple of shysters!" and the rest laughed, I was abashed all they could have wished, and was not restored to myself till one of them said that the thought of Boston made him as ugly as sin; then I began to hope again that men who took themselves so seriously as that need not be taken very seriously by me.

In fact I had heard things almost as desperately cynical in other newspaper offices before that, and I could not see what was so distinctively Bohemian in these *anime prave,* these souls so baleful by their own showing. But apparently Bohemia was not a state that you could well imagine from one encounter, and since my stay in New York was to be very short, I lost no time in acquainting myself further with it. That

very night I went to the beer-cellar, once very far
up Broadway, where I was given to know that the bohemian nights were smoked and quaffed away. It was
said, so far West as Ohio, that the queen of Bohemia
sometimes came to Pfaff's: a young girl of a sprightly
gift in letters, whose name or pseudonym had made
itself pretty well known at that day, and whose fate,
pathetic at all times, out-tragedies almost any other in
the history of letters. She was seized with hydrophobia
from the bite of her dog, on a railroad train; and made
a long journey home in the paroxysms of that agoniz-
ing disease, which ended in her death after she reached
New York. But this was after her reign had ended,
and no such black shadow was cast forward upon
Pfaff's, whose name often figured in the verse and the
epigrammatically paragraphed prose of the *Saturday
Press*. I felt that as a contributor and at least a bre-
vet Bohemian I ought not to go home without visiting
the famous place, and witnessing if I could not share
the revels of my comrades. As I neither drank beer
nor smoked, my part in the carousal was limited to a
German pancake, which I found they had very good
at Pfaff's, and to listening to the whirling words of
my commensals, at the long board spread for the bohemians in a cavernous space under the pavement.
There were writers for the *Saturday Press* and for
Vanity Fair (a hopefully comic paper of that day),
and some of the artists who drew for the illustrated
periodicals. Nothing of their talk remains with me,
but the impression remains that it was not so good talk
as I had heard in Boston. At one moment of the orgy,
which went but slowly for an orgy, we were joined by
some belated bohemians whom the others made a great
clamor over; I was given to understand they were just
recovered from a fearful debauch; their locks were

still damp from the wet towels used to restore them, and their eyes were very frenzied. I was presented to these types, who neither said nor did anything worthy of their awful appearance, but dropped into seats at the table, and ate of the supper with an appetite that seemed poor. I stayed hoping vainly for worse things till eleven o'clock, and then I rose and took my leave of a literary condition that had distinctly disappointed me. I do not say that it may not have been wickeder and wittier than I found it; I only report what I saw and heard in Bohemia on my first visit to New York, and I know that my acquaintance with it was not exhaustive. When I came the next year the *Saturday Press* was no more, and the editor and his contributors had no longer a common centre. The best of the young fellows whom I met there confessed, in a pleasant exchange of letters which we had afterwards, that he thought the pose a vain and unprofitable one; and when the *Press* was revived, after the war, it was without any of the old Bohemian characteristics except that of not paying for material. It could not last long upon these terms, and again it passed away, and still waits its second palingenesis.

The editor passed away too, not long after, and the thing that he had inspired altogether ceased to be. He was a man of a certain sardonic power, and used it rather fiercely and freely, with a joy probably more apparent than real in the pain it gave. In my last knowledge of him he was much milder than when I first knew him, and I have the feeling that he too came to own before he died that man cannot live by snapping-turtle alone. He was kind to some neglected talents, and befriended them with a vigor and a zeal which he would have been the last to let you call generous. The chief of these was Walt Whitman, who, when the

Saturday Press took it up, had as hopeless a cause with the critics on either side of the ocean as any man could have. It was not till long afterwards that his English admirers began to discover him, and to make his countrymen some noisy reproaches for ignoring him; they were wholly in the dark concerning him when the *Saturday Press,* which first stood his friend, and the young men whom the *Press* gathered about it, made him their cult. No doubt he was more valued because he was so offensive in some ways than he would have been if he had been in no way offensive, but it remains a fact that they celebrated him quite as much as was good for them. He was often at Pfaff's with them, and the night of my visit he was the chief fact of my experience. I did not know he was there till I was on my way out, for he did not sit at the table under the pavement, but at the head of one farther into the room. There, as I passed, some friendly fellow stopped me and named me to him, and I remember how he leaned back in his chair, and reached out his great hand to me, as if he were going to give it me for good and all. He had a fine head, with a cloud of Jovian hair upon it, and a branching beard and mustache, and gentle eyes that looked most kindly into mine, and seemed to wish the liking which I instantly gave him, though we hardly passed a word, and our acquaintance was summed up in that glance and the grasp of his mighty fist upon my hand. I doubt if he had any notion who or what I was beyond the fact that I was a young poet of some sort, but he may possibly have remembered seeing my name printed after some very Heinesque verses in the *Press.* I did not meet him again for twenty years, and then I had only a moment with him when he was reading the proofs of his poems in Boston. Some years later I saw him for the last time,

THE MEETING WITH WHITMAN

one day after his lecture on Lincoln, in that city, when he came down from the platform to speak with some hand-shaking friends who gathered about him. Then and always he gave me the sense of a sweet and true soul, and I felt in him a spiritual dignity which I will not try to reconcile with his printing in the forefront of his book a passage from a private letter of Emerson's, though I believe he would not have seen such a thing as most other men would, or thought ill of it in another. The spiritual purity which I felt in him no less than the dignity is something that I will no more try to reconcile with what denies it in his page; but such things we may well leave to the adjustment of finer balances than we have at hand. I will make sure only of the greatest benignity in the presence of the man. The apostle of the rough, the uncouth, was the gentlest person; his barbaric yawp, translated into the terms of social encounter, was an address of singular quiet, delivered in a voice of winning and endearing friendliness.

As to his work itself, I suppose that I do not think it so valuable in effect as in intention. He was a liberating force, a very "imperial anarch" in literature; but liberty is never anything but a means, and what Whitman achieved was a means and not an end, in what must be called his verse. I like his prose, if there is a difference, much better; there he is of a genial and comforting quality, very rich and cordial, such as I felt him to be when I met him in person. His verse seems to me not poetry, but the materials of poetry, like one's emotions; yet I would not misprize it, and I am glad to own that I have had moments of great pleasure in it. Some French critic quoted in the *Saturday Press* (I cannot think of his name) said the best thing of him when he said that he made you a partner of the enterprise, for that is precisely what he does, and that is what alienates and what endears in him, as you like or dislike the partnership. It is still something neighborly, brotherly, fatherly, and so I felt him to be when the benign old man looked on me and spoke to me.

III

That night at Pfaff's must have been the last of the Bohemians for me, and it was the last of New York authorship too, for the time. I do not know why I should not have imagined trying to see Curtis, whom I knew so much by heart, and whom I adored, but I may not have had the courage, or I may have heard that he was out of town; Bryant, I believe, was then out of the country; but at any rate I did not attempt him either. The bohemians were the beginning and the end of the story for me, and to tell the truth I did not like the story. I remember that as I sat at that table under the pavement, in Pfaff's beer-cellar, and listened to the wit that did not seem very funny, I thought of the dinner with Lowell, the breakfast with Fields, the supper at the Autocrat's, and felt that I had fallen very far. In fact it can do no harm at this distance of time to confess that it seemed to me then, and for a good while afterwards, that a person who had seen the men and had the things said before him that I had in Boston, could not keep himself too carefully in cotton; and this was what I did all the following winter, though of course it was a secret between me and me. I dare say it was not the worst thing I could have done, in some respects.

My sojourn in New York could not have been very long, and the rest of it was mainly given to viewing the monuments of the city from the windows of omnibuses

WILLIAM ALLEN BUTLER

and the platforms of horse-cars. The world was so simple then that there were perhaps only a half-dozen cities that had horse-cars in them, and I travelled in those conveyances at New York with an unfaded zest, even after my journeys back and forth between Boston and Cambridge. I have not the least notion where I went or what I saw, but I suppose that it was up and down the ugly east and west avenues, then lying open to the eye in all the hideousness now partly concealed by the elevated roads, and that I found them very stately and handsome. Indeed, New York was really handsomer then than it is now, when it has so many more pieces of beautiful architecture, for at that day the sky-scrapers were not yet, and there was a fine regularity in the streets that these brute bulks have robbed of all shapeliness. Dirt and squalor there were a plenty, but there was infinitely more comfort. The long succession of cross streets was yet mostly secure from business, after you passed Clinton Place; commerce was just beginning to show itself in Union Square, and Madison Square was still the home of the McFlimsies, whose kin and kind dwelt unmolested in the brownstone stretches of Fifth Avenue. I tried hard to imagine them from the acquaintance Mr. Butler's poem had given me, and from the knowledge the gentle satire of *The Potiphar Papers* had spread broadcast through a community shocked by the excesses of our best society; it was not half so bad then as the best now, probably. But I do not think I made very much of it, perhaps because most of the people who ought to have been in those fine mansions were away at the sea-side and the mountains.

The mountains I had seen on my way down from Canada, but the sea-side not, and it would never do to go home without visiting some famous summer resort.

77

I must have fixed upon Long Branch because I must have heard of it as then the most fashionable; and one afternoon I took the boat for that place. By this means I not only saw sea-bathing for the first time, but I saw a storm at sea: a squall struck us so suddenly that it blew away all the camp-stools of the forward prome-nade; it was very exciting, and I long meant to use in literature the black wall of cloud that settled on the water before us like a sort of portable midnight; I now throw it away upon the reader, as it were; it never would come in anywhere. I stayed all night at Long Branch, and I had a bath the next morning before break-fast: an extremely cold one, with a life-line to keep me against the undertow. In this rite I had the com-pany of a young New-Yorker, whom I had met on the boat coming down, and was of the light, hopeful, adventurous business type which seems peculiar to the city, and which has always attracted me. He told me much about his life, and how he lived, and what it cost him to live. He had a large room at a fashionable boarding-house, and he paid fourteen dollars a week. In Columbus I had such a room at such a house, and paid three and a half, and I thought it a good deal. But those were the days before the war, when America was the cheapest country in the world, and the West was incredibly inexpensive.

After a day of lonely splendor at this scene of fashion and gayety, I went back to New York, and took the boat for Albany on my way home. I noted that I had no longer the vivid interest in nature and human nature which I had felt in setting out upon my travels, and I said to myself that this was from having a mind so crowded with experiences and impressions that it could receive no more; and I really suppose that if the hap-piest phrase had offered itself to me at some moments, I should scarcely have looked about me for a landscape or a figure to fit it to. I was very glad to get back to my dear little city in the West (I found it seething in an August sun that was hot enough to have calcined the limestone State House), and to all the friends I was so fond of.

IV

I did what I could to prove myself unworthy of them by refusing their invitations, and giving myself wholly to literature, during the early part of the winter that followed; and I did not realize my error till the invitations ceased to come, and I found myself in an unbroken intellectual solitude. The worst of it was that an ungrateful Muse did little in return for the sacrifices I made her, and the things I now wrote were not liked by the editors I sent them to. The editorial taste is not always the test of merit, but it is the only one we have, and I am not saying the editors were wrong in my case. There were then such a very few places where you could market your work: the *Atlantic* in Boston and *Harper's* in New York were the magazines that paid, though the *Independent* newspaper bought literary material; the *Saturday Press* printed it without buying, and so did the old *Knickerbocker Magazine*, though there was pecuniary good-will in both these cases. I toiled much that winter over a story I had long been writing, and at last sent it to the *Atlantic,* which had published five poems for me the year before. After some weeks, or it may have been months, I got it back with a note saying that the editors had the less regret in returning it because they saw that in the May number of the *Knickerbocker* the first chapter of the story had appeared. Then I remembered that, years before, I had sent this chapter to that magazine, as a sketch to be printed by itself, and afterwards had continued the story from it. I had never heard of its acceptance, and supposed of course that it was rejected; but on my second visit to New York I called at the *Knickerbocker* office, and a new editor, of those that the magazine was always having in the days of its failing fortunes, told me that he had found my sketch in rummaging about in a barrel of his predecessors' manuscripts, and had liked it, and printed it. He said that there were fifteen dollars coming to me for that sketch, and might he send the money to me? I said that he might, though I do not see, to this day, why he did not give it me on the spot; and he made a very small minute in a very large sheet of paper (really like Dick Swiveller), and promised I should have it that night; but I sailed the next day for Liverpool without it. I sailed without the money for some verses that *Vanity Fair* bought of me, but I hardly expected that, for the editor, who was then Artemus Ward, had frankly told me in taking my address that ducats were few at that moment with *Vanity Fair*.

I was then on my way to be consul at Venice, where I spent the next four years in a vigilance for Confederate privateers which none of them ever surprised. I had asked for the consulate at Munich, where I hoped to steep myself yet longer in German poetry, but when my appointment came, I found it was for Rome. I was very glad to get Rome even; but the income of the office was in fees, and I thought I had better go on to Washington and find out how much the fees amounted to. People in Columbus who had been abroad said that on five hundred dollars you could live in Rome like a prince, but I doubted this; and when I learned at the State Department that the fees of the Roman consulate came to only three hundred, I perceived that I could not live better than a baron, probably, and I despaired. The kindly chief of the consular bureau said that the President's secretaries, Mr. John Nicolay and Mr. John Hay, were interested in my appointment, and he advised my going over to the White House and seeing them. I lost no time in doing that, and I learned that as young Western men they were interested in me because I was a young Western man who had done something in literature, and they were willing to help me for that reason, and for no other that I ever knew. They proposed my going to Venice; the salary was then seven hundred and fifty, but they thought they could get it put up to a thousand. In the end they got it put up to fifteen hundred, and so I went to Venice, where if I did not live like a prince on that income, I lived a good deal more like a prince than I could have done at Rome on a fifth of it.

If the appointment was not present fortune, it was the beginning of the best luck I have had in the world, and I am glad to owe it all to those friends of my verse, who could have been no otherwise friends of me. They were then beginning very early careers of distinction which have not been wholly divided. Mr. Nicolay could have been about twenty-five, and Mr. Hay nineteen or twenty. No one dreamed as yet of the opportunity opening to them in being so constantly near the man whose life they have written, and with whose fame they have imperishably interwrought their names. I remember the sobered dignity of the one, and the humorous gayety of the other, and how we had some young men's joking and laughing together, in the anteroom where they received me, with the great soul entering upon its travail beyond the closed door. They asked me if I had ever seen the President, and I said that I had seen him at Columbus, the year before; but I could not say how much I should like to see him again, and thank

F

him for the favor which I had no claim to at his hands, except such as the slight campaign biography I had written could be thought to have given me. That day or another, as I left my friends, I met him in the corridor without, and he looked at the space I was part of with his ineffably melancholy eyes, without knowing that I was the indistinguishable person in whose "integrity and abilities he had reposed such special confidence " as to have appointed him consul for Venice and the ports of the Lombardo-Venetian Kingdom, though he might have recognized the terms of my commission if I had reminded him of them. I faltered a moment in my longing to address him, and then I decided that every one who forebore to speak needlessly to him, or to shake his hand, did him a kindness; and I wish I could be as sure of the wisdom of all my past behavior as I am of that piece of it. He walked up to the water-cooler that stood in the corner, and drew himself a full goblet from it, which he poured down his throat with a backward tilt of his head, and then went wearily within doors. The whole affair, so simple, has always remained one of a certain pathos in my memory, and I would rather have seen Lincoln in that unconscious moment than on some statelier occasion.

V

I went home to Ohio, and sent on the bond I was to file in the Treasury Department; but it was mislaid there, and to prevent another chance of that kind I carried on the duplicate myself. It was on my second visit that I met the generous young Irishman William D. O'Connor, at the house of my friend Piatt, and heard his ardent talk. He was one of the promising men of that day, and he had written an anti-slavery novel in

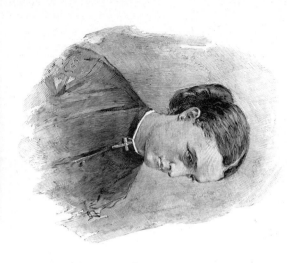

the heroic mood of Victor Hugo, which greatly took my fancy; and I believe he wrote poems too. He had not yet risen to be the chief of Walt Whitman's champions outside of the *Saturday Press,* but he had already espoused the theory of Bacon's authorship of Shakespeare, then newly exploited by the poor lady of Bacon's name, who died constant to it in an insane asylum. He used to speak of the reputed dramatist as " the fat peasant of Stratford," and he was otherwise picturesque of speech in a measure that consoled, if it did not convince. The great war was then full upon us, and when in the silences of our literary talk its awful breath was heard, and its shadow fell upon the hearth where we gathered round the first fires of autumn, O'Connor would lift his beautiful head with a fine effect of prophecy, and say, " Friends, I feel a sense of victory in the air." He was not wrong; only the victory was for the other side.

Who beside O'Connor shared in these saddened symposiums I cannot tell now; but probably other young journalists and office-holders, intending littérateurs, since more or less extinct. I make certain only of the young Boston publisher who issued a very handsome edition of *Leaves of Grass,* and then failed promptly if not consequently. But I had already met, in my first sojourn at the capital, a young journalist who had given hostages to poetry, and whom I was very glad to see and proud to know. · Mr. Stedman and I were talking over that meeting the other day, and I can be surer than I might have been without his memory, that I found him at a friend's house, where he was nursing himself for some slight sickness, and that I sat by his bed while our souls launched together into the joyful realms of hope and praise. In him I found the quality of Boston, the honor and passion of literature, and not a mere

pose of the literary life; and the world knows without
my telling how true he has been to his ideal of it.
His earthly mission then was to write letters from
Washington for the New York *World,* which started in
life as a good young evening paper, with a decided religious tone, so that the *Saturday Press* could call it the
Night-blooming Serious. I think Mr. Stedman wrote
for its editorial page at times, and his relation to it as a
Washington correspondent had an authority which is
wanting to the function in these days of perfected tele-
graphing. He had not yet achieved that seat in the
Stock Exchange whose possession has justified his re-
course to business, and has helped him to mean something more single in literature than many more singly
devoted to it. I used sometimes to speak about that
with another eager young author in certain middle
years when we were chafing in editorial harness, and we
always decided that Stedman had the best of it in being
able to earn his living in a sort so alien to literature
that he could come to it unjaded, and with a gust un-
spoiled by kindred savors. But no man shapes his own
life, and I dare say that Stedman may have been all the
time envying us our tripods from his high place in the
Stock Exchange. What is certain is that he has come
to stand for literature and to embody New York in it
as no one else does. In a community which seems never
to have had a conscious relation to letters, he has kept
the faith with dignity and fought the fight with constant
courage. Scholar and poet at once, he has spoken to
his generation with authority which we can forget only
in the charm which makes us forget everything else.

But his fame was still before him when we met,
and I could bring to him an admiration for work
which had not yet made itself known to so many, but
any admirer was welcome. We talked of what we had

MRS. R. H. STODDARD

done, and each said how much he liked certain things of the other's; I even seized my advantage of his help-lessness to read him a poem of mine which I had in my pocket; he advised me where to place it; and if the reader will not think it an unfair digression, I will tell here what became of that poem, for I think its varied fortunes were amusing, and I hope my own sufferings and final triumph with it will not be without encourage-ment to the young literary endeavorer. It was a poem called, with no prophetic sense of fitness, "Forlorn," and I tried it first with the *Atlantic Monthly*, which would not have it. Then I offered it in person to a former editor of this Magazine, but he could not see his ad-vantage in it, and I carried it overseas to Venice with me. From that point I sent it to all the English maga-zines as steadily as the post could carry it away and bring it back. On my way home, four years later, I took it to London with me, where a friend who knew Lewes, then just beginning with the *Fortnightly Re-view*, sent it to him for me. It was promptly returned, with a letter wholly reserved as to its quality, but full of a poetic gratitude for my wish to contribute to the *Fortnightly*. Then I heard that a certain Mr. Lucas was about to start a magazine, and I offered the poem to him. The kindest letter of acceptance followed me to America, and I counted upon fame and fortune as usual, when the news of Mr. Lucas's death came. I will not poorly joke an effect from my poem in the fact; but the fact remains. By this time I was a writer in the office of the *Nation* newspaper, and after I left this place to be Mr. Fields's assistant on the *Atlantic,* I sent my poem to the *Nation,* where it was printed at last. In such scant measure as my verses have pleased it has found rather unusual favor, and I need not say that its misfortunes endeared it to its author.

But all this is rather far away from my first meeting with Stedman in Washington. Of course I liked him, and I thought him very handsome and fine, with a full beard cut in the fashion he has always worn it, and with poet's eyes lighting an aquiline profile. Afterwards, when I saw him afoot, I found him of a worldly splendor in dress, and envied him, as much as I could envy him anything, the New York tailor whose art had clothed him: I had a New York tailor too, but with a difference. He had a worldly dash along with his supermundane gifts, which took me almost as much, and all the more because I could see that he valued himself nothing upon it. He was all for literature, and for literary men as the superiors of every one. I must have opened my heart to him a good deal, for when I told him how the newspaper I had written for from Canada and New England had ceased to print my letters, he said, " Think of a man like —— sitting in judgment on a man like *you!*" I thought of it, and was avenged if not comforted; and at any rate I liked Stedman's standing up so stiffly for the honor of a craft that is rather too limp in some of its votaries.

I suppose it was he who introduced me to the Stoddards, whom I met in New York just before I sailed, and who were then in the glow of their early fame as poets. They knew about my poor beginnings, and they were very, very good to me. Stoddard went with me to Franklin Square, and gave the sanction of his presence to the ineffectual offer of my poem there. But what I relished most was the long talks I had with them both about authorship in all its phases, and the exchange of delight in this poem and that, this novel and that, with gay, wilful runs away to make some wholly irrelevant joke, or fire puns into the air at no mark whatever. Stoddard had then a fame, with the sweet-

R. H. STODDARD

ness of personal affection in it, from the lyrics and the odes that will perhaps best keep him known, and Mrs. Stoddard was beginning to make her distinct and special quality felt in the magazines, in verse and fiction. In both it seems to me that she has failed of the recognition which her work merits. Her tales and novels have in them a foretaste of realism, which was too strange for the palate of their day, and is now too familiar, perhaps. It is a peculiar fate, and would form the scheme of a pretty study in the history of literature. But in whatever she did she left the stamp of a talent like no other, and of a personality disdainful of literary environment. In a time when most of us had to write like Tennyson, or Longfellow, or Browning, she never would write like any one but herself.

I remember very well the lodging over a corner of Fourth Avenue and some downtown street where I visited these winning and gifted people, and tasted the pleasure of their racy talk, and the hospitality of their good-will toward all literature, which certainly did not leave me out. We sat before their grate in the chill of the last October days, and they set each other on to one wild flight of wit after another, and again I bathed my delighted spirit in the atmosphere of a realm where for the time at least no

> " — rumor of oppression or defeat,
> Of unsuccessful or successful war,"

could penetrate. I liked the Stoddards because they were frankly not of that Bohemia which I disliked so much, and thought it of no promise or validity; and because I was fond of their poetry and found them in it. I liked the absolutely literary keeping of their lives. He had then, and for long after, a place in the Custom-house, but he was no more of that than Lamb was of

India House. He belonged to that better world where there is no interest but letters, and which was as much like heaven for me as anything I could think of.

The meetings with the Stoddards repeated themselves when I came back to sail from New York, early in November. Mixed up with the cordial pleasure of them in my memory is a sense of the cold and wet outdoors, and the misery of being in those infamous New York streets, then as for long afterwards the squalidest in the world. The last night I saw my friends they told me of the tragedy which had just happened at the camp in the City Hall Park. Fitz James O'Brien, the brilliant young Irishman who had dazzled us with his story of "The Diamond Lens," and frozen our blood with his ingenious tale of a ghost—"What was It?"—a ghost that could be felt and heard, but not seen—had enlisted for the war, and risen to be an officer with the swift process of the first days of it. In that camp he had just then shot and killed a man for some infraction of discipline, and it was uncertain what the end would be. He was acquitted, however, and it is known how he afterwards died of lockjaw from a wound received in battle.

VI

Before this last visit in New York there was a second visit to Boston, which I need not dwell upon, because it was chiefly a revival of the impressions of the first. Again I saw the Fieldses in their home; again the Autocrat in his, and Lowell now beneath his own roof, beside the study fire where I was so often to sit with him in coming years. At dinner (which we had at two o'clock) the talk turned upon my appointment, and he said of me to his wife: "Think of his having got Stillman's place! We ought to put poison in his wine," and he told me of the wish the painter had to go to Venice and follow up Ruskin's work there in a book of his own. But he would not let me feel very guilty, and I will not pretend that I had any personal regret for my good fortune.

The place was given me perhaps because I had not nearly so many other gifts as he who lost it, and who was at once artist, critic, journalist, traveller, and eminently each. I met him afterwards in Rome, which the powers bestowed upon him instead of Venice, and he forgave me, though I do not know whether he forgave the powers. We walked far and long over the Campagna, and I felt the charm of a most uncommon mind in talk which came out richest and fullest in the presence of the wild nature which he loved and knew so much better than most other men. I think that the book he would have written about Venice is forever to be regretted, and I do not at all console myself for its loss with the book I have written myself.

At Lowell's table that day they spoke of what sort of winter I should find in Venice, and he inclined to the belief that I should want a fire there. On his study hearth a very brisk one burned when we went back to it, and kept out the chill of a cold easterly storm. We looked through one of the windows at the rain, and he said he could remember standing and looking out of that window at such a storm when he was a child; for he was born in that house, and his life had kept coming back to it. He died in it, at last.

In a lifting of the rain he walked with me down to the village, as he always called the denser part of the town about Harvard Square, and saw me aboard a horse-car for Boston. Before we parted he gave me two charges: to open my mouth when I began to speak Italian, and to think well of women. He said that our race spoke its own tongue with its teeth shut, and so failed to master the languages that wanted freer utterance. As to women, he said there were unworthy ones, but a good woman was the best thing in the world, and a man was always the better for honoring women.

CASA FALIER, IN VENICE, WHERE MR. HOWELLS LIVED

Part Third

ROUNDABOUT TO BOSTON

DURING the four years of my life in Venice the literary intention was present with me at all times and in all places. I wrote many things in verse, which I sent to the magazines in every part of the English-speaking world, but they came unerringly back to me, except in three instances only, when they were kept by the editors who finally printed them. One of these pieces was published in the *Atlantic Monthly;* another in *Harper's Magazine;* the third was got into the New York *Ledger* through the kindness of Doctor Edward Everett Hale, who used I know not what mighty magic to that end. I had not yet met him; but he interested himself in my ballad as if it had been his own. His brother, Charles Hale, later Consul-General for Egypt, whom I saw almost every moment of the two visits he paid Venice in my time, had sent it to him, after copying it in his own large, fair hand, so that it could be read. He was not quite of that literary Boston which I so fondly remembered my glimpses of; he was rather of a journalistic and literary Boston which I had never known; but he was of Boston, after all. He had been in Lowell's classes at Harvard; he had often met Longfellow in Cambridge; he knew Doctor Holmes, of course; and he let me talk of my idols to my heart's content. I think he must have been amused by my raptures; most people would have been; but he was kind

91

and patient, and he listened to me with a sweet intelligence which I shall always gratefully remember. He died too young, with his life's possibilities mainly unfulfilled; but none who knew him could fail to imagine them, or to love him for what he was.

I

Besides those few pitiful successes, I had nothing but defeats in the sort of literature which I supposed was to be my calling, and the defeats threw me upon prose; for some sort of literary thing, if not one, then another, I must do if I lived; and I began to write those studies of Venetian life which afterwards became a book, and which I contributed as letters to the *Boston Advertiser,* after vainly offering them to more æsthetic periodicals. However, I do not imagine that it was a very smiling time for any literary endeavorer at home in the life-and-death civil war then waging. Some few young men arose who made themselves heard amid the din of arms even as far as Venice, but most of these were hushed long ago. I fancy Theodore Winthrop, who began to speak, as it were, from his soldier's grave, so soon did his death follow the earliest recognition by the public, and so many were his posthumous works, was chief of these; but there were others whom the present readers must make greater effort to remember. Forceythe Willson, who wrote *The Old Sergeant,* became known for the rare quality of his poetry; and now and then there came a poem from Aldrich, or Stedman, or Stoddard. The great new series of the *Biglow Papers* gathered volume with the force they had from the beginning. The Autocrat was often in the pages of the *Atlantic,* where one often found Whittier and Emerson, with many a fresh name

CHARLES HALE

THEODORE WINTHROP

now faded. In Washington the Piatts were writing some of the most beautiful verse of the war, and Brownell was sounding his battle lyrics like so many trumpet blasts. The fiction which followed the war was yet all to come. Whatever was done in any kind had some hint of the war in it, inevitably; though in the very heart of it Longfellow was setting about his great version of Dante peacefully, prayerfully, as he has told in the noble sonnets which register the mood of his undertaking.

At Venice, if I was beyond the range of literary recognition I was in direct relations with one of our greatest literary men, who was again of that literary Boston which mainly represented American literature to me. The official chief of the consul at Venice was the United States Minister at Vienna, and in my time this minister was John Lothrop Motley, the historian. He was removed, later, by that Johnson administration which followed Lincoln's so forgottenly that I name it with a sense of something almost prehistoric. Among its worst errors was the attempted discredit of a man who had given lustre to our name by his work, and who was an ardent patriot as well as accomplished scholar. He visited Venice during my first year, which was the darkest period of the civil war, and I remember with what instant security, not to say severity, he rebuked my scarcely whispered misgivings of the end, when I ventured to ask him what he thought it would be. Austria had never recognized the Secessionists as belligerents, and in the complications with France and England there was little for our minister but to share the home indignation at the sympathy of those powers with the South. In Motley this was heightened by that feeling of astonishment, of wounded faith, which all Americans with English friendships experienced in those days, and which he, whose English friendships were many, experienced in peculiar degree.

I drifted about with him in his gondola, and refreshed myself, long a-hungered for such talk, with his talk of literary life in London. Through some acquaintance I had made in Venice I was able to be of use to him in getting documents copied for him in the Venetian Archives, especially the Relations of the Venetian Ambassadors at different courts during the period and events he was studying. All such papers passed through my hands in transmission to the historian, though now I do not quite know why they need have done so; but perhaps he was willing to give me the pleasure of being a partner, however humble, in the enterprise. My recollection of him is of courtesy to a far younger man unqualified by patronage, and of a presence of singular dignity and grace. He was one of the handsomest men I ever saw, with beautiful eyes, a fine blond beard of modish cut, and a sensitive nose, straight and fine. He was altogether a figure of worldly splendor; and I had reason to know that he did not let the credit of our nation suffer at the most aristocratic court in Europe for want of a fit diplomatic costume, when some of our ministers were trying to make their office do its full effect upon all occasions in "the dress of an American gentleman." The morning after his arrival Mr. Motley came to me with a handful of newspapers which, according to the Austrian custom at that day, had been opened in the Venetian post-office. He wished me to protest against this on his behalf as an infringement of his diplomatic extra-territoriality, and I proposed to go at once to the director of the post: I had myself suffered in the same way, and though I knew that a mere consul was help-

JOHN LOTHROP MOTLEY

less, I was willing to see the double-headed eagle trodden under foot by a Minister Plenipotentiary. Mr. Motley said that he would go with me, and we put off in his gondola to the post-office. The director received us with the utmost deference. He admitted the irregularity which the minister complained of, and declared that he had no choice but to open every foreign newspaper, to whomsoever addressed. He suggested, however, that if the minister made his appeal to the Lieutenant-Governor of Venice, Count Toggenburg would no doubt instantly order the exemption of his newspapers from the general rule.

Mr. Motley said he would give himself the pleasure of calling upon the Lieutenant-Governor, and " How fortunate," he added, when we were got back into the gondola, " that I should have happened to bring my court dress with me!" I did not see the encounter of the high contending powers, but I know that it ended in a complete victory for our minister.

I had no further active relations of an official kind with Mr. Motley, except in the case of a naturalized American citizen, whose property was slowly but surely wasting away in the keeping of the Venetian courts. An order had at last been given for the surrender of the remnant to the owner; but the Lombardo-Venetian authorities insisted that this should be done through the United States Minister at Vienna, and Mr. Motley held as firmly that it must be done through the United States Consul at Venice. I could only report to him from time to time the unyielding attitude of the Civil Tribunal, and at last he consented, as he wrote, " to act officiously, not officially, in the matter," and the hapless claimant got what was left of his estate.

I had a glimpse of the historian afterwards in Boston, but it was only for a moment, just before his ap-

pointment to England, where he was made to suffer for
Sumner in his quarrel with Grant. That injustice
crowned the injuries his country had done a most faithful patriot and high-spirited gentleman, whose fame as
a historian once filled the ear of the English-speaking
world. His books seemed to have been written in a
spirit already no longer modern; and I did not find the
greatest of them so moving as I expected when I came
to it with all the ardor of my admiration for the historian. William the Silent seemed to me, by his
worshipper's own showing, scarcely level with the
popular movement which he did not so much direct as
follow; but it is a good deal for a prince to be able even
to follow his people; and it cannot be said that Motley
does not fully recognize the greatness of the Dutch
people, though he may see the Prince of Orange too
large. The study of their character made at least a
theoretical democrat of a scholar whose instincts were
not perhaps democratic, and his sympathy with that
brave little republic between the dikes strengthened him
in his fealty to the great commonwealth between the
oceans. I believe that so far as he was of any political
tradition, he was of the old Boston Whig tradition;
but when I met him at Venice he was in the glow of a
generous pride in our war as a war against slavery.
He spoke of the negroes and their simple-hearted,
single-minded devotion to the Union cause in terms
that an original abolitionist might have used, at a time
when original abolitionists were not so many as they
have since become.

For the rest, I fancy it was very well for us to be
represented at Vienna in those days by an ideal democrat who was also a real swell, and who was not likely
to discredit us socially when we so much needed to be
well thought of in every way. At a court where the

RICHARD HILDRETH

By permission of William Rutter & Co.

family of Count Schmerling, the Prime Minister, could not be received for want of the requisite descents, it was well to have a minister who would not commit the mistake of inviting the First Society to meet the Second Society, as a former Envoy Extraordinary had done, with the effect of finding himself left entirely to the Second Society during the rest of his stay in Vienna.

II

One of my consular colleagues under Motley was another historian, of no such popularity, indeed, nor even of such success, but perhaps not of inferior powers. This was Richard Hildreth, at Trieste, the author of one of the sincerest if not the truest histories of the United States, according to the testimony both of his liking and his misliking critics. I have never read his history, and I speak of it only at second hand; but I had read, before I met him, his novel of *Archy Moore, or The White Slave,* which left an indelible impression of his imaginative verity upon me. The impression is still so deep that after the lapse of nearly forty years since I saw the book, I have no misgiving in speaking of it as a powerful piece of realism. It treated passionately, intensely, though with a superficial coldness, of wrongs now so remote from us in the abolition of slavery that it is useless to hope it will ever be generally read hereafter, but it can safely be praised to any one who wishes to study that bygone condition, and the literature which grew out of it. I fancy it did not lack recognition in its time, altogether, for I used to see it in Italian and French translations on the bookstalls. I believe neither his history nor his novel brought the author more gain than fame. He had worn himself out on a newspaper when he got his appointment at Trieste, and I saw him in the shadow of the cloud that was wholly to darken him before he died. He was a tall thin man, absent, silent: already a phantom of himself, but with a scholarly serenity and dignity amidst the ruin, when the worst came.

I first saw him at the pretty villa where he lived in the suburbs of Trieste, and where I passed several days, and I remember him always reading, reading, reading. He could with difficulty be roused from his book by some strenuous appeal from his family to his conscience as a host. The last night he sat with *Paradise Lost* in his hand, and nothing could win him from it till he had finished it. Then he rose to go to bed. Would not he bid his parting guest good-bye? The idea of farewell perhaps dimly penetrated to him. He responded without looking round,

> "They, hand in hand, with wandering steps and slow,
> Through Eden took their solitary way,"

and so left the room.

I had earlier had some dealings with him as a fellow-consul concerning a deserter from an American ship whom I inherited from my predecessor at Venice. The man had already been four or five months in prison, and he was in a fair way to end his life there; for it is our law that a deserting sailor must be kept in the consul's custody till some vessel of our flag arrives, when the consul can oblige the master to take the deserter and let him work his passage home. Such a vessel rarely came to Venice even in times of peace, and in times of war there was no hope of any. So I got leave of the consul at Trieste to transfer my captive to that port, where now and then an American ship did touch. The flag determines the nationality of the sailor, and this unhappy wretch was theoretically our fellow-citizen; but when he got to Trieste he made a clean breast of it to the consul. He confessed that when he shipped under our flag he was a deserter from a British regiment at Malta; and he begged piteously not to be sent home to America, where he had never been in his life, nor ever wished to be. He wished to be sent back to his regiment at Malta, and to whatever fate awaited him there. The case certainly had its embarrassments; but the American consul contrived to let our presumptive compatriot slip into the keeping of the British consul, who promptly shipped him to Malta. In view of the strained relations between England and America at that time this was a piece of masterly diplomacy.

Besides my old Ohio-time friend Moncure D. Conway, who paid us a visit, and in his immediate relations with literary Boston seemed to bring the mountain to Mahomet, I saw no one else more literary than Henry Ward Beecher. He was passing through Venice on his way to those efforts in England in behalf of the Union which had a certain great effect at the time; and in the tiny parlor of our apartment on the Grand Canal, I can still see him sitting athletic, almost pugilistic, of presence, with his strong face, but kind, framed in long hair that swept above his massive forehead, and fell to the level of his humorously smiling mouth. His eyes quaintly gleamed at the things we told him of our life in the strange place; but he only partly relaxed from his strenuous pose, and the hands that lay upon his knees were clinched. Afterwards, as he passed our balcony in a gondola, he lifted the brave red fez he was wearing (many people wore the fez for one caprice or another) and saluted our eagle and us: we were often on the balcony behind the shield to attest the authenticity of the American eagle.

99

III

Before I left Venice, however, there came a turn in my literary luck, and from the hand I could most have wished to reverse the adverse wheel of fortune. I had labored out with great pains a paper on recent Italian comedy, which I sent to Lowell, then with his friend Professor Norton jointly editor of the *North American Review;* and he took it and wrote me one of his loveliest letters about it, consoling me in an instant for all the defeat I had undergone, and making it sweet and worthy to have lived through that misery. It is one of the hard conditions of this state that while we can mostly make out to let people taste the last drop of bitterness and ill-will that is in us, our love and gratitude are only semi-articulate at the best, and usually altogether tongue-tied. As often as I tried afterwards to tell Lowell of the benediction, the salvation, his letter was to me, I failed. But perhaps he would not have understood, if I had spoken out all that was in me with the fulness I could have given a resentment. His message came after years of thwarted endeavor, and reinstated me in the belief that I could still do something in literature. To be sure, the letters in the *Advertiser* had begun to make their impression; among the first great pleasures they brought me was a recognition from my diplomatic chief at Vienna; but I valued my admission to the *North American* peculiarly because it was Lowell let me in, and because I felt that in his charge it must be the place of highest honor. He spoke of the pay for my article, in his letter, and asked me where he should send it, and I answered, to my father-in-law, who put it in his savings-bank, where he lived, in Brattleboro, Vermont. There it remained, and I for-

BRATTLE STREET, CAMBRIDGE

got all about it, so that when his affairs were settled some years later and I was notified that there was a sum to my credit in the bank, I said, with the confidence I have nearly always felt when wrong, that I had no money there. The proof of my error was sent me in a check, and then I bethought me of the pay for "Recent Italian Comedy."

It was not a day when I could really afford to forget money due me, but then it was not a great deal of money. The *Review* was as poor as it was proud, and I had two dollars a printed page for my paper. But this was more than I got from the *Advertiser,* which gave me five dollars a column for my letters, printed in a type so fine that the money, when translated from greenbacks into gold at a discount of 2.80, must have been about a dollar a thousand words. However, I was richly content with that, and would gladly have let them have the letters for nothing.

Before I left Venice I had made my sketches into a book, which I sent on to Messrs. Trübner & Co., in London. They had consented to look at it to oblige my friend Conway, who during his sojourn with us in Venice, before his settlement in London, had been forced to listen to some of it. They answered me in due time that they would publish an edition of a thousand, at half profits, if I could get some American house to take five hundred copies. When I stopped in London I had so little hope of being able to do this that I asked the Trübners if I might, without losing their offer, try to get some other London house to publish my book. They said Yes, almost joyously; and I began to take my manuscript about. At most places they would not look at me or it, and they nowhere consented to read it. The house promptest in refusing to consider it afterwards pirated one of my novels, and with

101

some expressions of good intention in that direction, never paid me anything for it; though I believe the English still think that this sort of behavior was peculiar to the American publisher in the old buccaneering times. I was glad to go back to the Trübners with my book, and on my way across the Atlantic I met a publisher who finally agreed to take those five hundred copies. This was Mr. M. M. Hurd, of Hurd & Houghton, a house then newly established in New York and Cambridge. We played ring-toss and shuffleboard together, and became of a friendship which lasts to this day. But it was not till some months later, when I saw him in New York, that he consented to publish my book. I remember how he said, with an air of vague misgiving, and an effect of trying to justify himself in an imprudence, that it was not a great matter anyway. I perceived that he had no faith in it, and to tell the truth I had not much myself. But the book had an instant success, and it has gone on from edition to edition ever since. There was just then the interest of a not wholly generous surprise at American things among the English. Our success in putting down the great Confederate rebellion had caught the fancy of our cousins, and I think it was to this mood of theirs that I owed largely the kindness they showed my book. There were long and cordial reviews in all the great London journals, which I used to carry about with me like love-letters; when I tried to show them to other people, I could not understand their coldness concerning them.

At Boston, where we landed on our return home, there was a moment when it seemed as if my small destiny might be linked at once with that of the city which later became my home. I ran into the office of the *Advertiser* to ask what had become of some sketches of Italian travel I had sent the paper, and the managing editor made me promise not to take a place anywhere before I had heard from him. I gladly promised, but I did not hear from him, and when I returned to Boston a fortnight later, I found that a fatal partner had refused to agree with him in engaging me upon the paper. They even gave me back half a dozen unprinted letters of mine, and I published them in the *Nation,* of New York, and afterwards in the book called *Italian Journeys*.

But after I had encountered fortune in this frowning disguise, I had a most joyful little visit with Lowell, which made me forget there was anything in the world but the delight and glory of sitting with him in his study at Elmwood and hearing him talk. It must have been my freshness from Italy which made him talk chiefly of his own happy days in the land which so sympathetically brevets all its lovers fellow-citizens. At any rate he would talk of hardly anything else, and he talked late into the night, and early into the morning. About two o'clock, when all the house was still, he lighted a candle, and went down into the cellar, and came back with certain bottles under his arms. I had not a very learned palate in those days (or in these, for that matter), but I knew enough of wine to understand that these bottles had been chosen upon that principle which Longfellow put in verse, and used to repeat with a humorous lifting of the eyebrows and hollowing of the voice:

> " If you have a friend to dine,
>   Give him your best wine;
>   If you have two,
>   The second-best will do."

As we sat in their mellow afterglow, Lowell spoke to me of my own life and prospects, wisely and truly, as he always spoke. He said that it was enough for a man who had stuff in him to be known to two or three people, for they would not suffer him to be forgotten, and it would rest with himself to get on. I told him that though I had not given up my place at Venice, I was not going back, if I could find anything to do at home, and I was now on my way to Ohio, where I should try my best to find something; at the worst, I could turn to my trade of printer. He did not think it need ever come to that; and he said that he believed I should have an advantage with readers, if not with editors, in hailing from the West; I should be more of a novelty. I knew very well that even in my own West I should not have this advantage unless I appeared there with an Eastern imprint, but I could not wish to urge my misgiving against his faith. Was I not already richly successful? What better thing personally could befall me, if I lived forever after on milk and honey, than to be sitting there with my hero, my master, and having him talk to me as if we were equal in deed and in fame?

The cat-bird called in the syringa thicket at his door, before we said the good-night which was good-morning, using the sweet Italian words, and bidding each other the *Dorma bene* which has the quality of a benediction. He held my hand, and looked into my eyes with the sunny kindness which never failed me, worthy or unworthy; and I went away to bed. But not to sleep; only to dream such dreams as fill the heart of youth when the recognition of its endeavor has come from the achievement it holds highest and best.

IV

I found nothing to do in Ohio; some places that I heard of proved impossible one way or another, in Columbus and Cleveland, and Cincinnati; there was always the fatal partner; and after three weeks I was again in the East. I came to New York, resolved to fight my way in, somewhere, and I did not rest a moment before I began the fight.

My notion was that which afterwards became Bartley Hubbard's. " Get a basis," said the softening cynic of the *Saturday Press,* when I advised with him, among other acquaintances. " Get a salaried place, something regular on some paper, and then you can easily make up the rest." But it was a month before I achieved this vantage, and then I got it in a quarter where I had not looked for it. I wrote editorials on European and literary topics for different papers, but mostly for the *Times,* and they paid me well and more than well; but I was nowhere offered a basis, though once I got so far towards it as to secure a personal interview with the editor-in-chief, who made me feel that I had seldom met so busy a man. He praised some work of mine that he had read in his paper, but I was never recalled to his presence; and now I think he judged rightly that I should not be a lastingly good journalist. My point of view was artistic; I wanted time to prepare my effects.

There was another and clearer prospect opened to me on a literary paper, then newly come to the light, but long since gone out in the dark. Here again my work was taken, and liked so much that I was offered the basis (at twenty dollars a week) that I desired; I was even assigned to a desk where I should write in the office; and the next morning I came joyfully down to

Spruce Street to occupy it. But I was met at the door by one of the editors, who said lightly, as if it were a trifling affair, " Well, we've concluded to *waive* the idea of an engagement," and once more my bright hopes of a basis dispersed themselves. I said, with what calm I could, that they must do what they thought best, and I went on skirmishing baselessly about for this and the other papers which had been buying my material.

I had begun printing in the *Nation* those letters about my Italian journeys left over from the Boston *Advertiser;* they had been liked in the office, and one day the editor astonished and delighted me by asking how I would fancy giving up outside work to come there and write only for the *Nation*. We averaged my gains from all sources at forty dollars a week, and I had my basis as unexpectedly as if I had dropped upon it from the skies.

This must have been some time in November, and the next three or four months were as happy a time for me as I have ever known. I kept on printing my Italian material in the *Nation;* I wrote criticisms for it (not very good criticisms, I think now), and I amused myself very much with the treatment of social phases and events in a department which grew up under my hand. My associations personally were of the most agreeable kind. I worked with joy, with ardor, and I liked so much to be there, in that place and in that company, that I hated to have each day come to an end.

I believed that my lines were cast in New York for good and all; and I renewed my relations with the literary friends I had made before going abroad. I often stopped, on my way up town, at an apartment the Stoddards had in Lafayette Place, or near it; I saw Stedman, and reasoned high, to my heart's content, of literary things with them and him.

"IT'S LINCOLN'S HAND"

With the winter Bayard Taylor came on from his home in Kennett and took an apartment in East Twelfth Street, and once a week Mrs. Taylor and he received all their friends there, with a simple and charming hospitality. There was another house which we much resorted to—the house of James Lorrimer Graham, afterwards Consul-General at Florence, where he died. I had made his acquaintance at Venice three years before, and I came in for my share of that love for literary men which all their perversities could not extinguish in him. It was a veritable passion, which I used to think he could not have felt so deeply if he had been a literary man himself. There were delightful dinners at his house, where the wit of the Stoddards shone, and Taylor beamed with joyous good-fellowship and overflowed with invention; and Huntington, long Paris correspondent of the *Tribune,* humorously tried to talk himself into the resolution of spending the rest of his life in his own country. There was one evening when C. P. Cranch, always of a most pensive presence and aspect, sang the most killingly comic songs; and there was another evening when, after we all went into the library, something tragical happened. Edwin Booth was of our number, a gentle, rather silent person in company, or with at least little social initiative, who, as his fate would, went up to the cast of a huge hand that lay upon one of the shelves. " Whose hand is this, Lorry ?" he asked our host, as he took it up and turned it over in both his own hands. Graham feigned not to hear, and Booth asked again, " Whose hand is this ?" Then there was nothing for Graham but to say, " It's Lincoln's hand," and the man for whom it meant such unspeakable things put it softly down without a word.

107

V

It was one of the disappointments of a time which was nearly all joy that I did not then meet a man who meant hardly less than Lowell himself for me. George William Curtis was during my first winter in New York away on one of the long lecturing rounds to which he gave so many of his winters, and I did not see him till seven years afterwards, at Mr. Norton's in Cambridge. He then characteristically spent most of the evening in discussing an obscure point in Browning's poem of *My Lost Duchess*. I have long forgotten what the point was, but not the charm of Curtis's personality, his fine presence, his benign politeness, his almost deferential tolerance of difference in opinion. Afterwards I saw him again and again in Boston and New York, but always with a sense of something elusive in his graciousness, for which something in me must have been to blame. Cold, he was not, even to the youth that in those days was apt to shiver in any but the higher temperatures, and yet I felt that I made no advance in his kindness towards anything like the friendship I knew in the Cambridge men. Perhaps I was so thoroughly attuned to their mood that I could not be put in unison with another; and perhaps in Curtis there was really not the material of much intimacy.

He had the potentiality of publicity in the sort of welcome he gave equally to all men; and if I asked more I was not reasonable. Yet he was never far from any man of good - will, and he was the intimate of multitudes whose several existence he never dreamt of. In this sort he had become my friend when he made his first great speech on the Kansas question in 1855,

which will seem as remote to the young men of this day as the Thermopylæ question to which he likened it. I was his admirer, his lover, his worshipper before that for the things he had done in literature, for the *Howadji* books, and for the lovely fantasies of *Prue and I,* and for the sound-hearted satire of the *Potiphar Papers,* and now suddenly I learnt that this brilliant and graceful talent, this travelled and accomplished gentleman, this star of society who had dazzled me with his splendor far off in my Western village obscurity, was a man with the heart to feel the wrongs of men so little friended then as to be denied all the rights of men. I do not remember any passage of the speech, or any word of it, but I remember the joy, the pride with which the soul of youth recognizes in the greatness it has honored the goodness it may love. Mere politicians might be pro-slavery or anti-slavery without touching me very much, but here was the citizen of a world far greater than theirs, a light of the universal republic of letters, who was willing and eager to stand or fall with the just cause, and that was all in all to me. His country was my country, and his kindred my kindred, and nothing could have kept me from following after him.

His whole life taught the lesson that the world is well lost whenever the world is wrong; but never, I think, did any life teach this so sweetly, so winningly. The wrong world itself might have been entreated by him to be right, for he was one of the few reformers who have not in some measure mixed their love of man with hate of men; his quarrel was with error, and not with the persons who were in it. He was so gently steadfast in his opinions that no one ever thought of him as a fanatic, though many who held his opinions were assailed as fanatics, and suffered the shame if they

109

did not win the palm of martyrdom. In early life he was a communist, and then when he came out of Brook Farm into the world which he was so well fitted to adorn, and which would so gladly have kept him all its own, he became an abolitionist in the very teeth of the world which abhorred abolitionists. He was a believer in the cause of women's rights, which has no picturesqueness, and which chiefly appeals to the sense of humor in the men who never dreamt of laughing at him. The man who was in the last degree amiable was to the last degree unyielding where conscience was concerned; the soul which was so tender had no weakness in it; his lenity was the divination of a finer justice. His honesty made all men trust him when they doubted his opinions; his good sense made them doubt their own opinions, when they had as little question of their own honesty.

I should not find it easy to speak of him as a man of letters only, for humanity was above the humanities with him, and we all know how he turned from the fairest career in literature to tread the thorny path of politics because he believed that duty led the way, and that good citizens were needed more than good romancers. No doubt they are, and yet it must always be a keen regret with the men of my generation who witnessed with such rapture the early proofs of his talent, that he could not have devoted it wholly to the beautiful, and let others look after the true. Now that I have said this I am half ashamed of it, for I know well enough that what he did was best; but if my regret is mean, I will let it remain, for it is faithful to the mood which many have been in concerning him.

There can be no dispute, I am sure, as to the value of some of the results he achieved in that other path. He did indeed create anew for us the type of good-citizenship, wellnigh effaced in a sordid and selfish time, and of an honest politician and a pure-minded journalist. He never really forsook literature, and the world of actual interests and experiences afforded him outlooks and perspectives, without which æsthetic endeavor is self-limited and purblind. He was a great man of letters, he was a great orator, he was a great political journalist, he was a great citizen, he was a great philanthropist. But that last word with its conventional application scarcely describes the brave and gentle friend of men that he was. He was one that helped others by all that he did, and said, and was, and the circle of his use was as wide as his fame. There are other great men, plenty of them, common great men, whom we know as names and powers, and whom we willingly let the ages have when they die, for, living or dead, they are alike remote from us. They have never been with us where we live; but this great man was the neighbor, the contemporary, and the friend of all who read him or heard him; and even in the swift forgetting of this electrical age the stamp of his personality will not be effaced from their minds or hearts.

VI

Of those evenings at the Taylors's in New York, I can recall best the one which was most significant for me, and even fatefully significant. Mr. and Mrs. Fields were there, from Boston, and I renewed all the pleasure of my earlier meetings with them. At the end Fields said, mockingly, " Don't despise Boston!" and I answered, as we shook hands, " Few are worthy to live in Boston. It was New-Year's eve, and that night it came on to snow so heavily that my horse-car could hardly plough its way up to Forty-seventh Street through the drifts. The next day and the next, I wrote at home, because it was so hard to get down town. The third day I reached the office and found a letter on my desk from Fields, asking how I should like to come to Boston and be his assistant on the *Atlantic Monthly*. I submitted the matter at once to my chief on the *Nation,* and with his frank good-will I talked it over with Mr. Osgood, of Ticknor & Fields, who was to see me further about it if I wished, when he came to New York; and then I went to Boston to see Mr. Fields concerning details. I was to sift all the manuscripts and correspond with contributors; I was to do the literary proof-reading of the magazine; and I was to write the four or five pages of book-notices, which were then printed at the end of the periodical in finer type; and I was to have forty dollars a week. I said that I was getting that already for less work, and then Mr. Fields offered me ten dollars more. Upon these terms we closed, and on the 1st of March, which was my twenty-ninth birthday, I went to Boston and began my work. I had not decided to accept the place without advising with Lowell; he counselled the step, and gave me some shrewd and useful suggestions. The whole affair was conducted by Fields with his unfailing tact and kindness, but it could not be kept from me that the qualification I had as practical printer for the work was most valued, if not the most valued, and that as proof-reader I was expected to make it avail on the side of economy. Somewhere in life's feast the course of humble-pie must always come in; and if I did not wholly relish this bit of it, I dare say it was good for me, and I digested it perfectly.

ENGLISH ELMS AT LOWELL'S GATE

Part Fourth

LITERARY BOSTON AS I KNEW IT

AMONG my fellow-passengers on the train from New York to Boston, when I went to begin my work there in 1866, as the assistant editor of the *Atlantic Monthly,* was the late Samuel Bowles, of the *Springfield Republican,* who created in a subordinate city a journal of metropolitan importance. I had met him in Venice several years earlier, when he was suffering from the cruel insomnia which had followed his overwork on that newspaper, and when he told me that he was sleeping scarcely more than one hour out of the twenty-four. His worn face attested the misery which this must have been, and which lasted in some measure while he lived, though I believe that rest and travel relieved him in his later years. He was always a man of cordial friendliness, and he now expressed a most gratifying interest when I told him what I was going to do in Boston. He gave himself the pleasure of descanting upon the dramatic quality, of the fact that a young newspaper man from Ohio was about to share in the destinies of the great literary periodical of New England.

I

I do not think that such a fact would now move the fancy of the liveliest newspaper man, so much has the

H   113

West since returned upon the East in a refluent wave
of authorship. But then the West was almost an unknown quality in our literary problem; and in fact
there was scarcely any literature outside of New England. Even this was of New England origin, for it
was almost wholly the work of New England men
and women in the " splendid exile " of New York.
The *Atlantic Monthly,* which was distinctively literary, was distinctively a New England magazine,
though from the first it had been characterized
by what was more national, what was more
universal, in the New England temperament. Its
chief contributors for nearly twenty years were
Longfellow, Lowell, Holmes, Whittier, Emerson, Doctor Hale, Colonel Higginson, Mrs. Stowe, Whipple,
Rose Terry Cooke, Mrs. Julia Ward Howe, Mrs. Prescott Spofford, Mrs. Phelps Ward, and other New England writers who still lived in New England, and
largely in the region of Boston. Occasionally there
came a poem from Bryant, at New York, from Mr.
Stedman, from Mr. Stoddard and Mrs. Stoddard, from
Mr. Aldrich, and from Bayard Taylor. But all these,
except the last, were not only of New England race,
but of New England birth. I think there was no contributor from the South but Mr. M. D. Conway, and as
yet the West scarcely counted, though four young poets
from Ohio, who were not immediately or remotely of
Puritan origin, had appeared in early numbers; Alice
Cary, living with her sister in New York, had written
now and then from the beginning. Mr. John Hay
solely represented Illinois by a single paper, and he
was of Rhode Island stock. It was after my settlement at Boston that Mark Twain, of Missouri, became
a figure of world-wide fame at Hartford; and longer
after, that Mr. Bret Harte made that progress East-

JULIA WARD HOWE

ward from California which was telegraphed almost from hour to hour, as if it were the progress of a prince. Miss Constance F. Woolson had not yet begun to write. Mr. James Whitcomb Riley, Mr. Maurice Thompson, Miss Edith Thomas, Octave Thanet, Mr. Charles Warren Stoddard, Mr. H. B. Fuller, Mrs. Catherwood, Mr. Hamlin Garland, all whom I name at random among other Western writers, were then as unknown as Mr. Cable, Miss Murfree, Mrs. Rives Chanler, Miss Grace King, Mr. Joel Chandler Harris, Mr. Thomas Nelson Page, in the South, which they by no means fully represent.

The editors of the *Atlantic* had been eager from the beginning to discover any outlying literature; but, as I have said, there was in those days very little good writing done beyond the borders of New England. If the case is now different, and the best known among living American writers are no longer New-Englanders, still I do not think the South and West have yet trimmed the balance; and though perhaps the new writers now more commonly appear in those quarters, I should not be so very sure that they are not still characterized by New England ideals and examples. On the other hand, I am very sure that in my early day we were characterized by them, and wished to be so; we even felt that we failed in so far as we expressed something native quite in our own way. The literary theories we accepted were New England theories, the criticism we valued was New England criticism, or, more strictly speaking, Boston theories, Boston criticism.

II

Of those more constant contributors to the *Atlantic* whom I have mentioned, it is of course known that

Longfellow and Lowell lived in Cambridge, Emerson at Concord, and Whittier at Amesbury. Colonel Higginson was still and for many years afterwards at Newport; Mrs. Stowe was then at Andover; Miss Prescott of Newburyport had become Mrs. Spofford, and was presently in Boston, where her husband was a member of the General Court; Mrs. Phelps Ward, as Miss Elizabeth Stuart Phelps, dwelt in her father's house at Andover. The chief of the Bostonians were Mrs. Julia Ward Howe, Doctor Holmes, and Doctor Hale. Yet Boston stood for the whole Massachusetts group, and Massachusetts, in the literary impulse, meant New England. I suppose we must all allow, whether we like to do so or not, that the impulse seems now to have pretty well spent itself. Certainly the city of Boston has distinctly waned in literature, though it has waxed in wealth and population. I do not think there are in Boston to-day even so many talents with a literary coloring in law, science, theology, and journalism as there were formerly; though I have no belief that the Boston talents are fewer or feebler than before. I arrived in Boston, however, when all talents had more or less a literary coloring, and when the greatest talents were literary. These expressed with ripened fulness a civilization conceived in faith and brought forth in good works; but that moment of maturity was the beginning of a decadence which could only show itself much later. New England has ceased to be a nation in itself, and it will perhaps never again have anything like a national literature; but that was something like a national literature; and it will probably be centuries yet before the life of the whole country, the American life as distinguished from the New England life, shall have anything so like a national literature. It will be long before our

116

HARRIET PRESCOTT SPOFFORD

larger life interprets itself in such imagination as Hawthorne's, such wisdom as Emerson's, such poetry as Longfellow's, such prophecy as 'Whittier's, such wit and grace as Holmes's, such humor and humanity as Lowell's.

The literature of those great men was, if I may suffer myself the figure, the Socinian graft of a Calvinist stock. Their faith, in its varied shades, was Unitarian, but their art was Puritan. So far as it was imperfect—and great and beautiful as it was, I think it had its imperfections—it was marred by the intense ethicism that pervaded the New England mind for two hundred years, and that still characterizes it. They or their fathers had broken away from orthodoxy in the great schism at the beginning of the century, but, as if their heterodoxy were conscience-stricken, they still helplessly pointed the moral in all they did; some pointed it more directly, some less directly; but they all pointed it. I should be far from blaming them for their ethical intention, though I think they felt their vocation as prophets too much for their good as poets. Sometimes they sacrificed the song to the sermon, though not always, nor nearly always. It was in poetry and in romance that they excelled; in the novel, so far as they attempted it, they failed. I say this with the names of all the Bostonian group, and those they influenced, in mind, and with a full sense of their greatness. It may be ungracious to say that they have left no heirs to their peculiar greatness; but it would be foolish to say that they left an estate where they had none to bequeath. One cannot take account of such a fantasy as Judd's *Margaret*. The only New-Englander who has attempted the novel on a scale proportioned to the work of the New-Englanders in philosophy, in poetry, in romance, is Mr. De Forest, who is of New

Haven, and not of Boston. I do not forget the fictions of Doctor Holmes, or the vivid inventions of Doctor Hale, but I do not call them novels; and I do not forget the exquisitely realistic art of Miss Jewett or Miss Wilkins, which is free from the ethicism of the great New England group, but which has hardly the novelists's scope. New England, in Hawthorne's work, achieved supremacy in romance; but the romance is always an allegory, and the novel is a picture in which the truth to life is suffered to do its unsermonized office for conduct; and New England yet lacks her novelist, because it was her instinct and her conscience in fiction to be true to an ideal of life rather than to life itself.

Even when we come to the exception that proves the rule, even to such a signal exception as *Uncle Tom's Cabin,* I think that what I say holds true. That is almost the greatest work of imagination that we have produced in prose, and it is the work of a New England woman, writing from all the inspirations and traditions of New England. It is like begging the question to say that I do not call it a novel, however; but really, is it a novel, in the sense that *War and Peace* is a novel, or *Madame Flaubert,* or *L'Assommoir,* or *Phineas Finn,* or *Doña Perfecta,* or *Esther Waters,* or *Marta y María,* or *The Return of the Native,* or *Virgin Soil,* or *David Grieve?* In a certain way it is greater than any of these except the first; but its chief virtue, or its prime virtue, is in its address to the conscience, and not its address to the taste; to the ethical sense, not the æsthetical sense.

This does not quite say the thing, but it suggests it, and I should be sorry if it conveyed to any reader a sense of slight; for I believe no one has felt more deeply than myself the value of New England in literature.

118

PARK STREET CHURCH, BOSTON

The comparison of the literary situation at Boston to the literary situation at Edinburgh in the times of the reviewers has never seemed to me accurate or adequate, and it holds chiefly in the fact that both seem to be of the past. Certainly New York is yet no London in literature, and I think Boston was once vastly more than Edinburgh ever was, at least in quality. The Scotch literature of the palmy days was not wholly Scotch, and even when it was rooted in Scotch soil it flowered in the air of an alien speech. But the New England literature of the great day was the blossom of a New England root; and the language which the Bostonians wrote was the native English of scholars fitly the heirs of those who had brought the learning of the universities to Massachusetts Bay two hundred years before, and was of as pure a lineage as the English of the mother-country.

III

The literary situation which confronted me when I came to Boston was, then, as native as could well be; and whatever value I may be able to give a personal study of it will be from the effect it made upon me as one strange in everything but sympathy. I will not pretend that I saw it in its entirety, and I have no hope of presenting anything like a kinetoscopic impression of it. What I can do is to give here and there a glimpse of it; and I shall wish the reader to keep in mind the fact that it was in a "state of transition," as everything is always and everywhere. It was no sooner recognizably native than it ceased to be fully so; and I became a witness of it after the change had begun. The publishing house which so long embodied New England literature was already attempting enterprises out of the line of its traditions, and one of these had brought

119

Mr. T. B. Aldrich from New York, a few weeks before I arrived upon the scene in that dramatic quality which I think never impressed any one but Mr. Bowles. Mr. Aldrich was the editor of *Every Saturday* when I came to be assistant editor of the *Atlantic Monthly*. We were of nearly the same age, but he had a distinct and distinguished priority of reputation, insomuch that in my Western remoteness I had always ranged him with such elders and betters of mine as Holmes and Lowell, and never imagined him the blond, slight youth I found him, with every imaginable charm of contemporaneity. It is no part of the office which I have intended for these slight and sufficiently wandering glimpses of the past to show any writer in his final place; and above all I do not presume to assign any living man his rank or station. But I should be false to my own grateful sense of beauty in the work of this poet if I did not at all times recognize his constancy to an ideal which his name stands for. He is known in several kinds, but to my thinking he is best in a certain nobler kind of poetry; a serious sort in which the thought holds him above the scrupulosities of the art he loves and honors so much. Sometimes the file slips in his hold, as the file must and will; it is but an instrument at the best; but there is no mistouch in the hand that lays itself upon the reader's heart with the pulse of the poet's heart quick and true in it. There are sonnets of his, grave, and simple, and lofty, which I think of with the glow and thrill possible only from very beautiful poetry, and which impart such an emotion as we can feel only

> "When a great thought strikes along the brain
> And flushes all the cheek."

When I had the fortune to meet him first, I suppose that in the employ of the kindly house we were both so

LOOKING OUT OF BOYLSTON PLACE

eager to serve, our dignities were about the same; for if the *Atlantic Monthly* was a somewhat prouder affair than an eclectic weekly like *Every Saturday,* he was supreme in his place, and I was subordinate in mine. The house was careful, in the attitude of its senior partner, not to distinguish between us, and we were not slow to perceive the tact used in managing us; we had our own joke of it; we compared notes to find whether we were equally used in this thing or that; and we promptly shared the fun of our discovery with Fields himself.

We had another impartial friend (no less a friend of joy in the life which seems to have been pretty nearly all joy, as I look back upon it) in the partner who became afterwards the head of the house, and who forecast in his bold enterprises the change from a New England to an American literary situation. In the end James R. Osgood failed, though all his enterprises succeeded. The anomaly is sad, but it is not infrequent. They were greater than his powers and his means, and before they could reach their full fruition, they had to be enlarged to men of longer purse and longer patience. He was singularly fitted both by instinct and by education to become a great publisher; and he early perceived that if a leading American house were to continue at Boston, it must be hospitable to the talents of the whole country. He founded his future upon those generous lines; but he wanted the qualities as well as the resources for rearing the superstructure. Changes began to follow each other rapidly after he came into control of the house. Misfortune reduced the size and number of its periodicals. The *Young Folks* was sold outright, and the *North American Review* (long before Mr. Rice bought it and carried it to New York) was cut down one-half, so that Aldrich said, It looked as if

Destiny had sat upon it. His own periodical, *Every Saturday*, was first enlarged to a stately quarto and illustrated; and then, under stress of the calamities following the great Boston Fire, it collapsed to its former size. Then both the *Atlantic Monthly* and *Every Saturday* were sold away from their old ownership, and *Every Saturday* was suppressed altogether, and we two ceased to be of the same employ. There was some sort of evening rite (more funereal than festive) the day after they were sold, and we followed Osgood away from it, under the lamps. We all knew that it was his necessity that had caused him to part with the periodicals; but he professed that it was his pleasure, and he said, He had not felt so light-hearted since he was a boy. We asked him, How could he feel gay when he was no longer paying us our salaries, and how could he justify it to his conscience? He liked our mocking, and limped away from us with a rheumatic easing of his weight from one foot to another: a figure pathetic now that it has gone the way to dusty death, and dear to memory through benefactions unalloyed by one unkindness.

IV

But when I came to Boston early in 1866, the *Atlantic Monthly* and *Harper's* then divided our magazine world between them; the *North American Review*, in the control of Lowell and Professor Norton, had entered upon a new life; *Every Saturday* was an instant success in the charge of Mr. Aldrich, who was by taste and training one of the best editors; and *Our Young Folks* had the field of juvenile periodical literature to itself.

It was under the direction of Miss Lucy Larcom and of Mr. J. T. Trowbridge, who had come from western

JAMES R. OSGOOD

New York, where he was born, and must be noted as one of the first returners from the setting to the rising sun. He naturalized himself in Boston in his later boyhood, and he still breathes Boston air, where he dwells in the street called Pleasant, on the shore of Spy Pond, at Arlington, and still weaves the magic web of his satisfying stories for boys. He merges in their popularity the fame of a poet which I do not think will always suffer that eclipse, for his poems show him to have looked deeply into the heart of common humanity with a true and tender sense of it.

Miss Larcom scarcely seemed to change from date to date in the generation that elapsed between the time I first saw her and the time I saw her last, a year or two before her death. A goodness looked out of her comely face, which made me think of the Madonna's in Titian's " Assumption," and her whole aspect expressed a mild and friendly spirit which I find it hard to put in words. She was never of the fine world of literature; she dwelt where she was born, in that unfashionable Beverly which is not Beverly Farms, and was of a simple, sea-faring, God-fearing race, as she has told in one of the loveliest autobiographies I know, *A New England Girlhood*. She was the author of many poems, whose number she constantly enlarged, but she was chiefly, and will be most lastingly, famed for the one poem, *Hannah Binding Shoes,* which years before my days in Boston had made her so widely known. She never again struck so deep or so true a note; but if one has lodged such a note in the ear of time, it is enough; and if we are to speak of eternity, one might very well hold up one's head in the fields of asphodel, if one could say to the great others there, " I wrote *Hannah Binding Shoes.*" Her poem is very, very sad, as all who have read it will remember; but Miss Larcom herself was above everything cheerful, and she had a laugh of mellow richness which willingly made itself heard. She was not only of true New England stock, and a Boston author by right of race, but she came up to that city every winter from her native town.

By the same right and on the same terms, another New England poetess, whom I met those first days in Boston, was a Boston author. When I saw Celia Thaxter she was just beginning to make her effect with those poems and sketches which the sea sings and flashes through as it sings and flashes around the Isles of Shoals, her summer home, where her girlhood had been passed in a freedom as wild as the curlew's. She was a most beautiful creature, still very young, with a slender figure, and an exquisite perfection of feature; she was in presence what her work was: fine, frank, finished. I do not know whether other witnesses of our literary history feel that the public has failed to keep her as fully in mind as her work merited; but I do not think there can be any doubt but our literature would be sensibly the poorer without her work. It is interesting to remember how closely she kept to her native field, and it is wonderful to consider how richly she made those sea-beaten rocks to blossom. Something strangely full and bright came to her verse from the mystical environment of the ocean, like the luxury of leaf and tint that it gave the narrower flower-plots of her native isles. Her gift, indeed, could not satisfy itself with the terms of one art alone, however varied, and she learned to express in color the thoughts and feelings impatient of the pallor of words.

She remains in my memories of that far Boston a distinct and vivid personality; as the authoress of *Amber Gods,* and *In a Cellar,* and *Circumstance,* and those other wild romantic tales, remains

CELIA THAXTER

the gentle and somewhat evanescent presence I found her. Miss Prescott was now Mrs. Spofford, and her husband was a rising young politician of the day. It was his duties as member of the General Court that had brought them up from Newburyport to Boston for that first winter; and I remember that the evening when we met he was talking of their some time going to Italy that she might study for imaginative literature certain Italian cities he named. I have long since ceased to own those cities, but at the moment I felt a pang of expropriation which I concealed as well as I could; and now I heartily wish she could have fulfilled that purpose if it was a purpose, or realized that dream if it was only a dream. Perhaps, however, that sumptuous and glowing fancy of hers, which had taken the fancy of the young readers of that day, needed the cold New England background to bring out all its intensities of tint, all its splendors of light. Its effects were such as could not last, or could not be farther evolved; they were the expression of youth musing away from its environment and smitten with the glories of a world afar and beyond, the great world, the fine world, the impurpled world of romantic motives and passions. But for what they were, I can never think them other than what they appeared: the emanations of a rarely gifted and singularly poetic mind. I feel better than I can say how necessarily they were the emanations of a New England mind, and how to the subtler sense they must impart the pathos of revolt from the colorless rigidities which are the long result of puritanism in the physiognomy of New England life.

Their author afterwards gave herself to the stricter study of this life in many tales and sketches which showed an increasing mastery; but they could not have the flush, the surprise, the delight of a young talent trying itself in a kind native and, so far as I know, peculiar to it. From time to time I still come upon a poem of hers which recalls that earlier strain of music, of color, and I am content to trust it for my abiding faith in the charm of things I have not read for thirty years.

V

I speak of this one and that, as it happens, and with no thought of giving a complete prospect of literary Boston thirty years ago. I am aware that it will seem sparsely peopled in the effect I impart, and I would have the reader always keep in mind the great fames at Cambridge and at Concord, which formed so large a part of the celebrity of Boston. I would also like him to think of it as still a great town, merely, where every one knew every one else, and whose metropolitan liberation from neighborhood was just begun.

Most distinctly of that yet uncitified Boston was the critic Edwin P. Whipple, whose sympathies were indefinitely wider than his traditions. He was a most generous lover of all that was excellent in literature; and though I suppose we should call him an old-fashioned critic now, I suspect it would be with no distinct sense of what is newer fashioned. He was certainly as friendly to what promised well in the younger men as he was to what was done well in their elders; and there was no one writing in his day whose virtues failed of his recognition, though it might happen that his foibles would escape Whipple's censure. He wrote strenuously and of course conscientiously; his point of view was solely and always that which enabled him best to discern qualities. I doubt if he had any theory of criticism except to find out

E. P. WHIPPLE

what was good in an author and praise it; and he rather blamed what was ethically bad than what was æsthetically bad. In this he was strictly of New England, and he was of New England in a certain general intelligence, which constantly grew with an interrogative habit of mind.

He liked to talk to you of what he had found characteristic in your work, to analyze you to yourself; and the very modesty of the man, which made such a study impersonal as far as he was concerned, sometimes rendered him insensible to the sufferings of his subject. He had a keen perception of humor in others, but he had very little humor; he had a love of the beautiful in literature which was perhaps sometimes greater than his sense of it.

I write from a cursory acquaintance with his work, not recently renewed. Of the presence of the man I have a vivider remembrance: a slight, short, ecclesiasticized figure in black; with a white neckcloth and a silk hat of strict decorum, and between the two a square face with square features, intensified in their regard by a pair of very large glasses, and the prominent, myopic eyes staring through them. He was a type of out-dated New England scholarship in these aspects, but in the hospitable qualities of his mind and heart, the sort of man to be kept fondly in the memory of all who ever knew him.

Out of the vague of that far-off time another face and figure, as essentially New England as this, and yet so different, relieve themselves. Charles F. Browne, whose drollery wafted his pseudonym as far as the English speech could carry laughter, was a Westernized Yankee. He added an Ohio way of talking to the Maine way of thinking, and he so became a literary product of a rarer and stranger sort than our literature had otherwise known. He had gone from Cleveland to London, with intervals of New York and the lecture platform, four or five years before I saw him in Boston, shortly after I went there. We had met in Ohio, and he had personally explained to me the ducatless well-meaning of *Vanity Fair* in New York; but many men had since shaken the weary hand of Artemus Ward before I grasped it one day in front of the Tremont Temple. He did not recognize me, but he gave me at once a greeting of great impersonal cordiality, with " How do you do? When did you come?" and other questions that had no concern in them, till I began to dawn upon him through a cloud of other half-remembered faces. Then he seized my hand and wrung it all over again, and repeated his friendly demands with an intonation that was now " Why, *how* are you,—how *are* you?" for me alone. It was a bit of comedy, which had the fit pathetic relief of his impending doom: this was already stamped upon his wasted face, and his gay eyes had the death-look. His large, loose mouth was drawn, for all its laughter at the fact which he owned; his profile, which burlesqued an eagle's, was the profile of a drooping eagle; his lank length of limb trembled away with him when we parted. I did not see him again; I scarcely heard of him till I heard of his death, and this sad image remains with me of the humorist who first gave the world a taste of the humor which characterizes the whole American people.

VI

I was meeting all kinds of distinguished persons, in my relation to the magazine, and early that winter I met one who remains in my mind above all others a person of distinction. He was scarcely a celebrity,

128

GEORGE TICKNOR

but he embodied certain social traits which were so characteristic of literary Boston that it could not be approached without their recognition. The Muses have often been acknowledged to be very nice young persons, but in Boston they were really ladies: in Boston literature was of good family and good society in a measure it has never been elsewhere. It might be said even that reform was of good family in Boston; and literature, and reform equally shared the regard of Edmund Quincy, whose race was one of the most aristocratic in New England. I had known him by his novel of *Wensley* (it came so near being a first-rate novel), and by his *Life of Josiah Quincy,* then a new book, but still better by his Boston letters to the New York *Tribune*. These dealt frankly, in the old anti-slavery days between 1850 and 1860, with other persons of distinction in Boston, who did not see the right so clearly as Quincy did, or who at least let their interests darken them to the ugliness of slavery. Their fault was all the more comical because it was the error of men otherwise so correct, of characters so stainless, of natures so upright; and the Quincy letters got out of it all the fun there was in it. Quincy himself affected me as the finest patrician type I had ever met. He was charmingly handsome, with a nose of most fit aquilinity, smooth-shaven lips, "educated whiskers," and perfect glasses; his manner was beautiful, his voice delightful, when at our first meeting he made me his reproaches in terms of lovely kindness for having used in my *Venetian Life,* the Briticism *directly* for *as soon as.*

Lowell once told me that Quincy had never had any calling or profession, because when he found himself in the enjoyment of a moderate income on leaving college, he decided to be simply a gentleman. He was too

much of a man to be merely that, and he was an abolitionist, a journalist, and for conscience' sake a satirist.
Of that political mood of society which he satirized was
an eminent man whom it was also my good fortune to
meet in my early days in Boston; and if his great
sweetness and kindness had not instantly won my liking, I should still have been glad of the glimpse of the
older and statelier Boston which my slight acquaintance
with George Ticknor gave me. The historian of Spanish literature, the friend and biographer of Prescott,
and a leading figure of the intellectual society of an
epoch already closed, dwelt in the fine old square brick
mansion which yet stands at the corner of Park Street
and Beacon, though sunk now to a variety of business
uses, and lamentably changed in aspect. The interior
was noble, and there was an air of scholarly quiet and
of lettered elegance in the library, where the host received his guests, which seemed to pervade the whole
house, and which made its appeal to the imagination of
one of them most potently. It seemed to me that to
be master of such circumstance and keeping would be
enough of life in a certain way; and it all lingers in
my memory yet, as if it were one with the gentle courtesy which welcomed me.

Among my fellow-guests one night was George S.
Hillard, now a faded reputation, and even then a life
defeated of the high expectation of its youth. I do not
know whether his *Six Months in Italy* still keeps itself
in print; but it was a book once very well known; and
he was perhaps the more gracious to me, as our host
was, because of our common Italian background. He
was of the old Silver-gray Whig society too, and I suppose that order of things imparted its tone to what I
felt and saw in that place. The civil war had come
and gone, and that order accepted the result if not with

THE TICKNOR MANSION, BOSTON

faith, then with patience. There were two young English noblemen there that night, who had been travelling in the South, and whose stories of the wretched conditions they had seen moved our host to some open misgiving. But the Englishmen had no question; in spite of all, they defended the accomplished fact, and when I ventured to say that now at least there could be a hope of better things, while the old order was only the perpetuation of despair, he mildly assented, with a gesture of the hand that waived the point, and a deeply sighed, "Perhaps; perhaps."

He was a presence of great dignity, which seemed to recall the past with a steadfast allegiance, and yet to relax itself towards the present in the wisdom of the accumulated years. His whole life had been passed in devotion to polite literature and in the society of the polite world; and he was a type of scholar such as only the circumstances of Boston could form. Those circumstances could alone form such another type as Quincy; and I wish I could have felt then as I do now the advantage of meeting them so contemporaneously.

VII

The historian of Spanish literature was an old man nearer eighty than seventy when I saw him, and I recall of him personally his dark tint, and the scholarly refinement of his clean-shaven face, which seemed to me rather English than American in character. He was quite exterior to the *Atlantic* group of writers, and had no interest in me as one of it. Literary Boston of that day was not a solidarity, as I soon perceived; and I understood that it was only in my quality of stranger that I saw the different phases of it. I should not be just to a vivid phase if I failed to speak of Mrs. Julia

Ward Howe and the impulse of reform which she personified. I did not sympathize with this then so much as I do now, but I could appreciate it on the intellectual side. Once, many years later, I heard Mrs. Howe speak in public, and it seemed to me that she made one of the best speeches I had ever heard. It gave me for the first time a notion of what women might do in that sort if they entered public life; but when we met in those earlier days I was interested in her as perhaps our chief poetess. I believe she did not care much to speak of literature; she was alert for other meanings in life, and I remember how she once brought to book a youthful matron who had perhaps unduly lamented the hardships of housekeeping, with the sharp demand, " Child, where is your *religion?*" After the many years of an acquaintance which had not nearly so many meetings as years, it was pleasant to find her, at the latest, as strenuous as ever for the faith of works, and as eager to aid Stepniak as John Brown. In her beautiful old age she survives a certain literary impulse of Boston, but a still higher impulse of Boston she will not survive, for that will last while the city endures.

VIII

The Cambridge men were curiously apart from others that formed the great New England group, and with whom in my earlier ignorance I had always fancied them mingling. Now and then I met Doctor Holmes at Longfellow's table, but not oftener than now and then, and I never saw Emerson in Cambridge at all except at Longfellow's funeral. In my first years on the *Atlantic* I sometimes saw him, when he would address me some grave, rather retrorsive civilities, after I had been newly introduced to him, as I had always

WHITE ISLAND LIGHT, ISLES OF SHOALS, THE EARLY HOME OF CELIA THAXTER

to be on these occasions. I formed the belief that he did not care for me, either in my being or doing, and I am far from blaming him for that: on such points there might easily be two opinions, and I was myself often of the mind I imagined in him.

If Emerson forgot me, it was perhaps because I was not of those qualities of things which even then, it was said, he could remember so much better than things themselves. In his later years I sometimes saw him in the Boston streets with his beautiful face dreamily set, as he moved like one to whose vision

> " Heaven opens inward, chasm yawn,
> Vast images in glimmering dawn,
> Half shown, are broken and withdrawn."

It is known how before the end the eclipse became total and from moment to moment the record inscribed upon his mind was erased. Some years before he died I sat between him and Mrs. Rose Terry Cooke, at an *Atlantic* Breakfast where it was part of my editorial function to preside. When he was not asking me who she was, I could hear him asking her who I was. His great soul worked so independently of memory as we conceive it, and so powerfully and essentially, that one could not help wondering if, after all, our personal continuity, our identity hereafter, was necessarily trammeled up with our enduring knowledge of what happens here. His remembrance absolutely ceased with an event, and yet his character, his personality, his identity fully persisted.

I do not know whether the things that we printed for Emerson after his memory began to fail so utterly were the work of earlier years or not, but I know that they were of his best. There were certain poems which could not have been more electly, more exquisitely his, or fashioned with a keener and juster self-criticism. His vision transcended his time so far that some who have tired themselves out in trying to catch up with him have now begun to say that he was no seer at all; but I doubt if these form the last court of appeal in his case. In manner, he was very gentle, like all those great New England men, but he was cold, like many of them, to the new-comer, or to the old-comer who came newly. As I have elsewhere recorded, I once heard him speak critically of Hawthorne, and once he expressed his surprise at the late flowering brilliancy of Holmes's gift in the *Autocrat* papers after all his friends supposed it had borne its best fruit. But I recall no mention of Longfellow, or Lowell, or Whittier from him. At a dinner where the talk glanced upon Walt Whitman he turned to me as perhaps representing the interest posterity might take in the matter, and referred to Whitman's public use of his privately written praise as something altogether unexpected. He did not disown it or withdraw it, but seemed to feel (not indignantly) that there had been an abuse of it.

IX

The first time I saw Whittier was in Fields's room at the publishing office, where I had come upon some editorial errand to my chief. He introduced me to the poet: a tall, spare figure in black of Quaker cut, with a keen, clean-shaven face, black hair, and vivid black eyes. It was just after his poem, *Snow Bound,* had made its great success, in the modest fashion of those days, and had sold not two hundred thousand but twenty thousand, and I tried to make him my compliment. I contrived to say that I could not tell him how much I liked it; and he received the inadequate ex-

THOMAS BAILEY ALDRICH

pression of my feeling with doubtless as much effusion as he would have met something more explicit and abundant. If he had judged fit to take my contract off my hands in any way, I think he would have been less able to do so than any of his New England contemporaries. In him, as I have suggested, the Quaker calm was bound by the frosty Puritanic air, and he was doubly cold to the touch of the stranger, though he would thaw out to old friends, and sparkle in laugh and joke. I myself never got so far with him as to experience this geniality, though afterwards we became such friends as an old man and a young man could be who rarely met. Our better acquaintance began with some talk, at a second meeting, about Bayard Taylor's *Story of Kennett,* which had then lately appeared, and which he praised for its fidelity to Quaker character in its less amiable aspects. No doubt I had made much of my own Quaker descent (which I felt was one of the few things I had to be proud of), and he therefore spoke the more frankly of those traits of brutality into which the primitive sincerity of the sect sometimes degenerated. He thought the habit of plain-speaking had to be jealously guarded to keep it from becoming rude-speaking, and he matched with stories of his own some things I had heard my father tell of Friends in the backwoods who were Foes to good manners.

Whittier was one of the most generous of men towards the work of others, especially the work of a new man, and if I did anything that he liked, I could count upon him for cordial recognition. In the quiet of his country home at Danvers he apparently read all the magazines, and kept himself fully abreast of the literary movement, but I doubt if he so fully appreciated the importance of the social movement. Like some others of the great anti-slavery men, he seemed to imag-

ine that mankind had won itself a clear field by destroy-
ing chattel slavery, and he had no sympathy with those
who think that the man who may any moment be out of
work is industrially a slave. This is not strange; so
few men last over from one reform to another that the
wonder is that any should, not that one should not.
Whittier was prophet for one great need of the divine to
man, and he spoke his message with a fervor that at times
was like the trembling of a flame, or the quivering of
midsummer sunshine. It was hard to associate with the
man as one saw him, still, shy, stiff, the passion of his
verse. This imbued not only his anti-slavery utter-
ances, but equally his ballads of the old witch and
Quaker persecution, and flashed a far light into the
dimness where his interrogations of Mystery pierced.
Whatever doubt there can be of the fate of other New
England poets in the great and final account, it seems
to me that certain of these pieces make his place secure.

There is great inequality in his work, and I felt this
so strongly that when I came to have full charge of the
Magazine, I ventured once to distinguish. He sent me
a poem, and I had the temerity to return it, and beg him
for something else. He magnanimously refrained from
all show of offence, and after a while, when he had printed the poem elsewhere, he gave me another. By this time,
I perceived that I had been wrong, not as to the poem
returned, but as to my function regarding him and such
as he. I had made my reflections, and never again did
I venture to pass upon what contributors of his quality
sent me. I took it and printed it, and praised the gods;
and even now I think that with such men it was not
my duty to play the censor in the periodical which they
had made what it was. They had set it in authority
over American literature, and it was not for me to put
myself in authority over them. Their fame was in

their own keeping, and it was not my part to guard it against them.

After that experience I not only practised an eager acquiescence in their wish to reach the public through the *Atlantic,* but I used all the delicacy I was master of in bowing the way to them. Sometimes my utmost did not avail, or more strictly speaking it did not avail in one instance with Emerson. He had given me upon much entreaty a poem which was one of his greatest and best, but the proof-reader found a nominative at odds with its verb. We had some trouble in reconciling them, and some other delays, and meanwhile Doctor Holmes offered me a poem for the same number. I now doubted whether I should get Emerson's poem back in time for it, but unluckily the proof did come back in time, and then I had to choose between my poets, or acquaint them with the state of the case, and let them choose what I should do. I really felt that Doctor Holmes had the right to precedence, since Emerson had withheld his proof so long that I could not count upon it; but I wrote to Emerson, and asked (as nearly as I can remember) whether he would consent to let me put his poem over to the next number, or would prefer to have it appear in the same number with Doctor Holmes's; the subjects were cognate, and I had my misgivings. He wrote me back to " return the proofs and break up the forms." I could not go to this iconoclastic extreme with the electrotypes of the magazine, but I could return the proofs. I did so, feeling that I had done my possible, and silently grieving that there could be such ire in heavenly minds.

X

Emerson, as I say, I had once met in Cambridge, but Whittier never; and I have a feeling that poet as Cambridge felt him to be, she had her reservations concerning him. I cannot put these into words which would not oversay them, but they were akin to those she might have refined upon in regard to Mrs. Stowe. Neither of these great writers would have appeared to Cambridge of the last literary quality; their fame was with a world too vast to be the test that her own

"One entire and perfect crysolite"

would have formed. Whittier in fact had not arrived at the clear splendor of his later work without some earlier turbidity; he was still from time to time capable of a false rhyme, like *morn* and *dawn*. As for the author of *Uncle Tom's Cabin* her syntax was such a snare to her that it sometimes needed the combined skill of all the proof-readers and the assistant editor to extricate her. Of course, nothing was ever written into her work, but in changes of diction, in correction of solecisms, in transposition of phrases, the text was largely rewritten on the margin of her proofs. The soul of her art was present, but the form was so often absent, that when it was clothed on anew, it would have been hard to say whose cut the garment was of in many places. In fact, the proof-reading of the *Atlantic Monthly* was something almost fearfully scrupulous and perfect. The proofs were first read by the under proof-reader in the printing-office; then the head reader passed them to me perfectly clean as to typography, with his own abundant and most intelligent comments on the literature; and then I read them,

LUCY LARCOM

making what changes I chose, and verifying every quotation, every date, every geographical and biographical name, every foreign word to the last accent, every technical and scientific term. Where it was possible or at all desirable the proof was next submitted to the author. When it came back to me, I revised it, accepting or rejecting the author's judgment according as he was entitled by his ability and knowledge or not to have them. The proof now went to the printers for correction; they sent it again to the head reader, who carefully revised it and returned it again to me. I read it a second time, and it was again corrected. After this it was revised in the office and sent to the stereotyper, from whom it came to the head reader for a last revision in the plates.

It would not do to say how many of the first American writers owed their correctness in print to the zeal of our proof-reading, but I may say that there were very few who did not owe something. The wisest and ablest were the most patient and grateful, like Mrs. Stowe, under correction; it was only the beginners and the more ignorant who were angry; and almost always the proof-reading editor had his way on disputed points. I look back now, with respectful amazement at my proficiency in detecting the errors of the great as well as the little. I was able to discover mistakes even in the classical quotations of the deeply lettered Sumner, and I remember, in the earliest years of my service on the *Atlantic*, waiting in this statesman's study amidst the prints and engravings that attested his personal resemblance to Edmund Burke, with his proofs in my hand and my heart in my mouth, to submit my doubts of his latinity. I forget how he received them; but he was not a very gracious person.

139

Mrs. Stowe *was* a gracious person, and carried into age the inalienable charm of a woman who must have been very charming earlier. I met her only at the Fieldses' in Boston, where one night I witnessed a controversy between her and Doctor Holmes concerning homœopathy and allopathy which lasted well through dinner. After this lapse of time, I cannot tell how the affair ended, but I feel sure of the liking with which Mrs. Stowe inspired me. There was something very simple, very motherly in her, and something divinely sincere. She was quite the person to take *au grand serieux* the monstrous imaginations of Lady Byron's jealousy and to feel it on her conscience to make public report of them when she conceived that the time had come to do so.

XI

In Francis Parkman I knew much later than in some others a differentiation of the New England type which was not less characteristic. He, like so many other Boston men of letters, was of patrician family, and of those easy fortunes which Clio prefers her sons to be of; but he paid for these advantages by the suffering in which he wrought at what is, I suppose, our greatest history. He wrought at it piecemeal, and sometimes only by moments, when the terrible headaches which tormented him, and the disorder of the heart which threatened his life, allowed him a brief respite for the task which was dear to him. He must have been more than a quarter of a century in completing it, and in this time, as he once told me, it had given him a day-laborer's wages; but of course money was the least return he wished from it. I read the irregularly successive volumes of *The Jesuits in North*

J. T. TROWBRIDGE

America, The Old Régime in Canada, the *Wolfe and Montcalm,* and the others that went to make up the whole history with a sufficiently noisy enthusiasm, and our acquaintance began by his expressing his gratification with the praises of them that I had put in print. We entered into relations as contributor and editor, and I know that he was pleased with my eagerness to get as many detachable chapters from the book in hand as he could give me for the magazine, but he was of too fine a politeness to make this the occasion of his first coming to see me. He had walked out to Cambridge, where I then lived, in pursuance of a regimen which, I believe, finally built up his health; that it was unsparing, I can testify from my own share in one of his constitutionals in Boston, many years later.

His experience in laying the groundwork for his history, and his researches in making it thorough, were such as to have liberated him to the knowledge of other manners and ideals, but he remained strictly a Bostonian, and as immutably of the Boston social and literary faith as any I knew in that capital of accomplished facts. He had lived like an Indian among the wild Western tribes; he consorted with the Canadian archæologists in their mousings among the colonial archives of their fallen state; every year he went to Quebec or Paris to study the history of New France in the original documents; European society was open to him everywhere; but he had those limitations which I nearly always found in the Boston men. I remember his talking to me of *The Rise of Silas Lapham,* in a somewhat troubled and uncertain strain, and interpreting his rise as the achievement of social recognition, without much or at all liking it or me for it. I did not think it my part to point out that I had supposed the rise to be a moral one; and later I fell under his condemnation for certain high crimes and misdemeanors I had been guilty of against a well-known ideal in fiction. These in fact constituted lese-majesty of romanticism, which seemed to be disproportionately dear to a man who was in his own way trying to tell the truth of human nature as I was in mine. His displeasures passed, however, and my last meeting with our greatest historian, as I think him, was of unalloyed friendliness. He came to me during my final year in Boston for nothing apparently but to tell me of his liking for a book of mine describing boy-life in Southern Ohio a half-century ago. He wished to talk about many points of this, which he found the same as his own boy-life in the neighborhood of Boston; and we could agree that the life of the Anglo-Saxon boy was pretty much the same everywhere. He had helped himself into my apartment with a crutch, but I do not remember how he had fallen lame. It was the end of his long walks, I believe, and not long afterwards I had the grief to read of his death. I noticed that perhaps through his enforced quiet, he had put on weight; his fine face was full; whereas when I first knew him, he was almost delicately thin of figure and feature. He was always of a distinguished presence, and his face had a great distinction.

It had not the appealing charm I found in the face of James Parton, another historian I knew earlier in my Boston days. I cannot say how much his books, once so worthily popular, are now known, but I have an abiding sense of their excellence. I have not read the *Life of Voltaire,* which was the last, but all the rest, from the first, I have read, and if there are better American biographies than those of *Franklin* or of *Jefferson,* I could not say where to find them. The *Greeley* and the *Burr* were younger books, and so

142

was the *Jackson,* and they were not nearly so good; but to all the author had imparted the valuable humanity in which he abounded. He was never of the fine world of literature, the world that sniffs and sneers, and abashes the simpler-hearted reader. But he was a true artist, and English born as he was, he divined American character as few Americans have done. He was a man of eminent courage, and in the days when to be an agnostic was to be almost an outcast, he had the heart to say of the Mysteries, that he did not know. He outlived the condemnation that this brought, and I think that no man ever came near him without in some measure loving him. To me he was of a most winning personality, which his strong, gentle face expressed, and a cast in the eye which he could not bring to bear directly upon his *vis-à-vis,* endeared. I never met him without wishing more of his company, for he seldom failed to say something to whatever was most humane and most modern in me. Our last meeting was at Newburyport, whither he had long before removed from New York, and where in the serene atmosphere of the ancient Puritan town he found leisure and inspiration for his work. He was not then engaged upon any considerable task, and he had aged and broken somewhat. But the old geniality, the old warmth glowed in him, and made a summer amidst the storm of snow that blinded the wintry air without. A new light had then lately come into my life, by which I saw all things that did not somehow tell for human brotherhood dwarfish and ugly, and he listened, as I imagined, to what I had to say with the tolerant sympathy of a man who has been a long time thinking those things, and views with a certain amusement the zeal of the fresh discoverer.

There was yet another historian in Boston, whose

acquaintance I made later than either Parkman's or Parton's, and whose very recent death leaves me with the grief of a friend. No one, indeed, could meet John Codman Ropes without wishing to be his friend, or without finding a friend in him. He had his likes and his dislikes, but he could have had no enmities except for evil and meanness. I never knew a man of higher soul, of sweeter nature, and his whole life was a monument of character. It cannot wound him now to speak of the cruel deformity which came upon him in his boyhood, and haunted all his after days with suffering. His gentle face showed the pain which is always the part of the hunchback, but nothing else in him confessed a sense of his affliction, and the resolute activity of his mind denied it in every way. He was, as is well known, a very able lawyer, in full practice, while he was making his studies of military history, and winning recognition for almost unique insight and thoroughness in that direction, though I believe that when he came to embody the results in those extraordinary volumes recording the battles of our civil war, he retired from the law in some measure. He knew these battles more accurately than the generals who fought them, and he was of a like proficiency in the European wars from the time of Napoleon down to our own time. I have heard a story, which I cannot vouch for, that when foreknowledge of his affliction, at the outbreak of our civil war, forbade him to be a soldier, he became a student of soldiership, and wreaked in that sort the passion of his most gallant spirit. But whether this was true or not, it is certain that he pursued the study with a devotion which never blinded him to the atrocity of war. Some wars he could excuse and even justify, but for any war that seemed wanton or aggressive, he had only abhorrence.

The last summer of a score that I had known him,

144

SAMUEL BOWLES

we sat on the veranda of his cottage at York Harbor, and looked out over the moonlit sea, and he talked of the high and true things, with the inextinguishable zest for the inquiry which I always found in him, though he was then feeling the approaches of the malady which was so soon to end all groping in these shadows for him. He must have faced the fact with the same courage and the same trust with which he faced all facts. From the first I found him a deeply religious man, not only in the ecclesiastical sense, but in the more mystical meanings of the word, and he kept his faith as he kept his youth to the last. Every one who knew him, knows how young he was in heart, and how he liked to have those that were young in years about him. He wished to have his house in Boston, as well as his cottage at York, full of young men and young girls, whose joy of life he made his own, and whose society he preferred to his contemporaries'. One could not blame him for that, or for seeking the sun, wherever he could, but it would be a false notion of him to suppose that his sympathies were solely or chiefly with the happy. In every sort, as I knew him, he was fine and good. The word is not worthy of him, after some of its uses and associations, but if it were unsmutched by these, and whitened to its primitive significance, I should say he was one of the most perfect gentlemen I ever knew.

K

Part Fifth

OLIVER WENDELL HOLMES

ELSEWHERE we literary folk are apt to be such a common lot, with tendencies here and there to be a shabby lot; we arrive from all sorts of unexpected holes and corners of the earth, remote, obscure; and at the best we do so often come up out of the ground; but at Boston we were of ascertained and noted origin, and good part of us dropped from the skies. Instead of holding horses before the doors of theatres; or capping verses at the plough-tail; or tramping over Europe with nothing but a flute in the pocket; or walking up to the metropolis with no luggage but the MS. of a tragedy; or sleeping in doorways or under the arches of bridges; or serving as apothecaries' 'prentices—we were good society from the beginning. I think this was none the worse for us, and it was vastly the better for good society.

I

Literature in Boston, indeed, was so respectable, and often of so high a lineage, that to be a poet was not only to be good society, but almost to be good family. If one names over the men who gave Boston her supremacy in literature during that Unitarian harvest-time of the old Puritanic seed-time which was her Augustan age, one names the people who were and who had been socially first in the city ever since the self-exile of the

Tories at the time of the Revolution. To say Prescott, Motley, Parkman, Lowell, Norton, Higginson, Dana, Emerson, Channing, was to say patrician, in the truest and often the best sense, if not the largest. Boston was small, but these were of her first citizens, and their primacy, in its way, was of the same quality as that, say, of the chief families of Venice. But these names can never have the effect for the stranger that they had for one to the manner born. I say had, for I doubt whether in Boston they still mean all that they once meant, and that their equivalents meant in science, in law, in politics. The most famous, if not the greatest of all the literary men of Boston, I have not mentioned with them, for Longfellow was not of the place, though by his sympathies and relations he became of it; and I have not mentioned Oliver Wendell Holmes, because I think his name would come first into the reader's thought with the suggestion of social quality in the humanities.

Holmes was of the brahminical caste which his humorous recognition invited from its subjectivity in the New England consciousness into the light where all could know it and own it, and like Longfellow he was allied to the patriciate of Boston by the most intimate ties of life. For a long time, for the whole first period of his work, he stood for that alone, its tastes, its prejudices, its foibles even, and when he came to stand in his second period, for vastly, for infinitely more, and to make friends with the whole race, as few men have ever done, it was always, I think, with a secret shiver of doubt, a backward look of longing, and an eye askance. He was himself perfectly aware of this at times, and would mark his several misgivings with a humorous sense of the situation. He was essentially too kind to be of a narrow world, too human to be finally of less than humanity, too gentle to be of the finest gentility. But such limitations as he had were in the direction I have hinted, or perhaps more than hinted; and I am by no means ready to make a mock of them, as it would be so easy to do for some reasons that he has himself suggested. To value aright the affection which the old Bostonian had for Boston one must conceive of something like the patriotism of men in the times when a man's city was a man's country, something Athenian, something Florentine. The war that nationalized us liberated this love to the whole country, but its first tenderness remained still for Boston, and I suppose a Bostonian still thinks of himself first as a Bostonian and then as an American, in a way that no New-Yorker could deal with himself. The rich historical background dignifies and ennobles the intense public spirit of the place, and gives it a kind of personality.

II

In literature Doctor Holmes survived all the Bostonians who had given the city her primacy in letters, but when I first knew him there was no apparent ground for questioning it. I do not mean now the time when I visited New England, but when I came to live near Boston, and to begin the many happy years which I spent in her fine intellectual air. I found time to run in upon him, while I was there arranging to take my place on the *Atlantic Monthly,* and I remember that in this brief moment with him he brought me to book about some vaunting paragraph in the *Nation* claiming the literary primacy for New York. He asked me if I knew who wrote it, and I was obliged to own that I had written it myself, when with the kindness he always showed me he protested against my position. To tell

148

the truth, I do not think now I had any very good reasons for it, and I certainly could urge none that would
stand against his. I could only fall back upon the
saving clause that this primacy was claimed mainly if
not wholly for New York in the future. He was willing to leave me the connotations of prophecy, but I
think he did even this out of politeness rather than con-
viction, and I believe he had always a sensitiveness
where Boston was concerned, which could not seem un-

And if I should live to be
The last leaf upon the tree
In the Spring,
Let them smile as I do now
At the old forsaken bough
Where I cling.

1831.   1891.

Oliver Wendell Holmes.

DR. HOLMES' HANDWRITING

generous to any generous mind. Whatever lingering
doubt of me he may have had, with reference to Boston, seemed to satisfy itself when several years afterwards he happened to speak of a certain character in an
early novel of mine, who was not quite the kind of Bostonian one could wish to be. The thing came up in
talk with another person, who had referred to my Bostonian, and the doctor had apparently made his
acquaintance in the book, and not liked him. "I understood, of course," he said, "that he was a Bostonian,
not the Bostonian," and I could truthfully answer that
this was by all means my own understanding too.

His fondness for his city, which no one could appreciate better than myself, I hope, often found expression in a burlesque excess in his writings, and in his talk perhaps oftener still. Hard upon my return from Venice I had a half-hour with him in his old study on Charles Street, where he still lived in 1865, and while I was there a young man came in for the doctor's help as a physician, though he looked so very well, and was so lively and cheerful, that I have since had my doubts whether he had not made a pretext for a glimpse of him as the Autocrat. The doctor took him upon his word, however, and said he had been so long out of practice that he could not do anything for him, but he gave him the address of another physician, somewhere near Washington Street. "And if you don't know where Washington Street is," he said, with a gay burst at a certain vagueness which had come into the young man's face, " you don't know anything."

We had been talking of Venice, and what life was like there, and he made me tell him in some detail. He was especially interested in what I had to say of the minute subdivision and distribution of the necessaries, the small coins, and the small values adapted to their purchase, the intensely retail character, in fact, of household provisioning; and I could see how he pleased himself in formulating the theory that the higher a civilization the finer the apportionment of the demands and supplies. The ideal, he said, was a civilization in which you could buy two cents' worth of beef, and a divergence from this standard was towards barbarism.

The secret of the man who is universally interesting is that he is universally interested, and this was, above all, the secret of the charm that Doctor Holmes had for every one. No doubt he knew it, for what that most alert intelligence did not know of itself was scarcely worth knowing. (This knowledge was one of his chief pleasures, I fancy; he rejoiced in the consciousness which is one of the highest attributes of the highly organized man, and he did not care for the consequences in your mind, if you were so stupid as not to take him aright.) I remember the delight Henry James, the father of the novelist, had in reporting to me the frankness of the doctor, when he had said to him, "Holmes, you are intellectually the most alive man I ever knew." " I am, I am," said the doctor. " From the crown of my head to the sole of my foot, I'm alive, I'm alive!" Any one who ever saw him will imagine the vivid relish he had in recognizing the fact. He could not be with you a moment without shedding upon you the light of his flashing wit, his radiant humor, and he shone equally upon the rich and poor in mind. His gayety of heart could not withhold itself from any chance of response, but he did wish always to be fully understood, and to be liked by those he liked. He gave his liking cautiously, though, for the affluence of his sympathies left him without the reserves of colder natures, and he had to make up for these with careful circumspection. He wished to know the character of the person who made overtures to his acquaintance, for he was aware that his friendship lay close to it; he wanted to be sure that he was a nice person, and though I think he preferred social quality in his fellow-man, he did not refuse himself to those who had merely a sweet and wholesome humanity. He did not like anything that tasted or smelt of Bohemianism in the personnel of literature, but he did not mind the scent of the new-ploughed earth, or even of the barn-yard. I recall his telling me once that after two younger brothers-in-letters had called upon him in the odor of an habitual beeriness and smokiness, he opened the window; and the very last time I saw

him he remembered at eighty-five the offence he had
found on his first visit to New York, when a metropolitan poet had asked him to lunch in a basement restaurant.

III

He seemed not to mind, however, climbing to the little apartment we had in Boston when we came there in
1866, and he made this call upon us in due form,
bringing Mrs. Holmes with him as if to accent the
recognition socially. We were then incredibly young,
much younger than I find people ever are nowadays,
and in the consciousness of our youth we felt, to the last
exquisite value of the fact, what it was to have the
Autocrat come to see us; and I believe he was not dis-
pleased to perceive this; he liked to know that you felt
his quality in every way. That first winter, however,
I did not see him often, and in the spring we went to
live in Cambridge, and thereafter I met him chiefly at
Longfellow's, or when I came in to dine at the Fieldses',
in Boston. It was at certain meetings of the Dante
Club, when Longfellow read aloud his translation for
criticism, and there was supper later, that one saw the
doctor; and his voice was heard at the supper rather
than at the criticism, for he was no Italianate. He always seemed to like a certain turn of the talk toward the
mystical, but with space for the feet on a firm ground
of fact this side of the shadows; when it came to going
over among them, and laying hold of them with the
hand of faith, as if they were substance, he was not of
the excursion. It is well known how fervent, I cannot
say devout, a spiritualist Longfellow's brother-in-law,
Appleton, was; and when he was at the table too, it
took all the poet's delicate skill to keep him and the
Autocrat from involving themselves in a cataclysmal

controversy upon the matter of manifestations. With Doctor Holmes the inquiry was inquiry, to the last, I believe, and the burden of proof was left to the ghosts and their friends. His attitude was strictly scientific; he denied nothing, but he expected the supernatural to be at least as convincing as the natural.

There was a time in his history when the popular ignorance classed him with those who were once rudely called infidels; but the world has since gone so fast and so far that the mind he was of concerning religious belief would now be thought religious by a good half of the religious world. It is true that he had and always kept a grudge against the ancestral Calvinism which afflicted his youth; and he was through all rises and lapses of opinion essentially Unitarian; but of the honest belief of any one, I am sure he never felt or spoke otherwise than most tolerantly, most tenderly. As often as he spoke of religion, and his talk tended to it very often, I never heard an irreligious word from him, far less a scoff or sneer at religion; and I am certain that this was not merely because he would have thought it bad taste, though undoubtedly he would have thought it bad taste; I think it annoyed, it hurt him, to be counted among the iconoclasts, and he would have been profoundly grieved if he could have known how widely this false notion of him once prevailed. It can do no harm at this late day to impart from the secrets of the publishing house the fact that a supposed infidelity in the tone of his story *The Guardian Angel* cost the *Atlantic Monthly* many subscribers. Now, the tone of that story would not be thought even mildly agnostic, I fancy; and long before his death the author had outlived the error concerning him.

It was not the best of his stories, by any means, and it would not be too harsh to say that it was the poorest.

His novels all belonged to an order of romance which was as distinctly his own as the form of dramatized essay which he invented in the *Autocrat*. If he did not think poorly of them, he certainly did not think too proudly, and I heard him quote with relish the phrase of a lady who had spoken of them to him as his "medicated novels." That, indeed, was perhaps what they were; a faint, faint odor of the pharmacopœia clung to their pages; their magic was scientific. He knew this better than any one else, of course, and if any one had said it in his turn he would hardly have minded it. But what he did mind was the persistent misinterpretation of his intention in certain quarters where he thought he had the right to respectful criticism instead of the succession of sneers that greeted the successive numbers of his story; and it was no secret that he felt the persecution keenly. Perhaps he thought that he had already reached that time in his literary life when he was a fact rather than a question, and when reasons and not feelings must have to do with his acceptance or rejection. But he had to live many years yet before he reached this state. When he did reach it, happily a good while before his death, I do not believe any man ever enjoyed the like condition more. He loved to feel himself out of the fight, with much work before him still, but with nothing that could provoke ill-will in his activities. He loved at all times to take himself objectively, if I may so express my sense of a mental attitude that misled many. As I have said before, he was universally interested, and he studied the universe from himself. I do not know how one is to study it otherwise; the impersonal has really no existence; but with all his subtlety and depth he was of a make so simple, of a spirit so *naïve,* that he could not practise the feints some use to conceal that interest in

154

self which, after all, every one knows is only concealed. He frankly and joyously made himself the starting-point in all his inquest of the hearts and minds of other men, but so far from singling himself out in this, and standing apart in it, there never was any one who was more eagerly and gladly your fellow-being in the things of the soul.

IV

In the things of the world, he had fences, and looked at some people through palings and even over the broken bottles on the tops of walls; and I think he was the loser by this, as well as they. But then I think all fences are bad, and that God has made enough differences between men; we need not trouble ourselves to multiply them. Even behind his fences, however, Holmes had a heart kind for the outsiders, and I do not believe any one came into personal relations with him who did not experience this kindness. In that long and delightful talk I had with him on my return from Venice (I can praise the talk because it was mainly his), we spoke of the status of domestics in the Old World, and how fraternal the relation of high and low was in Italy, while in England, between master and man, it seemed without acknowledgment of their common humanity. " Yes," he said, " I always felt as if English servants expected to be trampled on; but I can't do that. If they want to be trampled on, they must get some one else." He thought that our American way was infinitely better; and I believe that in spite of the fences there was always an instinctive impulse with him to get upon common ground with his fellow-man. I used to notice in the neighborhood cabman who served our block on Beacon Street a sort of affectionate reverence for the Autocrat, which could have come from nothing but the kindly terms between them; if you went to him when he was engaged to Doctor Holmes, he told you so with a sort of implication in his manner that the thought of anything else for the time was profanation. The good fellow who took him his drives about the Beverly and Manchester shores seemed to be quite in the joke of the doctor's humor, and within the bounds of his personal modesty and his functional dignity permitted himself a smile at the doctor's sallies, when you stood talking with him, or listening to him at the carriage-side.

The civic and social circumstance that a man values himself on is commonly no part of his value, and certainly no part of his greatness. Rather, it is the very thing that limits him, and I think that Doctor Holmes appeared in the full measure of his generous personality to those who did not and could not appreciate his circumstance, and not to those who formed it, and who from life-long association were so dear and comfortable to him. Those who best knew how great a man he was were those who came from far to pay him their duty, or to thank him for some help they had got from his books, or to ask his counsel or seek his sympathy. With all such he was most winningly tender, most intelligently patient. I suppose no great author was ever more visited by letter and in person than he, or kept a faithfuler conscience for his guests. With those who appeared to him in the flesh he used a miraculous tact, and I fancy in his treatment of all the physician native in him bore a characteristic part. No one seemed to be denied access to him, but it was after a moment of preparation that one was admitted, and any one who was at all sensitive must have felt from the first moment in his presence that there could be no trespassing in point of time. If now and then some

insensitive began to trespass, there was a sliding-scale
of dismissal that never failed of its work, and that really saved the author from the effect of intrusion. He
was not bored because he would not be.

I transfer at random the impressions of many years
to my page, and I shall not try to observe a chron-
ological order in these memories. Vivid among them
is that of a visit which I paid him with Osgood the
publisher, then newly the owner of the *Atlantic Monthly,* when I had newly become the sole editor. We
wished to signalize our accession to the control of the
magazine by a stroke that should tell most in the public
eye, and we thought of asking Doctor Holmes to do
something again in the manner of the *Autocrat* and the
Professor at the Breakfast Table. Some letters had
passed between him and the management concerning
our wish, and then Osgood thought that it would be
right and fit for us to go to him in person. He proposed the visit, and Doctor Holmes received us with
a mind in which he had evidently formulated all his
thoughts upon the matter. His main question was
whether at his age of sixty years a man was justified
in seeking to recall a public of the past, or to create
a new public in the present. He seemed to have looked the ground over not only with a personal interest in
the question, but with a keen scientific zest for it as
something which it was delightful to consider in its
generic relations; and I fancy that the pleasure of
this inquiry more than consoled him for such pangs
of misgiving as he must have had in the personal question. As commonly happens in the solution of such
problems, it was not solved; he was very willing to take
our minds upon it, and to incur the risk, if we thought
it well and were willing to share it.

We came away rejoicing, and the new series began

with the new year following. It was by no means the
popular success that we had hoped; not because the
author had not a thousand new things to say, or
failed to say them with the gust and freshness of his
immortal youth, but because it was not well to disturb
a form associated in the public mind with an achievement which had become classic. It is of the *Autocrat
of the Breakfast Table* that people think, when they
think of the peculiar species of dramatic essay which
the author invented, and they think also of the *Professor at the Breakfast Table,* because he followed so
soon; but the *Poet at the Breakfast Table* came so long
after that his advent alienated rather than conciliated
liking. Very likely, if the *Poet* had come first he
would have had no second place in the affections of his
readers, for his talk was full of delightful matter; and
at least one of the poems which graced each instalment
was one of the finest and greatest that Doctor Holmes
ever wrote. I mean " Homesick in Heaven," which
seems to me not only what I have said, but one of the
most important, the most profoundly pathetic in the
language. Indeed, I do not know any other that in
the same direction goes so far with suggestion so penetrating.

The other poems were mainly of a cast which did
not win; the metaphysics in them were too much for
the human interest, and again there rose a foolish
clamor of the creeds against him on account of them.
The great talent, the beautiful and graceful fancy, the
eager imagination of the Autocrat could not avail
in this third attempt, and I suppose the *Poet at the
Breakfast Table* must be confessed as near a failure
as Doctor Holmes could come. It certainly was so in
the magazine which the brilliant success of the first
had availed to establish in the high place the periodical

must always hold in the history of American literature. Lowell was never tired of saying, when he recurred to the first days of his editorship, that the magazine could never have gone at all without the *Autocrat* papers. He was proud of having insisted upon
Holmes's doing something for the new venture, and he
was fond of recalling the author's misgivings concerning his contributions, which later repeated themselves
with too much reason, though not with the reason that
was in his own mind.

V

He lived twenty-five years after that self-question
at sixty, and after eighty he continued to prove that
threescore was not the limit of a man's intellectual
activity or literary charm. During all that time the
work he did in mere quantity was the work that a man
in the prime of life might well have been vain of doing,
and it was of a quality not less surprising. If I asked him with any sort of fair notice I could rely upon
him always for something for the January number,
and throughout the year I could count upon him for
those occasional pieces in which he so easily excelled
all former writers of occasional verse, and which he
liked to keep from the newspapers for the magazine.
He had a pride in his promptness with copy, and you
could always trust his promise. The printer's toe
never galled the author's kibe in his case; he wished to
have an early proof, which he corrected fastidiously,
but not overmuch, and he did not keep it long. He
had really done all his work in the manuscript, which
came print-perfect and beautifully clear from his pen,
in that flowing, graceful hand which to the last kept a
suggestion of the pleasure he must have had in it. Like

all wise contributors, he was not only patient, but very glad of all the queries and challenges that proof-reader and editor could accumulate on the margin of his proofs, and when they were both altogether wrong he was still grateful. In one of his poems there was some Latin-Quarter French, which our collective purism questioned, and I remember how tender of us he was in maintaining that in his Parisian time, at least, some ladies beyond the Seine said " Eh, b'en," instead of " Eh, bien." He knew that we must be always on the lookout for such little matters, and he would not wound our ignorance.

I do not think any one enjoyed praise more than he. Of course he would not provoke it, but if it came of itself, he would not deny himself the pleasure, as long as a relish of it remained. He used humorously to recognize his delight in it, and to say of the lecture audiences which in earlier times hesitated applause, " Why don't they give me three times three? I can stand it!" He himself gave in the generous fulness he desired. He did not praise foolishly or dishonest-ly, though he would spare an open dislike; but when a thing pleased him he knew how to say so cordially and skilfully, so that it might help as well as delight. I suppose no great author has tried more sincerely and faithfully to befriend the beginner than he; and from time to time he would commend something to me that he thought worth looking at, but never insistently. In certain cases, where he had simply to ease a burden from his own to the editorial shoulders, he would ask that the aspirant might be delicately treated. There might be personal reasons for this, but usually his kindness of heart moved him. His tastes had their geographical limit, but his sympathies were boundless, and the hopeless creature for whom he interceded was oftener remote from Boston and New England than otherwise.

It seems to me that he had a nature singularly affectionate, and that it was this which was at fault if he gave somewhat too much of himself to the celebration of the Class of '29, and all the multitude of Boston occasions, large and little, embalmed in the clear amber of his verse, somewhat to the disadvantage of the amber. If he were asked he could not deny the many friendships and fellowships which united in the asking; the immediate reclame from these things was sweet to him; but he loved to comply as much as he loved to be praised. In the pleasure he got he could feel himself a prophet in his own country, but the country which owned him prophet began perhaps to feel rather too much as if it owned him, and did not prize his vaticinations at all their worth. Some polite Bostonians knew him chiefly on this side, and judged him to their own detriment from it.

VI

After we went to live in Cambridge, my life and the delight in it were so wholly there that in ten years I had hardly been in as many Boston houses. As I have said, I met Doctor Holmes at the Fieldses', and at Longfellow's, when he came out to a Dante supper, which was not often, and somewhat later at the Saturday Club dinners. One parlous time at the publisher's I have already recalled, when Mrs. Harriet Beecher Stowe and the Autocrat clashed upon homœopathy, and it required all the tact of the host to lure them away from the dangerous theme. As it was, a battle waged in the courteous forms of Fontenoy, went on pretty well through the dinner, and it was only over the coffee that a truce was called. I need not say which was heterodox, or that each had a deep and strenuous conscience in the matter. I have always felt it a proof of his extreme leniency to me, unworthy, that the doctor was able to tolerate my own defection from the elder faith in medicine; and I could not feel his kindness less caressing because I knew it a concession to an infirmity. He said something like, After all a good physician was the great matter; and I eagerly turned his clemency to praise of our family doctor.

He was very constant at the Saturday Club, as long as his strength permitted, and few of its members missed fewer of its meetings. He continued to sit at its table until the ghosts of Hawthorne, of Agassiz, of Emerson, of Longfellow, of Lowell, out of others less famous, bore him company there among the younger men in the flesh. It must have been very melancholy, but nothing could deeply cloud his most cheerful spirit. His strenuous interest in life kept him alive to all the things of it, after so many of his friends were dead. The questions which he was wont to deal with so fondly, so wisely, the great problems of the soul, were all the more vital, perhaps, because the personal concern in them was increased by the translation to some other being of the men who had so often tried with him to fathom them here. The last time I was at that table he sat alone there among those great memories; but he was as gay as ever I saw him; his wit sparkled, his humor gleamed; the poetic touch was deft and firm as of old; the serious curiosity, the instant sympathy remained. To the witness he was pathetic, but to himself he could only have been interesting, as the figure of a man surviving, in an alien but not unfriendly present, the past which held so vast a part of all that had constituted him. If he had thought of himself in this way, it would have been without one emotion of self-pity, such as more maudlin souls indulge, but with a love of knowledge and wisdom as keenly alert as in his prime.

For three privileged years I lived all but next-door neighbor of Doctor Holmes in that part of Beacon Street whither he removed after he left his old home in Charles Street, and during these years I saw him rather often. We were both on the water side, which means so much more than the words say, and our library windows commanded the same general view of the Charles rippling out into the Cambridge marshes and the sunsets, and curving eastward under Long Bridge, through shipping that increased onward to the sea. He said that you could count fourteen towns and villages in the compass of that view, with the three conspicuous monuments accenting the different attractions of it: the tower of Memorial Hall at Harvard; the obelisk on Bunker Hill; and in the centre of the picture that bulk of Tufts College which he said he expected to greet his eyes the first thing when he opened them in the other world. But the prospect, though generally the same, had certain precious differences for each of us, which I have no doubt he valued himself as much upon as I did. I have a notion that he fancied these were to be enjoyed best in his library through two oval panes let into the bay there apart from the windows, for he was apt to make you come and look out of them if you got to talking of the view before you left. In this pleasant study he lived among the books, which seemed to multiply from case to case and shelf to shelf, and climb from floor to ceiling. Everything was in exquisite order, and the desk where he wrote was as scrupulously neat as if the sloven disarray of most authors' desks were impossible to him. He had a number of ingenious little contrivances for helping his work, which he liked to show you; for a time a revolving book-case at the

163

corner of his desk seemed to be his pet; and after that came his fountain-pen, which he used with due observance of its fountain principle, though he was tolerant of me when I said I always dipped mine in the inkstand; it was a merit in his eyes to use a fountain-pen in anywise. After you had gone over these objects with him, and perhaps taken a peep at something he was examining through his microscope, he sat down at one corner of his hearth, and invited you to an easy-chair at the other. His talk was always considerate of your wish to be heard, but the person who wished to talk when he could listen to Doctor Holmes was his own victim, and always the loser. If you were well advised you kept yourself to the question and response which manifested your interest in what he was saying, and let him talk on, with his sweet smile, and that husky laugh he broke softly into at times. Perhaps he was not very well when you came in upon him; then he would name his trouble, with a scientific zest and accuracy, and pass quickly to other matters. As I have noted, he was interested in himself only on the universal side; and he liked to find his peculiarity in you better than to keep it his own; he suffered a visible disappointment if he could not make you think or say you were so and so too. The querulous note was not in his most cheerful register; he would not dwell upon a specialized grief; though sometimes I have known him touch very lightly and currently upon a slight annoyance, or disrelish for this or that. As he grew older, he must have had, of course, an old man's disposition to speak of his infirmities; but it was fine to see him catch himself up in this, when he became conscious of it, and stop short with an abrupt turn to something else. With a real interest, which he gave humorous excess, he would celebrate some little ingenious thing that had fallen in his way,

OLIVER WENDELL HOLMES IN 1860

and I have heard him expatiate with childlike delight upon the merits of a new razor he had got: a sort of mower, which he could sweep recklessly over cheek and chin without the least danger of cutting himself. The last time I saw him he asked me if he had ever shown me that miraculous razor; and I doubt if he quite liked my saying I had seen one of the same kind.

It seemed to me that he enjoyed sitting at his chimney-corner rather as the type of a person having a good time than as such a person; he would rather be up and about something, taking down a book, making a note, going again to his little windows, and asking you if you had seen the crows yet that sometimes alighted on the shoals left bare by the ebb-tide behind the house. The reader will recall his lovely poem, " My Aviary," which deals with the winged life of that pleasant prospect. I shared with him in the flock of wild-ducks which used to come into our neighbor waters in spring, when the ice broke up, and stayed as long as the smallest space of brine remained unfrozen in the fall. He was graciously willing I should share in them, and in the cloud of gulls which drifted about in the currents of the sea and sky there, almost the whole year round. I did not pretend an original right to them, coming so late as I did to the place, and I think my deference pleased him.

VII

As I have said, he liked his fences, or at least liked you to respect them, or to be sensible of them. As often as I went to see him I was made to wait in the little reception-room below, and never shown at once to his study. My name would be carried up, and I would hear him verifying my presence from the maid through the opened door; then there came a cheery cry of welcome: " Is that you ? Come up, come up !" and I found him sometimes half-way down the stairs to meet me. He would make an excuse for having kept me below a moment, and say something about the rule he had to observe in all cases, as if he would not have me feel his fence a personal thing. I was aware how thoroughly his gentle spirit pervaded the whole house; the Irish maid who opened the door had the effect of being a neighbor too, and of being in the joke of the little formality; she apologized in her turn for the reception-room; there was certainly nothing trampled upon in her manner, but affection and reverence for him whose gate she guarded, with something like the sentiment she would have cherished for a dignitary of the Church, but nicely differenced and adjusted to the Autocrat's peculiar merits.

The last time I was in that place, a visitant who had lately knocked at my own door was about to enter. I met the master of the house on the landing of the stairs outside his study, and he led me in for the few moments we could spend together. He spoke of the shadow so near, and said he supposed there could be no hope, but he did not refuse the cheer I offered him from my ignorance against his knowledge, and at something that was thought or said he smiled, with even a breath of laughter, so potent is the wont of a lifetime, though his eyes were full of tears, and his voice broke with his words. Those who have sorrowed deepest will understand this best.

It was during the few years of our Beacon Street neighborhood that he spent those hundred days abroad in his last visit to England and France. He was full of their delight when he came back, and my propinquity gave me the advantage of hearing him speak of them at first hand. He whimsically pleased himself most with his Derby-day experiences, and enjoyed contrasting the crowd and occasion with that of forty or fifty years earlier, when he had seen some famous race of the Derby won; nothing else in England seemed to have moved him so much, though all that royalties, dignities, and celebrities could well do for him had been done. Of certain things that happened to him, characteristic of the English, and interesting to him in their relation to himself through his character of universally interested man, he spoke freely; but he has said what he chose to the public about them, and I have no right to say more. The thing that most vexed him during his sojourn apparently was to have been described in one of the London papers as quite deaf; and I could truly say to him that I had never imagined him at all deaf, or heard him accused of it before. "Oh, yes," he said, "I am a little hard of hearing on one side. But it isn't deafness."

He had, indeed, few or none of the infirmities of age that make themselves painfully or inconveniently evident. He carried his slight figure erect, and until his latest years his step was quick and sure. Once he spoke of the lessened height of old people, apropos of something that was said, and " They *will shrink,* you know," he added, as if he were not at all concerned in the fact himself. If you met him in the street, you encountered a spare, carefully dressed old gentleman, with a clean-shaven face and a friendly smile, qualified by the involuntary frown of his thick, senile brows; well coated, lustrously shod, well gloved, in a silk hat, latterly wound with a mourning-weed. Sometimes he did not know you when he knew you quite well, and at such times I think it was kind to spare his years the fatigue of recalling your identity; at any rate, I am glad of the times when I did so. In society he had the

167

same vagueness, the same dimness; but after the moment he needed to make sure of you, he was as vivid as ever in his life. He made me think of a bed of embers on which the ashes have thinly gathered, and which, when these are breathed away, sparkles and tinkles keenly up with all the freshness of a newly kindled fire. He did not mind talking about his age, and I fancied rather enjoyed doing so. Its approaches interested him; if he was going, he liked to know just how and when he was going. Once he spoke of his lasting strength in terms of imaginative humor: he was still so intensely interested in nature, the universe, that it seemed to him he was not like an old man so much as a lusty infant which struggles against having the breast snatched from it. He laughed at the notion of this, with that impersonal relish, which seemed to me singularly characteristic of the self-consciousness so marked in him. I never heard one lugubrious word from him in regard to his years. He liked your sympathy on all grounds where he could have it self-respectfully, but he was a most manly spirit, and he would not have had it even as a type of the universal decay. Possibly he would have been interested to have you share in that analysis of himself which he was always making, if such a thing could have been.

He had not much patience with the unmanly craving for sympathy in others, and chiefly in our literary craft, which is somewhat ignobly given to it, though he was patient, after all. He used to say, and I believe he has said it in print, that unless a man could show a good reason for writing verse, it was rather against him, and a proof of weakness. I suppose this severe conclusion was something he had reached after dealing with innumerable small poets who sought the light in him with verses that no editor would admit to print. Yet of morbidness he was often very tender; he knew it to be disease, something that must be scientifically rather than ethically treated. He was in the same degree kind to any sensitiveness, for he was himself as sensitive as he was manly, and he was most delicately sensitive to any rightful social claim upon him. I was once at a dinner with him, where he was in some sort my host, in a company of people whom he had not seen me with before, and he made a point of acquainting me with each of them. It did not matter that I knew most of them already; the proof of his thoughtfulness was precious, and I was sorry when I had to disappoint it by confessing a previous knowledge.

VIII

I had three memorable meetings with him not very long before he died: one a year before, and the other two within a few months of the end. The first of these was at luncheon in the summer-house of a friend whose hospitality made it summer the year round, and we all went out to meet him, when he drove up in his open carriage, with the little sunshade in his hand, which he took with him for protection against the heat, and also, a little, I think, for the whim of it. He sat a moment after he arrived, as if to orient himself in respect to each of us. Beside the gifted hostess, there was the most charming of all the American essayists, and the Autocrat seemed at once to find himself singularly at home with the people who greeted him. There was no interval needed for fanning away the ashes; he tinkled up before he entered the house, and at the table he was as vivid and scintillant as I ever saw him, if indeed I ever saw him as much so. The talk began at once, and we had made him believe that there was nothing ego-

tistic in his taking the word, or turning it in illustration
from himself upon universal matters. I spoke among
other things of some humble ruins on the road to
Gloucester, which gave the way-side a very aged look;
the tumbled foundation-stones of poor bits of houses,
and "Ah," he said, "the cellar and the well?" He
added, to the company generally, "Do you know what
I think are the two lines of mine that go as deep as any
others, in a certain direction?" and he began to repeat
stragglingly certain verses from one of his earlier
poems, until he came to the closing couplet. But I will
give them in full, because in going to look them up I
have found them so lovely, and because I can hear his
voice again in every fondly accented syllable:

> "Who sees unmoved, a ruin at his feet,
> The lowliest home where human hearts have beat?
> The hearth-stone, shaded with the bistre stain,
> A century's showery torrents wash in vain;
> Its starving orchard where the thistle blows,
> And mossy trunks still mark the broken rows;
> Its chimney-loving poplar, oftenest seen
> Next an old roof, or where a roof has been;
> Its knot-grass, plantain,—all the social weeds,
> Man's mute companions following where he leads;
> Its dwarfed pale flowers, that show their straggling
> heads,
> Sown by the wind from grass-choked garden beds;
> Its woodbine creeping where it used to climb;
> Its roses breathing of the olden time;
> All the poor shows the curious idler sees,
> As life's thin shadows waste by slow degrees,
> *Till naught remains, the saddening tale to tell,*
> *Save last life's wrecks—the cellar and the well!"*

The poet's chaunting voice rose with a triumphant
swell in the climax, and "There," he said, "isn't it so?
The cellar and the well—they can't be thrown down or
burnt up; they are the human monuments that last
longest, and defy decay." He rejoiced openly in the

sympathy that recognized with him the divination of a most pathetic, most signal fact, and he repeated the last couplet again at our entreaty, glad to be entreated for it. I do not know whether all will agree with him concerning the relative importance of the lines, but I think all must feel the exquisite beauty of the picture to which they give the final touch.

He said a thousand witty and brilliant things that day, but his pleasure in this gave me the most pleasure, and I recall the passage distinctly out of the dimness that covers the rest. He chose to figure us younger men, in touching upon the literary circumstance of the past and present, as representative of modern feeling and thinking, and himself as no longer contemporary. We knew he did this to be contradicted, and we protested, affectionately, fervently, with all our hearts and minds; and indeed there were none of his generation who had lived more widely into ours. He was not a prophet like Emerson, nor ever a voice crying in the wilderness like Whittier or Lowell. His note was heard rather amid the sweet security of streets, but it was always for a finer and gentler civility. He imagined no new rule of life, and no philosophy or theory of life will be known by his name. He was not constructive; he was essentially observant, and in this he showed the scientific nature. He made his reader known to himself, first in the little, and then in the larger things. From first to last he was a censor, but a most winning and delightful censor, who could make us feel that our faults were other people's, and who was not wont

"To bait his homilies with his brother worms."

At one period he sat in the seat of the scorner, as far as Reform was concerned, or perhaps reformers, who are so often tedious and ridiculous; but he seemed to get a new heart with the new mind which came to him when he began to write the Autocrat papers, and the light mocker of former days became the serious and compassionate thinker, to whom most truly nothing that was human was alien. His readers trusted and loved him; few men have ever written so intimately with so much dignity, and perhaps none has so endeared himself by saying just the thing for his reader that his reader could not say for himself. He sought the universal through himself in others, and he found to his delight and theirs that the most universal thing was often, if not always, the most personal thing.

In my later meetings with him I was struck more and more by his gentleness. I believe that men are apt to grow gentler as they grow older, unless they are of the curmudgeon type, which rusts and crusts with age, but with Doctor Holmes the gentleness was peculiarly marked. He seemed to shrink from all things that could provoke controversy, or even difference; he waived what might be a matter of dispute, and rather sought the things that he could agree with you upon. In the last talk I had with him he appeared to have no grudge left, except for the puritanic orthodoxy in which he had been bred as a child. This he was not able to forgive, though its tradition was interwoven with what was tenderest and dearest in his recollections of childhood. We spoke of puritanism, and I said I sometimes wondered what could be the mind of a man towards life who had not been reared in its awful shadow, say an English Churchman, or a Continental Catholic; and he said he could not imagine, and that he did not believe such a man could at all enter into our feelings; puritanism, he seemed to think, made an essential and ineradicable difference. I do not believe

172

THE WATER-SIDE AT BEVERLY

he had any of that false sentiment which attributes virtue of character to severity of creed, while it owns the creed to be wrong.

He differed from Longfellow in often speaking of his contemporaries. He spoke of them frankly, but with an appreciative rather than a censorious criticism. Of Longfellow himself he said that day, when I told him I had been writing about him, and he seemed to me a man without error, that he could think of but one error in him, and that was an error of taste, of almost merely literary taste. It was at an earlier time that he talked of Lowell, after his death, and told me that Lowell once in the fever of his antislavery apostolate had written him, urging him strongly, as a matter of duty, to come out for the cause he had himself so much at heart. Afterwards Lowell wrote again, owning himself wrong in his appeal, which he had come to recognize as invasive. "He was ten years younger than I," said the doctor.

I found him that day I speak of in his house at Beverly Farms, where he had a pleasant study in a corner by the porch, and he met me with all the cheeriness of old. But he confessed that he had been greatly broken up by the labor of preparing something that might be read at some commemorative meeting, and had suffered from finding first that he could not write something specially for it. Even the copying and adapting an old poem had overtaxed him, and in this he showed the failing powers of age. But otherwise he was still young, intellectually; that is, there was no failure of interest in intellectual things, especially literary things. Some new book lay on the table at his elbow, and he asked me if I had seen it, and made some joke about his having had the good luck to read it, and have it lying by him a few days before when the author called. I do not know whether he schooled himself against an old man's tendency to revert to the past or not, but I know that he seldom did so. That morning, however, he made several excursions into it, and told me that his youthful satire of the *Spectre Pig* had been provoked by a poem of the eldest Dana's, where a phantom horse had been seriously employed, with an effect of anticlimax which he had found irresistible. Another foray was to recall the oppression and depression of his early religious associations, and to speak with moving tenderness of his father, whose hard doctrine as a minister was without effect upon his own kindly nature.

In a letter written to me a few weeks after this time, upon an occasion when he divined that some word from him would be more than commonly dear, he recurred to the feeling he then expressed: "Fifty-six years ago— more than half a century—I lost my own father, his age being seventy-three years. As I have reached that period of life, passed it, and now left it far behind, my recollections seem to brighten and bring back my boyhood and early manhood in a clearer and fairer light than it came to me in my middle decades. I have often wished of late years that I could tell him how I cherished his memory; perhaps I may have the happiness of saying all I long to tell him on the other side of that thin partition which I love to think is all that divides us."

Men are never long together without speaking of women, and I said how inevitably men's lives ended where they began, in the keeping of women, and their strength failed at last and surrendered itself to their care. I had not finished before I was made to feel that I was poaching, and "Yes," said the owner of the preserve, "I have spoken of that," and he went on to tell me just where. He was not going to have me suppose

I had invented those notions, and I could not do less than own that I must have found them in his book, and forgotten it.

He spoke of his pleasant summer life in the air, at once soft and fresh, of that lovely coast, and of his drives up and down the country roads. Sometimes this lady and sometimes that came for him, and one or two habitually, but he always had his own carriage ordered, if they failed, that he might not fail of his drive in any fair weather. His cottage was not immediately on the sea, but in full sight of it, and there was a sense of the sea about it, as there is in all that incomparable region, and I do not think he could have been at home anywhere beyond the reach of its salt breath.

I was anxious not to outstay his strength, and I kept my eye on the clock in frequent glances. I saw that he followed me in one of these, and I said that I knew what his hours were, and I was watching so that I might go away in time, and then he sweetly protested. Did I like that chair I was sitting in? It was a gift to him, and he said who gave it, with a pleasure in the fact that was very charming, as if he liked the association of the thing with his friend. He was disposed to excuse the formal look of his bookcases, which were filled with sets, and presented some phalanxes of fiction in rather severe array.

When I rose to go, he was concerned about my being able to find my way readily to the station, and he told me how to go, and what turns to take, as if he liked realizing the way to himself. I believe he did not walk much of late years, and I fancy he found much the same pleasure in letting his imagination make this excursion to the station with me that he would have found in actually going.

I saw him once more, but only once, when a day or

two later he drove up by our hotel in Magnolia towards the cottage where his secretary was lodging. He saw us from his carriage, and called us gayly to him, to make us rejoice with him at having finally got that commemorative poem off his mind. He made a jest of the trouble it had cost him, even some sleeplessness, and said he felt now like a convalescent. He was all brightness, and friendliness, and eagerness to make us feel his mood, through what was common to us all; and I am glad that this last impression of him is so one with the first I ever had, and with that which every reader receives from his work.

That is bright, and friendly and eager too, for it is throughout the very expression of himself. I think it is a pity if an author disappoints even the unreasonable expectation of the reader, whom his art has invited to love him; but I do not believe that Doctor Holmes could inflict this disappointment. Certainly he could disappoint no reasonable expectation, no intelligent expectation. What he wrote, that he was, and every one felt this who met him. He has therefore not died, as some men die, the remote impersonal sort, but he is yet thrillingly alive in every page of his books. The quantity of his literature is not great, but the quality is very surprising, and surprising first of all as equality. From the beginning to the end he wrote one man, of course in his successive consciousnesses. Perhaps every one does this, but his work gives the impression of an uncommon continuity, in spite of its being the effect of a later and an earlier impulse so very marked as to have made the later an astonishing revelation to those who thought they knew him.

IX

It is not for me in such a paper as this to attempt any judgment of his work. I have loved it, as I loved him, with a sense of its limitations which is by no means a censure of its excellences. He was not a man who cared to transcend; he liked bounds, he liked horizons, the constancy of shores. If he put to sea, he kept in sight of land, like the ancient navigators. He did not discover new continents; and I will own that I, for my part, should not have liked to sail with Columbus. I think one can safely affirm that as great and as useful men stayed behind, and found an America of the mind without stirring from their thresholds.

Part Sixth

THE WHITE MR. LONGFELLOW

W E had expected to stay in Boston only until we
could find a house in Old Cambridge. This
was not so simple a matter as it might seem; for the
ancient town had not yet quickened its scholarly pace
to the modern step. Indeed, in the spring of 1866 the
impulse of expansion was not yet visibly felt anywhere; the enormous material growth that followed the
civil war had not yet begun. In Cambridge the houses
to be let were few, and such as there were fell either below our pride or rose above our purse. I wish I might
tell how at last we bought a house; we had no money, but
we were rich in friends, who are still alive to shrink
from the story of their constant faith in a financial future which we sometimes doubted, and who backed their
credulity with their credit. It is sufficient for the present record, which professes to be strictly literary, to
notify the fact that on the first day of May, 1866, we
went out to Cambridge and began to live in a house
which we owned in fee if not in deed, and which was
none the less valuable for being covered with mort-
gages. Physically, it was a carpenter's box, of a sort
which is readily imagined by the Anglo-American genius for ugliness, but which it is not so easy to impart a
just conception of. A trim hedge of arbor-vitæ tried to
hide it from the world in front, and a tall board fence
behind; the little lot was well planted (perhaps too

178

well planted) with pears, grapes, and currants, and there was a small open space which I lost no time in digging up for a kitchen-garden. On one side of us were the open fields; on the other a brief line of neighbor-houses; across the street before us was a grove of stately oaks, which I never could persuade Aldrich had painted leaves on them in the fall. We were really in a poor suburb of a suburb; but such is the fascination of ownership, even the ownership of a fully mortgaged property, that we calculated the latitude and longitude of the whole earth from the spot we called ours. In our walks about Cambridge we saw other places where we might have been willing to live; only, we said, they were too far off. We even prized the architecture of our little box, though we had but so lately lived in a Gothic palace on the Grand Canal in Venice, and were not uncritical of beauty in the possessions of others. Positive beauty we could not have honestly said we thought our cottage had as a whole, though we might have held out for something of the kind in the brackets of turned wood under its eaves. But we were richly content with it; and with life in Cambridge, as it began to open itself to us, we were infinitely more than content. This life, so refined, so intelligent, so gracefully simple, I do not suppose has anywhere else had its parallel.

I

It was the moment before the old American customs had been changed by European influences among people of easier circumstances; and in Cambridge society kept what was best of its village traditions, and chose to keep them in the full knowledge of different things. Nearly every one had been abroad; and nearly every one had acquired the taste for olives without losing a relish for native sauces; through the intellectual life there was an entire democracy, and I do not believe that since the capitalistic era began there was ever a community in which money counted for less. There was little show of what money could buy; I remember but one private carriage (naturally, a publisher's); and there was not one livery, except a livery in the larger sense kept by the stableman Pike, who made us pay now a quarter and now a half dollar for a seat in his carriages, according as he lost or gathered courage for the charge. We thought him extortionate, and we mostly walked through snow and mud of amazing depth and thickness.

The reader will imagine how acceptable this circumstance was to a young literary man beginning life with a fully mortgaged house and a salary of untried elasticity. If there were distinctions made in Cambridge they were not against literature, and we found ourselves in the midst of a charming society, indifferent, apparently, to all questions but those of the higher education which comes so largely by nature. That is to say, in the Cambridge of that day (and, I dare say, of this) a mind cultivated in some sort was essential, and after that came civil manners, and the willingness and ability to be agreeable and interesting; but the question of riches or poverty did not enter. Even the question of family, which is of so great concern in New England, was in abeyance. Perhaps it was taken for granted that every one in Old Cambridge society must be of good family, or he could not be there; perhaps his mere residence tacitly ennobled him; certainly his acceptance was an informal patent of gentility. To my mind, the structure of society was almost ideal, and until we have a perfectly socialized condition of things I do not believe we shall ever have a more perfect soci-

ety. The instincts which governed it were not such as
can arise from the sordid competition of interests; they
flowed from a devotion to letters, and from a self-sacrifice in material things which I can give no better notion of than by saying that the outlay of the richest
college magnate seemed to be graduated to the income of
the poorest.

In those days, the men whose names have given
splendor to Cambridge were still living there. I shall
forget some of them in the alphabetical enumeration of
Louis Agassiz, Francis J. Child, Richard Henry Dana,
Jun., John Fiske, Dr. Asa Gray, the family of the
Jameses, father and sons, Lowell, Longfellow, Charles
Eliot Norton, Dr. John G. Palfrey, James Pierce, Dr.
Peabody, Professor Parsons, Professor Sophocles. The
variety of talents and of achievements was indeed so
great that Mr. Bret Harte, when fresh from his Pacific
slope, justly said, after listening to a partial rehearsal
of them, " Why, you couldn't fire a revolver from your
front porch anywhere without bringing down a two-
volumer!" Everybody had written a book, or an article,
or a poem; or was in the process or expectation of doing
it, and doubtless those whose names escape me will
have greater difficulty in eluding fame. These kindly,
these gifted folk each came to see us and to make us at
home among them; and my home is still among them,
on this side and on that side of the line between the
living and the dead, which invisibly passes through all
the streets of the cities of men.

II

We had the whole summer for the exploration of
Cambridge before society returned from the mountains
and the sea-shore, and it was not till October that I saw

Longfellow. I heard again, as I heard when I first came to Boston, that he was at Nahant, and though Nahant was no longer so far away, now, as it was then, I did not think of seeking him out even when we went for a day to explore that coast during the summer. It seems strange that I cannot recall just when and where I saw him, but early after his return to Cambridge I had a message from him asking me to come to a meeting of the Dante Club at Craigie House.

Longfellow was that winter (1866–7) revising his translation of the *Paradiso,* and the Dante Club was the circle of Italianate friends and scholars whom he invited to follow him and criticize his work from the original, while he read his version aloud. Those who were most constantly present were Lowell and Professor Norton, but from time to time others came in, and we seldom sat down at the nine-o'clock supper that followed the reading of the canto in less number than ten or twelve.

The criticism, especially from the accomplished Danteists I have named, was frank and frequent. I believe they neither of them quite agreed with Longfellow as to the form of version he had chosen, but waiving that, the question was how perfectly he had done his work upon the given lines. I myself, with whatever right, great or little, I may have to an opinion, believe thoroughly in Longfellow's plan. When I read his version my sense aches for the rhyme which he rejected, but my admiration for his fidelity to Dante otherwise is immeasurable. I remember with equal admiration the subtle and sympathetic scholarship of his critics, who scrutinized every shade of meaning in a word or phrase that gave them pause, and did not let it pass till all the reasons and facts had been considered. Sometimes, and even often, Longfellow yielded to their censure, but for the most part, when he was of another mind, he held to his mind, and the passage had to go as he said. I make a little haste to say that in all the meetings of the Club, during a whole winter of Wednesday evenings, I myself, though I faithfully followed in an Italian Dante with the rest, ventured upon one suggestion only. This was kindly, even seriously, considered by the poet, and gently rejected. He could not do anything otherwise than gently, and I was not suffered to feel that I had done a presumptuous thing. I can see him now, as he looked up from the proof-sheets on the round table before him, and over at me, growing consciously smaller and smaller, like something through a reversed opera-glass. He had a shaded drop-light in front of him, and in its glow his beautiful and benignly noble head had a dignity peculiar to him.

All the portraits of Longfellow are likenesses more or less bad and good, for there was something as simple in the physiognomy as in the nature of the man. His head, after he allowed his beard to grow and wore his hair long in the manner of elderly men, was leonine, but mildly leonine, as the old painters conceived the lion of St. Mark. Once Sophocles, the ex-monk of Mount Athos, so long a Greek professor at Harvard, came in for supper, after the reading was over, and he was leonine too, but of a fierceness that contrasted finely with Longfellow's mildness. I remember the poet's asking him something about the punishment of impaling, in Turkey, and his answering, with an ironical gleam of his fiery eyes, " Unhappily, it is obsolete." I dare say he was not so leonine, either, as he looked.

When Longfellow read verse, it was with a hollow, with a mellow resonant murmur, like the note of some deep-throated horn. His voice was very lulling in quality, and at the Dante Club it used to have early effect with an old scholar who sat in a cavernous arm-chair at the corner of the fire, and who drowsed audibly in the soft tone and the gentle heat. The poet had a fat terrier who wished always to be present at the meetings of the Club, and he commonly fell asleep at the same moment with that dear old scholar, so that when they began to make themselves heard in concert, one could not tell which it was that most took our thoughts from the text of the *Paradiso*. When the duet opened, Longfellow would look up with an arch recognition of the fact, and then go gravely on to the end of the canto. At the close he would speak to his friend and lead him out to supper as if he had not seen or heard anything amiss.

III

In that elect company I was silent, partly because I was conscious of my youthful inadequacy, and partly because I preferred to listen. But Longfellow always behaved as if I were saying a succession of edifying and delightful things, and from time to time he addressed himself to me, so that I should not feel left out. He did not talk much himself, and I recall nothing that he said. But he always spoke both wisely and simply, without the least touch of pose, and with no intention of effect, but with something that I must call quality for want of a better word; so that at a table where Holmes sparkled, and Lowell glowed, and Agassiz beamed, he cast the light of a gentle gayety, which seemed to dim all those vivider luminaries. While he spoke you did not miss Fields's story or Tom Appleton's wit, or even the gracious amity of Mr. Norton, with his unequalled intuitions.

The supper was very plain: a cold turkey, which the host carved, or a haunch of venison, or some braces of grouse, or a platter of quails, with a deep bowl of salad, and the sympathetic companionship of those elect vintages which Longfellow loved, and which he chose with the inspiration of affection. We usually began with oysters, and when some one who was expected did not come promptly, Longfellow invited us to raid his plate, as a just punishment of his delay. One evening Lowell remarked, with the cayenne poised above his bluepoints, " It's astonishing how fond these fellows are of pepper."

The old friend of the cavernous arm-chair was perhaps not wide enough awake to repress an " Ah ?" of deep interest in this fact of natural history, and Lowell was provoked to go on. " Yes, I've dropped a red pepper pod into a barrel of them, before now, and then taken them out in a solid mass, clinging to it like a swarm of bees to their queen."

" Is it possible?" cried the old friend; and then Longfellow intervened to save him from worse, and turned the talk.

I reproach myself that I made no record of the talk, for I find that only a few fragments of it have caught in my memory, and that the sieve which should have kept the gold has let it wash away with the gravel. I remember once Doctor Holmes's talking of the physician as the true seer, whose awful gift it was to behold with the fatal second sight of science the shroud gathering to the throat of many a doomed man apparently in perfect health, and happy in the promise of unnumbered days. The thought may have been suggested by some of the toys of superstition which intellectual people like to play with.

I never could be quite sure at first that Longfellow's brother-in-law, Appleton, was seriously a spiritualist, even when he disputed the most strenuously with the unbelieving Autocrat. But he really was in earnest about it, though he relished a joke at the expense of his doctrine, like some clerics when they are in the safe company of other clerics. He told me once of having recounted to Agassiz the facts of a very remarkable séance, where the souls of the departed outdid themselves in the athletics and acrobatics they seem so fond of over there, throwing large stones across the room, moving pianos, and lifting dinner-tables and setting them a-twirl under the chandelier. " And now," he demanded, " what do you say to that ?" " Well, Mr. Appleton," Agassiz answered, to Appleton's infinite delight, *" I say that it did not happen."*

One night they began to speak at the Dante supper of the unhappy man whose crime is a red stain in the Cambridge annals, and one and another recalled their impressions of Professor Webster. It was possibly with a retroactive sense that they had all felt something uncanny in him, but, apropos of the deep salad-bowl in the centre of the table, Longfellow remembered a supper Webster was at, where he lighted some chemical in such a dish and held his head over it, with a handkerchief noosed about his throat and lifted above it with one hand, while his face, in the pale light, took on the livid ghastliness of that of a man hanged by the neck.

Another night the talk wandered to the visit which an English author (now with God) paid America at the height of a popularity long since toppled to the ground, with many another. He was in very good humor with our whole continent, and at Longfellow's table he found the champagne even surprisingly fine. " But," he said to his host, who now told the story, " it cawn't be *genuine,* you know!"

Many years afterwards this author revisited our

shores, and I dined with him at Longfellow's, where
he was anxious to constitute himself a guest during
his sojourn in our neighborhood. Longfellow was
equally anxious that he should not do so, and he took
a harmless pleasure in outmanœuvring him. He seized
a chance to speak with me alone, and plotted to deliver him over to me without apparent unkindness,
when the latest horse-car should be going in to Boston,
and begged me to walk him to Harvard Square and put
him aboard. " Put him aboard, and don't leave him
till the car starts, and then watch that he doesn't get
off."

These instructions he accompanied with a lifting of
the eyebrows, and a pursing of the mouth, in an anxiety not altogether burlesque. He knew himself the
prey of any one who chose to batten on him, and his
hospitality was subject to frightful abuse. Perhaps
Mr. Norton has somewhere told how, when he asked
if a certain person who had been outstaying his time
was not a dreadful bore, Longfellow answered, with
angelic patience, " Yes; but then you know I have
been bored so often!"

There was one fatal Englishman whom I shared
with him during the great part of a season: a poor
soul, not without gifts, but always ready for more,
especially if they took the form of meat and drink.
He had brought letters from one of the best Englishmen alive, who withdrew them too late to save his
American friends from the sad consequences of welcoming him. So he established himself impregnably
in a Boston club, and came out every day to dine with
Longfellow in Cambridge, beginning with his return
from Nahant in October and continuing far into De-
cember. That was the year of the great horse-dis-
temper, when the plague disabled the transportation

187

in Boston, and cut off all intercourse between the suburb and the city on the street railways. "I did think," Longfellow pathetically lamented, "that when the horse-cars stopped running, I should have a little respite from L., *but he walks out.*"

In the midst of his own suffering he was willing to advise with me concerning some poems L. had offered to the *Atlantic Monthly,* and after we had desperately read them together he said, with inspiration, "I think these things are more adapted to music than the magazine," and this seemed so good a notion that when L. came to know their fate from me, I answered, confidently, "I think they are rather more adapted to music."

He calmly asked, "Why?" and as this was an exigency which Longfellow had not forecast for me, I was caught in it without hope of escape. I really do not know what I said, but I know that I did not take the poems, such was my literary conscience in those days; I am afraid I should be weaker now.

IV

The suppers of the Dante Club were a relaxation from the severity of their toils on criticism, and I will not pretend that their table-talk was of that seriousness which duller wits might have given themselves up to. The passing stranger, especially if a light or jovial person, was always welcome, and I never knew of the enforcement of the rule I heard of, that if you came in without question on the Club nights, you were a guest; but if you rang or knocked, you could not get in.

Any sort of diversion was hailed, and once Appleton proposed that Longfellow should show us his wine-

cellar. He took up the candle burning on the table
for the cigars, and led the way into the basement of the
beautiful old Colonial mansion, doubly memorable as
Washington's headquarters while he was in Cambridge, and as the home of Longfellow for so many
years. The taper cast just the right gleams on the
darkness, bringing into relief the massive piers of
brick, and the solid walls of stone, which gave the cellar the effect of a casemate in some fortress, and leaving the corners and distances to a romantic gloom.
This basement was a work of the days when men built
more heavily if not more substantially than now, but
I forget, if I ever knew, what date the wine-cellar was
of. It was well stored with precious vintages, aptly
cobwebbed and dusty; but I could not find that it had
any more charm than the shelves of a library: it is the
inside of bottles and of books that makes its appeal.
The whole place witnessed a bygone state and luxury,
which otherwise lingered in a dim legend or two.
Longfellow once spoke of certain old love-letters which
dropped down on the basement stairs from some
place overhead; and there was the fable or the fact of
a subterranean passage under the street from Craigie
House to the old Batchelder House, which I relate
to these letters with no authority I can allege. But in
Craigie House dwelt the proud fair lady who was
buried in the Cambridge church-yard with a slave at
her head and a slave at her feet.

" Dust is in her beautiful eyes,"

and whether it was they that smiled or wept in their
time over those love-letters, I will leave the reader to
say. The fortunes of her Tory family fell with those
of their party, and the last Vassal ended his days a
prisoner from his creditors in his own house, with a

weekly enlargement on Sundays, when the law could not reach him. It is known how the place took Longfellow's fancy when he first came to be professor in Harvard, and how he was a lodger of the last Mistress Craigie there, long before he became its owner. The house is square, with Longfellow's study where he read and wrote on the right of the door, and a statelier library behind it; on the left is the drawing-room, with the dining-room in its rear; from its square hall climbs a beautiful stairway with twisted banisters, and a tall clock in their angle.

The study where the Dante Club met, and where I mostly saw Longfellow, was a plain, pleasant room, with broad panelling in white painted pine; in the centre before the fireplace stood his round table, laden with books, papers, and proofs; in the farthest corner by the window was a high desk which he sometimes stood at to write. In this room Washington held his councils and transacted his business with all comers; in the chamber overhead he slept. I do not think Longfellow associated the place much with him, and I never heard him speak of Washington in relation to it except once, when he told me with peculiar relish what he called the true version of a pious story concerning the aide-de-camp who blundered in upon him while he knelt in prayer. The father of his country rose and rebuked the young man severely, and then resumed his devotions. "He rebuked him," said Longfellow, lifting his brows and making rings round the pupils of his eyes, "by throwing his scabbard at his head."

All the front windows of Craigie House look out over the open fields across the Charles, which is now the Longfellow Memorial Garden. The poet used to be amused with the popular superstition that he was holding this vacant ground with a view to a rise in the price of lots, while all he wanted was to keep a feature of his beloved landscape unchanged. Lofty elms drooped at the corners of the house; on the lawn billowed clumps of the lilac, which formed a thick hedge along the fence. There was a terrace part way down this lawn, and when a white-painted balustrade was set some fifteen years ago upon its brink, it seemed always to have been there. Long verandas stretched on either side of the mansion; and behind was an old-fashioned garden with beds primly edged with box after a design of the poet's own. Longfellow had a ghost story of this quaint plaisance, which he used to tell with an artful reserve of the catastrophe. He was coming home one winter night, and as he crossed the garden he was startled by a white figure swaying before him. But he knew that the only way was to advance upon it. He pushed boldly forward, and was suddenly caught under the throat—by the clothes-line with a long night-gown on it.

Perhaps it was at the end of a long night of the Dante Club that I heard him tell this story. The evenings were sometimes mornings before the reluctant break-up came, but they were never half long enough for me. I have given no idea of the high reasoning of vital things which I must often have heard at that table, and that I have forgotten it is no proof that I did not hear it. The memory will not be ruled as to what it shall bind and what it shall loose, and I should entreat mine in vain for record of those meetings other than what I have given. Perhaps it would be well, in the interest of some popular conceptions of what the social intercourse of great wits must be, for me to invent some ennobling and elevating passages of conversation at Longfellow's; perhaps I ought to do it for

191

the sake of my own repute as a serious and adequate witness. But I am rather helpless in the matter; I must set down what I remember, and surely if I can remember no phrase from Holmes that a reader could live or die by, it is something to recall how, when a certain potent cheese was passing, he leaned over to gaze at it, and asked: "Does it kick? Does it kick?" No strain of high poetic thinking remains to me from Lowell, but he made me laugh unforgettably with his passive adventure one night going home late, when a man suddenly leaped from the top of a high fence upon the sidewalk at his feet, and after giving him the worst fright of his life, disappeared peaceably into the darkness. To be sure, there was one most memorable supper, when he read the "Bigelow Paper" he had finished that day, and enriched the meaning of his verse with the beauty of his voice. There lingers yet in my sense his very tone in giving the last line of the passage lamenting the waste of the heroic lives which in those dark hours of Johnson's time seemed to have been

"Butchered to make a blind man's holiday."

The hush that followed upon his ceasing was of that finest quality which spoken praise always lacks; and I suppose that I could not give a just notion of these Dante Club evenings without imparting the effect of such silences. This I could not hopefully undertake to do; but I am tempted to some effort of the kind by my remembrance of Longfellow's old friend George Washington Greene, who often came up from his home in Rhode Island, to be at those sessions, and who was a most interesting and amiable fact of those delicate silences. A full half of his earlier life had been passed in Italy, where he and Longfellow met and loved each other in their youth with an affection which the

192

poet was constant to in his age, after many vicissitudes, with the beautiful fidelity of his nature. Greene was like an old Italian house-priest in manner, gentle, suave, very suave, smooth as creamy curds, cultivated in the elegancies of literary taste, and with a certain meek abeyance. I think I never heard him speak, in all those evenings, except when Longfellow addressed him, though he must have had the Dante scholarship for an occasional criticism. It was at more recent dinners, where I met him with the Longfellow family alone, that he broke now and then into a quotation from some of the modern Italian poets he knew by heart (preferably Giusti), and syllabled their verse with an exquisite Roman accent and a bewitching Florentine rhythm. Now and then at these times he brought out a faded Italian anecdote, faintly smelling of civet, and threadbare in its ancient texture. He liked to speak of Goldoni and of Nota, of Niccolini and Manzoni, of Monti and Leopardi; and if you came to America, of the Revolution and his grandfather, the Quaker General Nathaniel Greene, whose life he wrote (and I read) in three volumes. He worshipped Longfellow, and their friendship continued while they lived, but towards the last of his visits at Craigie House it had a pathos for the witness which I should grieve to wrong. Greene was then a quivering paralytic, and he clung tremulously to Longfellow's arm in going out to dinner, where even the modern Italian poets were silent upon his lips. When we rose from table, Longfellow lifted him out of his chair, and took him upon his arm again for their return to the study.

He was of lighter metal than most other members of the Dante Club, and he was not of their immediate intimacy, living away from Cambridge, as he did, and I shared his silence in their presence with full sympathy. I was by far the youngest of their number, and I cannot yet quite make out why I was of it at all. But at every moment I was as sensible of my good fortune as of my ill desert. They were the men whom of all men living I most honored, and it seemed to be impossible that I at my age should be so perfectly fulfilling the dream of my life in their company. Often the nights were very cold, and as I returned home from Craigie House to the carpenter's box on Sacramento Street, a mile or two away, I was as if soul-borne through the air by my pride and joy, while the frozen blocks of snow clinked and tinkled before my feet stumbling along the middle of the road. I still think that was the richest moment of my life, and I look back at it as the moment, in a life not unblessed by chance, which I would most like to live over again—if I must live any.

The next winter the sessions of the Dante Club were transferred to the house of Mr. Norton, who was then completing his version of the *Vita Nuova*. This has always seemed to me a work of not less graceful art than Longfellow's translation of the *Commedia*. In fact, it joins the effect of a sympathy almost mounting to divination with a patient scholarship and a delicate skill unknown to me elsewhere in such work. I do not know whether Mr. Norton has satisfied himself better in his prose version of the *Commedia* than in this of the *Vita Nuova,* but I do not believe he could have satisfied Dante better, unless he had rhymed his sonnets and canzonets. I am sure he might have done this if he had chosen. He has always pretended that it was impossible, but miracles are never impossible in the right hands.

V

After three or four years we sold the carpenter's box on Sacramento Street, and removed to a larger house near Harvard Square, and in the immediate neighborhood of Longfellow. He gave me an easement across that old garden behind his house, through an opening in the high board fence which enclosed it, and I saw him oftener than ever, though the meetings of the Dante Club had come to an end. At the last of them, Lowell had asked him, with fond regret in his jest, " Longfellow, why don't you do that Indian poem in forty thousand verses?" The demand but feebly expressed the reluctance in us all, though I suspect the Indian poem existed only by the challenger's invention. Before I leave my faint and unworthy record of these great times I am tempted to mention an incident poignant with tragical associations. The first night after Christmas the holly and the pine wreathed about the chandelier above the supper-table took fire from the gas, just as we came out from the reading, and Longfellow ran forward and caught the burning garlands down and bore them out. No one could speak for thinking what he must be thinking of when the ineffable calamity of his home befell it. Curtis once told me that a little while before Mrs. Longfellow's death he was driving by Craigie House with Holmes, who said he trembled to look at it, for those who lived there had their happiness so perfect that no change, of all the changes which must come to them, could fail to be for the worse.

I did not know Longfellow before that fatal time, and I shall not say that his presence bore record of it except in my fancy. He may always have had that look of one who had experienced the utmost harm that fate can do, and henceforth could possess himself of what was left of life in peace. He could never have been a man of the flowing ease that makes all comers at home; some people complained of a certain *gêne* in him; and he had a reserve with strangers, which never quite lost itself in the abandon of friendship, as Lowell's did. He was the most perfectly modest man I ever saw, ever imagined, but he had a gentle dignity which I do not believe any one, the coarsest, the obtusest, could tres- pass upon. In the years when I began to know him, his long hair and the beautiful beard which mixed with it were of one iron-gray, which I saw blanch to a per- fect silver, while that pearly tone of his complexion, which Appleton so admired, lost itself in the wanness of age and pain. When he walked, he had a kind of spring in his gait, as if now and again a buoyant thought lifted him from the ground. It was fine to meet him coming down a Cambridge street; you felt that the en- counter made you a part of literary history, and set you apart with him for the moment from the poor and mean. When he appeared in Harvard Square, he beat- ified if not beautified the ugliest and vulgarest looking spot on the planet outside of New York. You could meet him sometimes at the market, if you were of the same provision-man as he; and Longfellow remained as constant to his tradespeople as to any other friends. He rather liked to bring his proofs back to the printer's himself, and we often found ourselves together at the University Press, where the *Atlantic Monthly* used to be printed. But outside of his own house Longfellow seemed to want a fit atmosphere, and I love best to think of him in his study, where he wrought at his lovely art with a serenity expressed in his smooth, regular, and scrupulously perfect handwriting. It was quite vertical, and rounded, with a slope neither to the right nor left, and at the time I knew him first, he was fond of using a soft pencil on printing paper, though commonly he wrote with a quill. Each letter was distinct in shape, and between the verses was always the exact space of half an inch. I have a good many of his poems written in this fashion, but whether they were the first drafts or not I cannot say; very likely not. Towards the last he no longer sent his poems to the magazines in his own hand, but they were always signed in autograph.

I once asked him if he were not a great deal interrupted, and he said, with a faint sigh, Not more than was good for him, he fancied; if it were not for the interruptions, he might overwork. He was not a friend to stated exercise, I believe, nor fond of walking, as Lowell was; he had not, indeed, the childish associations of the younger poet with the Cambridge neighborhoods; and I never saw him walking for pleasure except on the east veranda of his house, though I was told he loved walking in his youth. In this and in some other things Longfellow was more European than American, more Latin than Saxon. He once said quaintly that one got a great deal of exercise in putting on and off one's overcoat and overshoes.

I suppose no one who asked decently at his door was denied access to him, and there must have been times when he was overrun with volunteer visitors; but I never heard him complain of them. He was very charitable in the immediate sort which Christ seems to have meant; but he had his preferences, humorously owned, among beggars. He liked the German beggars least, and the Italian beggars most, as having most *savoir-faire;* in fact, we all loved the Italians in Cambridge. He was pleased with the accounts I could give him of the love and honor I had known for him in

Italy, and one day there came a letter from an Italian admirer, addressed to " Mr. Greatest Poet Longfellow," which he said was the very most amusing superscription he had ever seen.

It is known that the King of Italy offered Longfellow the cross of San Lazzaro, which is the Italian literary decoration. It came through the good offices of my old acquaintance Professor Messadaglia, then a deputy in the Italian Parliament, whom, for some reason I cannot remember, I had put in correspondence with Longfellow. The honor was wholly unexpected, and it brought Longfellow a distress which was chiefly for the gentleman who had procured him the impossible distinction. He showed me the pretty collar and cross, not, I think, without a natural pleasure in it. No man was ever less a bigot in things civil or religious than he, but he said, firmly, " Of course, as a republican and a Protestant, I can't accept a decoration from a Catholic prince." His decision was from his conscience, and I think that all Americans who think duly about it will approve his decision.

VI

Such honors as he could fitly permit himself he did not refuse, and I recall what zest he had in his election to the Arcadian Academy, which had made him a shepherd of its Roman Fold, with the title, as he said, of " Olimipico something." But I fancy his sweetest pleasure in his vast renown came from his popular recognition everywhere. Few were the lands, few the languages he was unknown to: he showed me a version of the " Psalm of Life " in Chinese. Apparently even the poor lost autograph-seeker was not denied by his universal kindness; I know that he kept a store of auto-

graphs ready written on small squares of paper for all
who applied by letter or in person; he said it was no
trouble; but perhaps he was to be excused for refusing
the request of a lady for fifty autographs, which she
wished to offer as a novel attraction to her guests at a
lunch party.

Foreigners of all kinds thronged upon him at their
pleasure, apparently, and with perfect impunity. Sometimes he got a little fun, very, very kindly, out of their
excuses and reasons; and the Englishman who came to
see him because there were no ruins to visit in America
was no fable, as I can testify from the poet himself.
But he had no prejudice against Englishmen, and even
at a certain time when the coarse-handed British criticism began to blame his delicate art for the universal
acceptance of his verse, and to try to sneer him into
the rank of inferior poets, he was without rancor for
the clumsy misliking that he felt. He could not understand rudeness; he was too finely framed for that; he
could know it only as Swedenborg's most celestial angels
perceived evil, as something distressful, angular. The
ill-will that seemed nearly always to go with adverse
criticism made him distrust criticism, and the discomfort which mistaken or blundering praise gives
probably made him shy of all criticism. He said
that in his early life as an author he used to seek
out and save all the notices of his poems, but in his
latter days he read only those that happened to fall
in his way; these he cut out and amused his leisure
by putting together in scrap - books. He was reluctant to make any criticism of other poets; I do not
remember ever to have heard him make one; and his
writings show no trace of the literary dislikes or con-
tempts which we so often mistake in ourselves for right-
eous judgments. No doubt he had his resentments, but

he hushed them in his heart, which he did not suffer them to embitter. While Poe was writing of " Longfellow and other Plagiarists," Longfellow was helping to keep Poe alive by the loans which always made themselves gifts in Poe's case. He very, very rarely spoke of himself at all, and almost never of the grievances which he did not fail to share with all who live.

He was patient, as I said, of all things, and gentle beyond all mere gentlemanliness. But it would have been a great mistake to mistake his mildness for softness. It was most manly and firm; and of course it was braced with the New England conscience he was born to. If he did not find it well to assert himself, he was prompt in behalf of his friends, and one of the fine things told of him was his resenting some censures of Sumner at a dinner in Boston during the old pro-slavery times: he said to the gentlemen present that Sumner was his friend, and he must leave their company if they continued to assail him.

But he spoke almost as rarely of his friends as of himself. He liked the large, impersonal topics which could be dealt with on their human side, and involved characters rather than individuals. This was rather strange in Cambridge, where we were apt to take our instances from the environment. It was not the only thing he was strange in there; he was not to that manner born; he lacked the final intimacies which can come only of birth and lifelong association, and which make the men of the Boston breed seem exclusive when they least feel so; he was Longfellow to the friends who were James, and Charles, and Wendell to one another. He and Hawthorne were classmates at college, but I never heard him mention Hawthorne; I never heard him mention Whittier or Emerson. I think his reticence about his contemporaries was largely due to his reluctance from criticism: he was the finest artist of them all, and if he praised he must have praised with the reservations of an honest man. Of younger writers he was willing enough to speak. No new contributor made his mark in the magazine unnoted by him, and sometimes I showed him verse in manuscript which gave me peculiar pleasure. I remember his liking for the first piece that Mr. Maurice Thompson sent me, and how he tasted the fresh flavor of it, and inhaled its wild new fragrance. He admired the skill of some of the young story-tellers; he praised the subtlety of one in working out an intricate character, and said modestly that he could never have done that sort of thing himself. It was entirely safe to invite his judgment when in doubt, for he never suffered it to become aggressive, or used it to urge upon me the manuscripts that must often have been urged upon him.

Longfellow had a house at Nahant where he went every summer for more than a quarter of a century. He found the slight transition change enough from Cambridge, and liked it perhaps because it did not take him beyond the range of the friends and strangers whose company he liked. Agassiz was there, and Appleton; Sumner came to sojourn with him; and the tourists of all nations found him there in half an hour after they reached Boston. His cottage was very plain and simple, but was rich in the sight of the illimitable sea, and it had a luxury of rocks at the foot of its garden, draped with sea-weed, and washed with the indefatigable tides. As he grew older and feebler he ceased to go to Nahant; he remained the whole year round at Cambridge; he professed to like the summer which he said warmed him through there, better than the cold spectacle of summer which had no such effect at Nahant.

The hospitality which was constant at either house

was not merely of the worldly sort. Longfellow loved
good cheer; he tasted history and poetry in a precious
wine; and he liked people who were acquainted with
manners and men, and brought the air of capitals with
them. But often the man who dined with Longfellow
was the man who needed a dinner; and from what I
have seen of the sweet courtesy that governed at that
board, I am sure that such a man could never have felt
himself the least honored guest. The poet's heart was
open to all the homelessness of the world; and I remember how once when we sat at his table and I spoke of his
poem of " The Challenge," then a new poem, and said
how I had been touched by the fancy of

> " The poverty-stricken millions
> Who challenge our wine and bread,
> And impeach us all as traitors,
> Both the living and the dead,"

his voice sank in grave humility as he answered, " Yes,
I often think of those things." He had thought of them
in the days of the slave, when he had taken his place
with the friends of the hopeless and hapless, and as long
as he lived he continued of the party which had freed
the slave. He did not often speak of politics, but when
the movement of some of the best Republicans away
from their party began, he said that he could not see the
wisdom of their course. But this was said without
censure or criticism of them, and so far as I know he
never permitted himself anything like denunciation of
those who in any wise differed from him. On a matter
of yet deeper interest, I do not feel authorized to speak
for him, but I think that as he grew older, his hold upon
anything like a creed weakened, though he remained of
the Unitarian philosophy concerning Christ. He did
not latterly go to church, I believe; but then, very few
of his circle were church-goers. Once he said some-

thing very vague and uncertain concerning the doctrine of another life when I affirmed my hope of it, to the effect that he wished he could be sure, with the sigh that so often clothed the expression of a misgiving with him.

VII

When my acquaintance with Longfellow began he had written the things that made his fame, and that it will probably rest upon: " Evangeline," " Hiawatha," and the " Courtship of Miles Standish " were by that time old stories. But during the eighteen years that I knew him he produced the best of his minor poems, the greatest of his sonnets, the sweetest of his lyrics. His art ripened to the last, it grew richer and finer, and it never knew decay. He rarely read anything of his own aloud, but in three or four cases he read to me poems he had just finished, as if to give himself the pleasure of hearing them with the sympathetic sense of another. The hexameter piece, " Elizabeth," in the third part of " Tales of a Wayside Inn," was one of these, and he liked my liking its rhythmical form, which I believed one of the measures best adapted to the English speech, and which he had used himself with so much pleasure and success.

About this time he was greatly interested in the slight experiments I was beginning to make in dramatic form, and he said that if he were himself a young man he should write altogether for the stage; he thought the drama had a greater future with us. He was pleased when a popular singer wished to produce his " Masque of Pandora," with music, and he was patient when it failed of the effect hoped for it as an opera. When the late Lawrence Barrett, in the enthusiasm which was one of the fine traits of his generous character, had taken my play of " A Counterfeit Presentment," and came to the Boston Museum with it, Longfellow could not apparently have been more zealous for its popular acceptance if it had been his own work. He invited himself to one of the rehearsals with me, and he sat with me on the stage through the four acts with a forti-tude which I still wonder at, and with the keenest zest for all the details of the performance. No finer testi-mony to the love and honor which all kinds of people had for him could have been given than that shown by the actors and employees of the theatre, high and low. They thronged the scenery, those who were not upon the stage, and at the edge of every wing were faces peering round at the poet, who sat unconscious of their adora-tion, intent upon the play. He was intercepted at every step in going out, and made to put his name to the pho-tographs of himself which his worshippers produced from their persons.

He came to the first night of the piece, and when it seemed to be finding favor with the public, he leaned forward out of his line to nod and smile at the author; when they had the author up, it was the sweetest flat-tery of the applause which abused his fondness that Longfellow clapped first and loudest.

Where once he had given his kindness he could not again withhold it, and he was anxious no fact should be interpreted as withdrawal. When the Emperor Dom Pedro of Brazil, who was so great a lover of Longfel-low, came to Boston, he asked himself out to dine with the poet, who had expected to offer him some such hos-pitality. Soon after, Longfellow met me, and as if eager to forestall a possible feeling in me, said, " I wanted to ask *you* to dinner with the Emperor, but he not only sent word he was coming, he named his fellow-guests !" I answered that though I should probably never come so near dining with an emperor again, I prized his wish to ask me much more than the chance I had missed; and with this my great and good friend seemed a little consoled. I believe that I do not speak too confidently of our relation. He was truly the friend of all men, but I had certainly the advantage of my propinquity. We were near neighbors, as the pleonasm has it, both when I lived on Berkeley Street and after I had built my own house on Concord Avenue; and I suppose he found my youthful informality convenient. He always asked me to dinner when his old friend Greene came to visit him, and then we had an Italian time together, with more or less repetition in our talk, of what we had said before of Italian poetry and Italian character. One day there came a note from him saying, in effect, " Salvini is coming out to dine with me to-morrow night, and I want you to come too. There will be no one else but Greene and myself, and we will have an Italian dinner."

Unhappily I had accepted a dinner in Boston for that night, and this invitation put me in great misery. I must keep my engagement, but how could I bear to miss meeting Salvini at Longfellow's table on terms like these? We consulted at home together and questioned whether I might not rush into Boston, seek out my host there, possess him of the facts, and frankly throw myself on his mercy. Then a sudden thought struck us: Go to Longfellow, and submit the case to him! I went, and he entered with delicate sympathy into the affair. But he decided that, taking the large view of it, I must keep my engagement, lest I should run even a remote risk of wounding my friend's susceptibilities. I obeyed, and I had a very good time, but I still feel that I missed the best time of my life, and that I ought to be rewarded for my sacrifice, somewhere.

Longfellow so rarely spoke of himself in any way that one heard from him few of those experiences of the distinguished man in contact with the undistinguished, which he must have had so abundantly. But he told, while it was fresh in his mind, an incident that happened to him one day in Boston at a tobacconist's, where a certain brand of cigars was recommended to him as the kind Longfellow smoked. "Ah, then I must have some of them; and I will ask you to send me a box," said Longfellow, and he wrote down his name and address. The cigar-dealer read it with the smile of a worsted champion, and said, "Well, I guess you *had* me, *that* time." At a funeral a mourner wished to open conversation, and by way of suggesting a theme of common interest, began, "*You've* buried, I believe?"

Sometimes people were shown by the poet through Craigie House who had no knowledge of it except that it had been Washington's headquarters. Of course Longfellow was known by sight to every one in Cambridge. He was daily in the streets, while his health endured, and as he kept no carriage, he was often to be met in the horse-cars, which were such common ground in Cambridge that they were often like small invited parties of friends when they left Harvard Square, so that you expected the gentlemen to jump up and ask the ladies whether they would have chicken salad. In civic and political matters he mingled so far as to vote regularly, and he voted with his party, trusting it for a general regard to the public welfare.

I fancy he was somewhat shy of his fellow-men, as the scholar seems always to be, from the sequestered habit of his life; but I think Longfellow was incapable of marking any difference between himself and them. I never heard from him anything that was *de haut en*

bas, when he spoke of people, and in Cambridge, where
there was a good deal of contempt for the less lettered,
and we liked to smile though we did not like to sneer,
and to analyze if we did not censure, Longfellow and
Longfellow's house were free of all that. Whatever
his feeling may have been towards other sorts and conditions of men, his effect was of an entire democracy.
He was always the most unassuming person in any
company, and at some large public dinners where I saw
him I found him patient of the greater attention that
more public men paid themselves and one another.
He was not a speaker, and I never saw him on his feet
at dinner, except once, when he read a poem for Whittier, who was absent. He disliked after-dinner speaking, and made conditions for his own exemption from
it.

VIII

Once your friend, Longfellow was always your
friend; he would not think evil of you, and if he knew
evil of you, he would be the last of all that knew it to
judge you for it. This may have been from the impersonal habit of his mind, but I believe it was also
the effect of principle, for he would do what he could
to arrest the delivery of judgment from others, and
would soften the sentences passed in his presence.
Naturally this brought him under some condemnation
with those of a severer cast; and I have heard him
criticised for his benevolence towards all, and his constancy to some who were not quite so true to themselves, perhaps. But this leniency of Longfellow's
was what constituted him great as well as good, for it
is not our wisdom that censures others. As for his
goodness, I never saw a fault in him. I do not mean
to say that he had no faults, or that there were no bet-

LITERARY FRIENDS AND ACQUAINTANCE

ter men, but only to give the witness of my knowledge concerning him. I claim in no wise to have been his intimate; such a thing was not possible in my case for quite apparent reasons; and I doubt if Longfellow was capable of intimacy in the sense we mostly attach to the word. Something more of egotism than I ever found in him must go to the making of any intimacy which did not come from the tenderest affections of his heart. But as a man shows himself to those often with him, and in his noted relations with other men, he showed himself without blame. All men that I have known, besides, have had some foible (it often endeared them the more), or some meanness, or pettiness, or bitterness; but Longfellow had none, nor the suggestion of any. No breath of evil ever touched his name; he went in and out among his fellow-men without the reproach that follows wrong; the worst thing I ever heard said of him was that he had *gêne,* and this was said by one of those difficult Cambridge men who would have found *gêne* in a celestial angel. Something that Björnstjerne Björnson wrote to me when he was leaving America after a winter in Cambridge, comes nearer suggesting Longfellow than all my talk. The Norsemen, in the days of their stormy and reluctant conversion, used always to speak of Christ as the White Christ, and Björnson said in his letter, " Give my love to the White Mr. Longfellow."

A good many years before Longfellow's death he began to be sleepless, and he suffered greatly. He said to me once that he felt as if he were going about with his heart in a kind of mist. The whole night through he would not be aware of having slept. " But," he would add, with his heavenly patience, " I always get a good deal of rest from lying down so long." I cannot say whether these conditions persisted, or how

THE WASHINGTON ELM, CAMBRIDGE

much his insomnia had to do with his breaking health; three or four years before the end came, we left Cambridge for a house farther in the country, and I saw him less frequently than before. He did not allow our meetings to cease; he asked me to dinner from time to time, as if to keep them up, but it could not be with the old frequency. Once he made a point of coming to see us in our cottage on the hill west of Cambridge, but it was with an effort not visible in the days when he could end one of his brief walks at our house on Concord Avenue; he never came but he left our house more luminous for his having been there. Once he came to supper there to meet Garfield (an old family friend of mine in Ohio), and though he was suffering from a heavy cold, he would not scant us in his stay. I had some very bad sherry which he drank with the serenity of a martyr, and I shudder to this day to think what his kindness must have cost him. He told his story of the clothes-line ghost, and Garfield matched it with the story of an umbrella ghost who sheltered a friend of his through a midnight storm, but was not cheerful company to his beneficiary, who passed his hand through him at one point in the effort to take his arm.

After the end of four years I came to Cambridge to be treated for a long sickness, which had nearly been my last, and when I could get about I returned the visit Longfellow had not failed to pay me. But I did not find him, and I never saw him again in life. I went into Boston to finish the winter of 1881–2, and from time to time I heard that the poet was failing in health. As soon as I felt able to bear the horse-car journey I went out to Cambridge to see him. I had knocked once at his door, the friendly door that had so often opened to his welcome, and stood with the knocker in my hand when the door was suddenly set ajar, and a maid showed her face wet with tears. "How is Mr. Longfellow?" I palpitated, and with a burst of grief she answered, "Oh, the poor gentleman has just departed!" I turned away as if from a help-less intrusion at a death-bed.

At the services held in the house before the obsequies at the cemetery, I saw the poet for the last time, where

"Dead he lay among his books,"

in the library behind his study. Death seldom fails to bring serenity to all, and I will not pretend that there was a peculiar peacefulness in Longfellow's noble mask, as I saw it then. It was calm and benign as it had been in life; he could not have worn a gentler aspect in going out of the world than he had always worn in it; he had not to wait for death to dignify it with "the peace of God." All who were left of his old Cambridge were present, and among those who had come farther was Emerson. He went up to the bier, and with his arms crossed on his breast, and his elbows held in either hand, stood with his head patheti-cally fallen forward, looking down at the dead face. Those who knew how his memory was a mere blank, with faint gleams of recognition capriciously coming and going in it, must have felt that he was struggling to remember who it was lay there before him; and for me the electly simple words confessing his failure will always be pathetic with his remembered aspect: "The gentleman we have just been burying," he said, to the friend who had come with him, "was a sweet and beau-tiful soul; but I forget his name."

I had the privilege and honor of looking over the unprinted poems Longfellow left behind him, and of helping to decide which of them should be published.

210

There were not many of them, and some of these few were quite fragmentary. I gave my voice for the publication of all that had any sort of completeness, for in every one there was a touch of his exquisite art, the grace of his most lovely spirit. We have so far had two men only who felt the claim of their gift to the very best that the most patient skill could give its utterance: one was Hawthorne and the other was Longfellow. I shall not undertake to say which was the greater artist of these two; but I am sure that every one who has studied it must feel with me that the art of Longfellow held out to the end with no touch of decay in it, and that it equalled the art of any other poet of his time. It knew when to give itself, and more and more it knew when to withhold itself.

What Longfellow's place in literature will be, I shall not offer to say; that is Time's affair, not mine; but I am sure that with Tennyson and Browning he fully shared in the expression of an age which more completely than any former age got itself said by its poets.

STUDIES OF LOWELL

I HAVE already spoken of my earliest meetings with Lowell at Cambridge when I came to New England on a literary pilgrimage from the West in 1860. I saw him more and more after I went to live in Cambridge in 1866; and I now wish to record what I knew of him during the years that passed between this date and that of his death. If the portrait I shall try to paint does not seem a faithful likeness to others who knew him, I shall only claim that so he looked to me, at this moment and at that. If I do not keep myself quite out of the picture, what painter ever did?

I

It was in the summer of 1865 that I came home from my consular post at Venice; and two weeks after I landed in Boston, I went out to see Lowell at Elmwood, and give him an inkstand that I had brought him from Italy. The bronze lobster whose back opened and disclosed an inkpot and a sand-box was quite ugly; but I thought it beautiful then, and if Lowell thought otherwise he never did anything to let me know it. He put the thing in the middle of his writing-table (he nearly always wrote on a pasteboard pad resting upon his knees), and there it remained as long as I knew the place—a matter of twenty-five years;

JAMES RUSSELL LOWELL AT FORTY

but in all that time I suppose the inkpot continued as dry as the sand-box.

My visit was in the heat of August, which is as fervid in Cambridge as it can well be anywhere, and I still have a sense of his study windows lifted to the summer night, and the crickets and grasshoppers crying in at them from the lawns and the gardens outside. Other people went away from Cambridge in the summer to the sea and to the mountains, but Lowell always stayed at Elmwood, in an impassioned love for his home and for his town. I must have found him there in the afternoon, and he must have made me sup with him (dinner was at two o'clock) and then go with him for a long night of talk in his study. He liked to have some one help him idle the time away, and keep him as long as possible from his work; and no doubt I was impersonally serving his turn in this way, aside from any pleasure he might have had in my company as some one he had always been kind to, and as a fresh arrival from the Italy dear to us both.

He lighted his pipe, and from the depths of his easy-chair, invited my shy youth to all the ease it was capable of in his presence. It was not much; I loved him, and he gave me reason to think that he was fond of me, but in Lowell I was always conscious of an older and closer and stricter civilization than my own, an unbroken tradition, a more authoritative status. His democracy was more of the head and mine more of the heart, and his denied the equality which mine affirmed. But his nature was so noble and his reason so tolerant that whenever in our long acquaintance I found it well to come to open rebellion, as I more than once did, he admitted my right of insurrection, and never resented the outbreak. I disliked to differ with him, and perhaps he subtly felt this so much that he would not

213

dislike me for doing it. He even suffered being taxed with inconsistency, and where he saw that he had not been quite just, he would take punishment for his error, with a contrition that was sometimes humorous and always touching.

Just then it was the dark hour before the dawn, with Italy, and he was interested but not much encouraged by what I could tell him of the feeling in Venice against the Austrians. He seemed to reserve a like scepticism concerning the fine things I was hoping for the Italians in literature, and he confessed an interest in the facts treated which in the retrospect, I am aware, was more tolerant than participant of my enthusiasm. That was always Lowell's attitude towards the opinions of people he liked, when he could not go their lengths with them, and nothing was more characteristic of his affectionate nature and his just intelligence. He was a man of the most strenuous convictions, but he loved many sorts of people whose convictions he disagreed with, and he suffered even prejudices counter to his own if they were not ignoble. In the whimsicalities of others he delighted as much as in his own.

II

Our associations with Italy held over until the next day, when after breakfast he went with me towards Boston as far as " the village " : for so he liked to speak of Cambridge in the custom of his younger days when wide tracts of meadow separated Harvard Square from his life-long home at Elmwood. We stood on the platform of the horse-car together, and when I objected to his paying my fare in the American fashion, he allowed that the Italian usage of each paying for himself was the politer way. He would not commit himself about

214

my returning to Venice (for I had not given up my place, yet, and was away on leave), but he intimated his distrust of the flattering conditions of life abroad. He said it was charming to be treated *da signore,* but he seemed to doubt whether it was well; and in this as in all other things he showed his final fealty to the American ideal.

It was that serious and great moment after the successful close of the civil war when the republican consciousness was more robust in us than ever before or since; but I cannot recall any reference to the historical interest of the time in Lowell's talk. It had been all about literature and about travel; and now with the suggestion of the word village it began to be a little about his youth. I have said before how reluctant he was to let his youth go from him; and perhaps the touch with my juniority had made him realize how near he was to fifty, and set him thinking of the past which had sorrows in it to age him beyond his years. He would never speak of these, though he often spoke of the past. He told once of having been on a brief journey when he was six years old, with his father, and of driving up to the gate of Elmwood in the evening, and his father saying, " Ah, this is a pleasant place! I wonder who lives here—what little boy?" At another time he pointed out a certain window in his study, and said he could see himself standing by it when he could only get his chin on the window-sill. His memories of the house, and of everything belonging to it, were very tender; but he could laugh over an escapade of his youth when he helped his fellow-students pull down his father's fences, in the pure zeal of good-comradeship.

III

My fortunes took me to New York, and I spent most of the winter of 1865--6 writing in the office of *The Nation*. I contributed several sketches of Italian travel to that paper; and one of these brought me a precious letter from Lowell. He praised my sketch, which he said he had read without the least notion who had written it, and he wanted me to feel the full value of such an impersonal pleasure in it. At the same time he did not fail to tell me that he disliked some pseudo-cynical verses of mine which he had read in another place; and I believe it was then that he bade me " sweat the Heine out of " me, " as men sweat the mercury out of their bones."

When I was asked to be assistant editor of the *Atlantic Monthly,* and came on to Boston to talk the matter over with the publishers, I went out to Cambridge and consulted Lowell. He strongly urged me to take the position (I thought myself hopefully placed in New York on *The Nation*); and at the same time he seemed to have it on his heart to say that he had recommended some one else for it, never, he owned, having thought of me.

He was most cordial, but after I came to live in Cambridge (where the magazine was printed, and I could more conveniently look over the proofs), he did not call on me for more than a month, and seemed quite to have forgotten me. We met one night at Mr. Norton's, for one of the Dante readings, and he took no special notice of me till I happened to say something that offered him a chance to give me a little humorous snub. I was speaking of a paper in the Magazine on the " Claudian Emissary," and I demanded (no doubt a little too airily) something like " Who in the world

216

ever heard of the Claudian Emissary?" "*You are in Cambridge,* Mr. Howells," Lowell answered, and laughed at my confusion. Having put me down, he seemed to soften towards me, and at parting he said, with a light of half-mocking tenderness in his beautiful eyes, "Good-night, fellow-townsman." "I hardly knew we were fellow-townsmen," I returned. He liked that, apparently, and said he had been meaning to call upon me, and that he was coming very soon.

He was as good as his word, and after that hardly a week of any kind of weather passed but he mounted the steps to the door of the ugly little house in which I lived, two miles away from him, and asked me to walk. These walks continued, I suppose, until Lowell went abroad for a winter in the early seventies. They took us all over Cambridge, which he knew and loved every inch of, and led us afield through the straggling, unhandsome outskirts, bedrabbled with squalid Irish neighborhoods, and fraying off into marshes and salt meadows. He liked to indulge an excess of admiration for the local landscape, and though I never heard him profess a preference for the Charles River flats to the finest Alpine scenery, I could well believe he would do so under provocation of a fit listener's surprise. He had always so much of the boy in him that he liked to tease the over-serious or over-sincere. He liked to tease and he liked to mock, especially his juniors, if any touch of affectation, or any little exuberance of manner gave him the chance; when he once came to fetch me, and the young mistress of the house entered with a certain excessive elasticity, he sprang from his seat, and minced towards her, with a burlesque of her buoyant carriage —which made her laugh. When he had given us his heart in trust of ours, he used us like a younger brother and sister, or like his own children. He included our

217

children in his affection, and he enjoyed our fondness
for them as if it were something that had come back
to him from his own youth. I think he had also a sort
of artistic, a sort of ethical pleasure in it, as being of
the good tradition, of the old honest, simple material,
from which pleasing effects in literature and civilization were wrought. He liked giving the children books,
and writing tricksy fancies in these, where he masked
as a fairy prince; and as long as he lived he remembered
his early kindness for them.

IV

In those walks of ours I believe he did most of the
talking, and from his talk then and at other times there
remains to me an impression of his growing conserva-
tism. I had in fact come into his life when it had spent
its impulse towards positive reform, and I was to be
witness of its increasing tendency towards the negative
sort. He was quite past the storm and stress of his anti-
slavery age; with the close of the war which had broken
for him all his ideals of inviolable peace, he had reached
the age of misgiving. I do not mean that I ever heard
him express doubt of what he had helped to do, or regret
for what he had done; but I know that he viewed with
critical anxiety what other men were doing with the
accomplished facts. His anxiety gave a cast of what
one may call reluctance from the political situation, and
turned him back towards those civic and social defences
which he had once seemed willing to abandon. I do not
mean that he lost faith in democracy; this faith he constantly then and signally afterwards affirmed; but he
certainly had no longer any faith in insubordination as
a means of grace. He preached a quite Socratic reverence for law, as law, and I remember that once when I

had got back from Canada in the usual disgust for the
American custom-house, and spoke lightly of smug-
gling as not an evil in itself, and perhaps even a right
under our vexatious tariff, he would not have it, but
held that the illegality of the act made it a moral offence. This was not the logic that would have justified
the attitude of the antislavery men towards the fugitive
slave act; but it was in accord with Lowell's feeling
about John Brown, whom he honored while always con-
demning his violation of law; and it was in the line of
all his later thinking. In this, he wished you to agree
with him, or at least he wished to make you; but he did
not wish you to be more of his mind than he was himself. In one of those squalid Irish neighborhoods I
confessed a grudge (a mean and cruel grudge, I now
think it) for the increasing presence of that race among
us, but this did not please him; and I am sure that
whatever misgiving he had as to the future of America,
he would not have had it less than it had been the
refuge and opportunity of the poor of any race or color.
Yet he would not have had it this alone. There was a
line in his poem on Agassiz which he left out of the
printed version, at the fervent entreaty of his friends,
as saying too bitterly his disappointment with his
country. Writing at the distance of Europe, and with
America in the perspective which the alien environment clouded, he spoke of her as " The Land of Broken
Promise." It was a splendid reproach, but perhaps too
dramatic to bear the full test of analysis, and yet it had
the truth in it, and might, I think, have usefully stood,
to the end of making people think. Undoubtedly it expressed his sense of the case, and in the same measure
it would now express that of many who love their country most among us. It is well to hold one's country to
her promises, and if there are any who think she is for-

219

getting them it is their duty to say so, even to the point
of bitter accusation. I do not suppose it was the " common man " of Lincoln's dream that Lowell thought
America was unfaithful to, though as I have suggested
he could be tender of the common man's hopes in her;
but he was impeaching in that blotted line her sincerity
with the uncommon man: the man who had expected of
her a constancy to the ideals of her youth and to the
high martyr-moods of the war which had given an un-
guarded and bewildering freedom to a race of slaves.
He was thinking of the shame of our municipal corruptions, the debased quality of our national statesman-
ship, the decadence of our whole civic tone, rather than
of the increasing disabilities of the hard-working poor,
though his heart when he thought of them was with
them, too, as it was in " the time when the slave would
not let him sleep."

He spoke very rarely of those times, perhaps because
their political and social associations were so knit up
with the saddest and tenderest personal memories, which
it was still anguish to touch. Not only was he

"—not of the race
That hawk their sorrows in the market place,"

but so far as my witness went he shrank from mention
of them. I do not remember hearing him speak of the
young wife who influenced him so potently at the most
vital moment, and turned him from his whole scholarly
and aristocratic tradition to an impassioned champion-
ship of the oppressed; and he never spoke of the children he had lost. I recall but one allusion to the days
when he was fighting the antislavery battle along the
whole line, and this was with a humorous relish of his
Irish servant's disgust in having to wait upon a negro
whom he had asked to his table.

He was rather severe in his notions of the subordina-

tion his domestics owed him. They were "to do as they were bid," and yet he had a tenderness for such as had been any time with him, which was wounded when once a hired man long in his employ greedily overreached him in a certain transaction. He complained of that with a simple grief for the man's indelicacy after so many favors from him, rather than with any resentment. His hauteur towards his dependents was theoretic; his actual behavior was of the gentle consideration common among Americans of good breeding, and that recreant hired man had no doubt never been suffered to exceed him in shows of mutual politeness. Often when the maid was about weightier matters, he came and opened his door to me himself, welcoming me with the smile that was like no other. Sometimes he said, "*Siete il benvenuto,*" or used some other Italian phrase, which put me at ease with him in the region where we were most at home together.

Looking back I must confess that I do not see what it was he found to make him wish for my company, which he presently insisted upon having once a week at dinner. After the meal we turned into his study where we sat before a wood fire in winter, and he smoked and talked. He smoked a pipe which was always needing tobacco, or going out, so that I have the figure of him before my eyes constantly getting out of his deep chair to rekindle it from the fire with a paper lighter. He was often out of his chair to get a book from the shelves that lined the walls, either for a passage which he wished to read, or for some disputed point which he wished to settle. If I had caused the dispute, he enjoyed putting me in the wrong; if he could not, he sometimes whimsically persisted in his error, in defiance of all authority; but mostly he had such reverence for the truth that he would not question it even in jest.

If I dropped in upon him in the afternoon I was apt to find him reading the old French poets, or the plays of Calderon, or the *Divina Commedia,* which he magnanimously supposed me much better acquainted with than I was because I knew some passages of it by heart. One day I came in quoting—

> " Io son, cantava, io son dolce Sirena,
>   Che i marinai in mezzo al mar dismago."

He stared at me in a rapture with the matchless music, and then uttered all his adoration and despair in one word. *" Damn!"* he said, and no more. I believe he instantly proposed a walk that day, as if his study walls with all their vistas into the great literatures cramped his soul liberated to a sense of ineffable beauty of the verse of the *sommo poeta*. But commonly he preferred to have me sit down with him there among the mute witnesses of the larger part of his life. As I have suggested in my own case, it did not matter much whether you brought anything to the feast or not. If he liked you he liked being with you, not for what he got, but for what he gave. He was fond of one man whom I recall as the most silent man I ever met. I never heard him say anything, not even a dull thing, but Lowell delighted in him, and would have you believe that he was full of quaint humor.

V

While Lowell lived there was a superstition which has perhaps survived him that he was an indolent man, wasting himself in barren studies and minor efforts instead of devoting his great powers to some monumental work worthy of them. If the robust body of literature, both poetry and prose, which lives after him does not yet correct this vain delusion, the time will

222

come when it must; and in the meantime the delusion cannot vex him now. I think it did vex him, then, and that he even shared it, and tried at times to meet such shadowy claim as it had. One of the things that people urged upon him was to write some sort of story, and it is known how he attempted this in verse. It is less known that he attempted it in prose, and that he went so far as to write the first chapter of a novel. He read this to me, and though I praised it then, I have a feeling now that if he had finished the novel it would have been a failure. " But I shall never finish it," he sighed, as if he felt irremediable defects in it, and laid the manuscript away, to turn and light his pipe. It was a rather old-fashioned study of a whimsical character, and it did not arrive anywhere, so far as it went; but I believe that it might have been different with a Yankee story in verse such as we have fragmentarily in *The Nooning* and *FitzAdam's Story*. Still, his gift was essentially lyrical and meditative, with the universal New England tendency to allegory. He was wholly undramatic in the actuation of the characters which he imagined so dramatically. He liked to deal with his subject at first hand, to indulge through himself all the whim and fancy which the more dramatic talent indulges through its personages.

He enjoyed writing such a poem as " The Cathedral," which is not of his best, but which is more immediately himself, in all his moods, than some better poems. He read it to me soon after it was written, and in the long walk which we went hard upon the reading (our way led us through the Port far towards East Cambridge, where he wished to show me a tupelo-tree of his acquaintance, because I said I had never seen one), his talk was still of the poem which he was greatly in conceit of. Later his satisfaction with it received a check from the reserves of other friends concerning some whimsical lines which seemed to them too great a drop from the higher moods of the piece. Their reluctance nettled him; perhaps he agreed with them; but he would not change the lines, and they stand as he first wrote them. In fact, most of his lines stand as he first wrote them; he would often change them in revision, and then, in a second revision go back to the first version.

He was very sensitive to criticism, especially from those he valued through his head or heart. He would try to hide his hurt, and he would not let you speak of it, as though your sympathy unmanned him, but you could see that he suffered. This notably happened in my remembrance from a review in a journal which he greatly esteemed; and once when in a notice of my own I had put one little thorny point among the flowers, he confessed a puncture from it. He praised the criticism hardily, but I knew that he winced under my recognition of the didactic quality which he had not quite guarded himself against in the poetry otherwise praised. He liked your liking, and he openly rejoiced in it; and I suppose he made himself believe that in trying his verse with his friends he was testing it; but I do not believe that he was, and I do not think he ever corrected his judgment by theirs, however he suffered from it.

In any matter that concerned literary morals he was more than eager to profit by another eye. One summer he sent me for the Magazine a poem which, when I read it, I trembled to find in motive almost exactly like one we had lately printed by another contributor. There was nothing for it but to call his attention to the resemblance, and I went over to Elmwood with the two poems. He was not at home, and I was obliged to leave the poems, I suppose with some sort of note, for the next morning's post brought me a delicious letter from him, all one cry of confession, the most complete, the most ample. He did not trouble himself to say that his poem was an unconscious reproduction of the other; that was for every reason unnecessary, but he had at once rewritten it upon wholly different lines; and I do not think any reader was reminded of Mrs. Akers's " Among the Laurels " by Lowell's " Foot-path." He was not only much more sensitive of others' rights than his own, but in spite of a certain severity in him, he was most tenderly regardful of their sensibilities when he had imagined them : he did not always imagine them.

VI

At this period, between the years 1866 and 1874, when he unwillingly went abroad for a twelvemonth, Lowell was seen in very few Cambridge houses, and in still fewer Boston houses. He was not an unsocial man, but he was most distinctly not a society man. He loved chiefly the companionship of books, and of men who loved books; but of women generally he had an amusing diffidence; he revered them and honored them, but he would rather not have had them about. This is oversaying it, of course, but the truth is in what I say. There was never a more devoted husband, and he was content to let his devotion to the sex end with that. He especially could not abide difference of opinion in women; he valued their taste, their wit, their humor, but he would have none of their reason. I was by one day when he was arguing a point with one of his nieces, and after it had gone on for some time, and the impartial witness must have owned that she was getting the better of him he closed the controversy by giving her a great kiss, with the words, " You are a very good girl, my dear," and practically putting her out of the

P

room. As to women of the flirtatious type, he did not dislike them; no man, perhaps, does; but he feared them, and he said that with them there was but one way, and that was to run.

I have a notion that at this period Lowell was more freely and fully himself than at any other. The passions and impulses of his younger manhood had mellowed, the sorrows of that time had softened; he could blamelessly live to himself in his affections and his sobered ideals. His was always a duteous life; but he had pretty well given up making man over in his own image, as we all wish some time to do, and then no longer wish it. He fulfilled his obligations to his fellow-men as these sought him out, but he had ceased to seek them. He loved his friends and their love, but he had apparently no desire to enlarge their circle. It was that hour of civic suspense, in which public men seemed still actuated by unselfish aims, and one not essentially a politician might contentedly wait to see what would come of their doing their best. At any rate, without occasionally withholding open criticism or acclaim Lowell waited among his books for the wounds of the war to heal themselves, and the nation to begin her healthfuller and nobler life. With slavery gone, what might not one expect of American democracy!

His life at Elmwood was of an entire simplicity. In the old colonial mansion in which he was born, he dwelt in the embowering leafage, amid the quiet of lawns and garden-plots broken by few noises ruder than those from the elms and the syringas where

"The oriole clattered and the cat-bird sang."

From the tracks on Brattle Street, came the drowsy tinkle of horse-car bells; and sometimes a funeral trailed its black length past the corner of his grounds, and

lost itself from sight under the shadows of the willows
that hid Mount Auburn from his study windows. In
the winter the deep New England snows kept their
purity in the stretch of meadow behind the house, which
a double row of pines guarded in a domestic privacy.
All was of a modest dignity within and without the
house, which Lowell loved but did not imagine of a
manorial presence; and he could not conceal his annoyance with an over-enthusiastic account of his home in
which the simple chiselling of some panels was vaunted
as rich wood-carving. There was a graceful staircase,
and a good wide hall, from which the dining-room and
drawing-room opened by opposite doors; behind the last,
in the southwest corner of the house, was his study.

There, literally, he lived during the six or seven
years in which I knew him after my coming to Cambridge. Summer and winter he sat there among his
books, seldom stirring abroad by day except for a walk,
and by night yet more rarely. He went to the monthly
mid-day dinner of the Saturday Club in Boston; he
was very constant at the fortnightly meetings of his
whist-club, because he loved the old friends who formed
it; he came always to the Dante suppers at Longfellow's,
and he was familiarly in and out at Mr. Norton's, of
course. But, otherwise, he kept to his study, except for
some rare and almost unwilling absences upon university lecturing at Johns Hopkins or at Cornell.

For four years I did not take any summer outing
from Cambridge myself, and my associations with Elmwood and with Lowell are more of summer than of
winter weather meetings. But often we went our walks
through the snows, trudging along between the horse-
car tracks which enclosed the only well-broken-out paths
in that simple old Cambridge. I date one memorable
expression of his from such a walk, when, as we were

passing Longfellow's house, in mid-street, he came as near the declaration of his religious faith as he ever did in my presence. He was speaking of the New Testament, and he said, The truth was in it; but they had covered it up with their hagiology. Though he had been bred a Unitarian, and had more and more liberated himself from all creeds, he humorously affected an abiding belief in hell, and similarly contended for the eternal punishment of the wicked. He was of a religious nature, and he was very reverent of other people's religious feelings. He expressed a special tolerance for my own inherited faith, no doubt because Mrs. Lowell was also a Swedenborgian; but I do not think he was interested in it, and I suspect that all religious formulations bored him. In his earlier poems are many intimations and affirmations of belief in an overruling providence, and especially in the God who declares vengeance His and will repay men for their evil deeds, and will right the weak against the strong. I think he never quite lost this, though when, in the last years of his life, I asked him if he believed there was a moral government of the universe, he answered gravely and with a sort of pain, The scale was so vast, and we saw such a little part of it.

As to the notion of a life after death, I never had any direct or indirect expression from him; but I incline to the opinion that his hold upon this weakened with his years, as it is sadly apt to do with men who have read much and thought much: they have apparently exhausted their potentialities of psychological life. Mystical Lowell was, as every poet must be, but I do not think he liked mystery. One morning he told me that when he came home the night before he had seen the *Doppelgänger* of one of his household: though, as he joked, he was not in a state to see double.

He then said he used often to see people's *Doppel-gänger;* at another time, as to ghosts, he said, He was like Coleridge: he had seen too many of 'em. Lest any weaker brethren should be caused to offend by the restricted oath which I have reported him using in a moment of transport it may be best to note here that I never heard him use any other imprecation, and this one seldom.

Any grossness of speech was inconceivable of him; now and then, but only very rarely, the human nature of some story "unmeet for ladies" was too much for his sense of humor, and overcame him with amusement which he was willing to impart, and did impart, but so that mainly the human nature of it reached you. In this he was like the other great Cambridge men, though he was opener than the others to contact with the commoner life. He keenly delighted in every native and novel turn of phrase, and he would not undervalue a vital word or a notion picked up out of the road even if it had some dirt sticking to it.

He kept as close to the common life as a man of his patrician instincts and cloistered habits could. I could go to him with any new find about it and be sure of delighting him; after I began making my involuntary and all but unconscious studies of Yankee character, especially in the country, he was always glad to talk them over with me. Still, when I had discovered a new accent or turn of speech in the fields he had cultivated, I was aware of a subtle grudge mingling with his pleasure; but this was after all less envy than a fine regret.

At the time I speak of there was certainly nothing in Lowell's dress or bearing that would have kept the common life aloof from him, if that life were not always too proud to make advances to any one. In this retrospect, I see him in the sack coat and rough suit which he wore upon all out-door occasions, with heavy shoes, and a round hat. I never saw him with a high hat on till he came home after his diplomatic stay in London; then he had become rather rigorously correct in his costume, and as conventional as he had formerly been indifferent. In both epochs he was apt to be gloved, and the strong, broad hands, which left the sensation of their vigor for some time after they had clasped yours, were notably white. At the earlier period, he still wore his auburn hair somewhat long; it was darker than his beard, which was branching and full, and more straw-colored than auburn, as were his thick eyebrows; neither hair nor beard was then touched with gray, as I now remember. When he uncovered, his straight, wide, white forehead showed itself one of the most beautiful that could be; his eyes were gay with humor, and alert with all intelligence. He had an enchanting smile, a laugh that was full of friendly joyousness, and a voice that was exquisite music. Everything about him expressed his strenuous physical condition: he would not wear an overcoat in the coldest Cambridge weather; at all times he moved vigorously, and walked with a quick step, lifting his feet well from the ground.

VII

It gives me a pleasure which I am afraid I cannot impart, to linger in this effort to materialize his presence from the fading memories of the past. I am afraid I can as little impart a due sense of what he spiritually was to my knowledge. It avails nothing for me to say that I think no man of my years and desert had ever so true and constant a friend. He was both younger and older than I by insomuch as he was a poet through and through, and had been out of college before I was born. But he had already come to the age of self-distrust when a man likes to take counsel with his juniors as with his elders, and fancies he can correct his perspective by the test of their fresher vision. Besides, Lowell was most simply and pathetically reluctant to part with youth, and was willing to cling to it wherever he found it. He could not in any wise bear to be left out. When Mr. Bret Harte came to Cambridge, and the talk was all of the brilliant character - poems with which he had then first dazzled the world, Lowell casually said, with a most touching, however ungrounded sense of obsolescence, He could remember when the *Biglow Papers* were all the talk. I need not declare that there was nothing ungenerous in that. He was only too ready to hand down his laurels to a younger man; but he wished to do it himself. Through the modesty that is always a quality of such a nature, he was magnanimously sensitive to the appearance of fading interest; he could not take it otherwise than as a proof of his fading power. I had a curious hint of this when one year in making up the prospectus of the Magazine for the next, I omitted his name because I had nothing special to promise from him, and because I was half ashamed to be always flourishing it in the eyes of the public. "I see that you have dropped me this year," he wrote, and I could see that it had hurt, and I knew that he was glad to believe the truth when I told him.

He did not care so much for popularity as for the praise of his friends. If he liked you he wished you not only to like what he wrote, but to say so. He was himself most cordial in his recognition of the things that pleased him. What happened to me from him, happened to others, and I am only describing his common habit when I say that nothing I did to his liking failed to bring me a spoken or oftener a written acknowledgment. This continued to the latest years of his life when the effort even to give such pleasure must have cost him a physical pang.

He was of a very catholic taste; and he was apt to be carried away by a little touch of life or humor, and to overvalue the piece in which he found it; but mainly his judgments of letters and men were just. One of the dangers of scholarship was a peculiar danger in the Cambridge keeping, but Lowell was almost as averse as Longfellow from contempt. He could snub, and pitilessly, where he thought there was presumption and apparently sometimes merely because he was in the mood; but I cannot remember ever to have heard him sneer. He was often wonderfully patient of tiresome people, and sometimes celestially insensible to vulgarity. In spite of his reserve, he really wished people to like him; he was keenly alive to neighborly good-will or ill-will; and when there was a question of widening Elmwood avenue by taking part of his grounds, he was keenly hurt by hearing that some one who lived near him had said he hoped the city would cut down Lowell's elms: his English elms, which his father had planted, and with which he was himself almost one blood!

VIII

In the period of which I am speaking, Lowell was constantly writing and pretty constantly printing, though still the superstition held that he was an idle man. To this time belongs the publication of some of his finest poems, if not their inception: there were cases

"A PLEASANT OLD-FASHIONED HOUSE NEAR THE DELTA"

in which their inception dated far back, even to ten or twenty years. He wrote his poems at a heat, and the manuscript which came to me for the magazine was usually the first draft, very little corrected. But if the cold fit took him quickly it might hold him so fast that he would leave the poem in abeyance till he could slowly live back to a liking for it.

The most of his best prose belongs to the time between 1866 and 1874, and to this time we owe the several volumes of essays and criticisms called *Among My Books* and *My Study Windows*. He wished to name these more soberly, but at the urgence of his publishers he gave them titles which they thought would be attractive to the public, though he felt that they took from the dignity of his work. He was not a good business man in a literary way, he submitted to others' judgment in all such matters. I doubt if he ever put a price upon anything he sold, and I dare say he was usually surprised at the largeness of the price paid him; but sometimes if his need was for a larger sum, he thought it too little, without reference to former payments. This happened with a long poem in the *Atlantic,* which I had urged the counting-room authorities to deal handsomely with him for. I did not know how many hundred they gave him, and when I met him I ventured to express the hope that the publishers had done their part. He held up four fingers, " *Quattro,*" he said in Italian, and then added with a disappointment which he tried to smile away, " I thought they might have made it *cinque.*"

Between me and me I thought *quattro* very well, but probably Lowell had in mind some end which *cinque* would have fitted better. It was pretty sure to be an unselfish end, a pleasure to some one dear to him, a gift that he had wished to make. Long afterwards when I

233

had been the means of getting him *cinque* for a poem one-tenth the length, he spoke of the payment to me. " It came very handily ; I had been wanting to give —— a watch."

I do not believe at any time Lowell was able to deal with money

> " Like wealthy men, not knowing what they give."

More probably he felt a sacredness in the money got by literature, which the literary man never quite rids himself of, even when he is not a poet, and which made him wish to dedicate it to something finer than the every-day uses. He lived very quietly, but he had by no means more than he needed to live upon, and at that time he had pecuniary losses. He was writing hard, and was doing full work in his Harvard professorship, and he was so far dependent upon his salary, that he felt its absence for the year he went abroad. I do not know quite how to express my sense of something unworldly, of something almost womanlike in his relation to money.

He was not only generous of money, but he was generous of himself, when he thought he could be of use, or merely of encouragement. He came all the way into Boston to hear certain lectures of mine on the Italian poets, which he could not have found either edifying or amusing, that he might testify his interest in me, and show other people that they were worth coming to. He would go carefully over a poem with me, word by word, and criticise every turn of phrase, and after all be magnanimously tolerant of my sticking to phrasings that he disliked. In a certain line :

> " The silvern chords of the piano trembled,"

he objected to *silvern*. Why not silver ? I alleged
234

leathern, golden, and like adjectives in defence of my word; but still he found an affectation in it, and suffered it to stand with extreme reluctance. Another line of another piece—

" And what she would, would rather that she would not "—

he would by no means suffer. He said that the stress falling on the last word made it " public-school English," and he mocked it with the answer a maid had lately given him when he asked if the master of the house was at home. She said, " No, sir, he is *not*," when she ought to have said " No, sir, he *isn't*." He was appeased when I came back the next day with the stanza amended so that the verse could read—

" And what she would, would rather she would not so "—

but I fancy he never quite forgave my word *silvern*. Yet, he professed not to have prejudices in such matters, but to use any word that would serve his turn, without wincing; and he certainly did use and defend words, as *undisprivacied* and *disnatured,* that made others wince.

He was otherwise such a stickler for the best diction that he would not have had me use slovenly vernacular even in the dialogue in my stories: my characters must not say they *wanted* to do so and so, but *wished,* and the like. In a copy of one of my books which I found him reading, I saw he had corrected my erring Western *woulds* and *shoulds;* as he grew old he was less and less able to restrain himself from setting people right to their faces. Once, in the vast area of my ignorance, he specified my small acquaintance with a certain period of English poetry, saying, " You're rather shady, there, old fellow." But he would not have had me too learned, holding that he had himself been hurt for literature by his scholarship.

His patience in analyzing my work with me might have been the easy effort of his habit of teaching; and his willingness to give himself and his own was no doubt more signally attested in his asking a brother man of letters who wished to work up a subject in the college library, to stay a fortnight in his house, and to share his study, his beloved study, with him. This must truly have cost him dear, as any author of fixed habits will understand. Happily the man of letters was a good fellow, and knew how to prize the favor done him, but if he had been otherwise, it would have been the same to Lowell. He not only endured, but did many things for the weaker brethren, which were amusing enough to one in the secret of his inward revolt. Yet in these things he was considerate also of the editor whom he might have made the sharer of his self-sacrifice, and he seldom offered me manuscripts for others. The only real burden of the kind that he put upon me was the diary of a Virginian who had travelled in New England during the early thirties, and had set down his impressions of men and manners there. It began charmingly, and went on very well under Lowell's discreet pruning, but after a while he seemed to fall in love with the character of the diarist so much that he could not bear to cut anything.

IX

He had a great tenderness for the broken and ruined South, whose sins he felt that he had had his share in visiting upon her, and he was willing to do what he could to ease her sorrows in the case of any particular Southerner. He could not help looking askance upon the dramatic shows of retribution which some of the Northern politicians were working, but with all his misgivings he continued to act with the Republican

party until after the election of Hayes; he was away
from the country during the Garfield campaign. He
was in fact one of the Massachusetts electors chosen by
the Republican majority in 1876, and in that most
painful hour when there was question of the policy and
justice of counting Hayes in for the presidency, it was
suggested by some of Lowell's friends that he should
use the original right of the electors under the constitution, and vote for Tilden, whom one vote would have
chosen president over Hayes. After he had cast his
vote for Hayes, he quietly referred to the matter one
day, in the moment of lighting his pipe, with perhaps
the faintest trace of indignation in his tone. He said
that whatever the first intent of the constitution was,
usage had made the presidential electors strictly the
instruments of the party which chose them, and that for
him to have voted for Tilden when he had been chosen
to vote for Hayes would have been an act of bad faith.

He would have resumed for me all the old kindness of our relations before the recent year of his absence, but this had inevitably worked a little estrange-
ment. He had at least lost the habit of me, and that
says much in such matters. He was not so perfectly
at rest in the Cambridge environment; in certain inde-
finable ways it did not so entirely suffice him, though
he would have been then and always the last to allow
this. I imagine his friends realized more than he, that
certain delicate but vital filaments of attachment had
frayed and parted in alien air, and left him heart-loose
as he had not been before.

I do not know whether it crossed his mind after the
election of Hayes that he might be offered some place
abroad, but it certainly crossed the minds of some of
his friends, and I could not feel that I was acting for
myself alone when I used a family connection with the

President, very early in his term, to let him know that I believed Lowell would accept a diplomatic mission. I could assure him that I was writing wholly without Lowell's privity or authority, and I got back such a letter as I could wish in its delicate sense of the situation. The President said that he had already thought of offering Lowell something, and he gave me the pleasure, a pleasure beyond any other I could imagine, of asking Lowell whether he would accept the mission to Austria. I lost no time carrying his letter to Elmwood, where I found Lowell over his coffee at dinner. He saw me at the threshold, and called to me through the open door to come in, and I handed him the letter, and sat down at table while he ran it through. When he had read it, he gave a quick " Ah!" and threw it over the length of the table to Mrs. Lowell. She read it in a smiling and loyal reticence, as if she would not say one word of all she might wish to say in urging his acceptance, though I could see that she was intensely eager for it. The whole situation was of a perfect New England character in its tacit significance; after Lowell had taken his coffee we turned into his study without further allusion to the matter.

A day or two later he came to my house to say that he could not accept the Austrian mission, and to ask me to tell the President so for him, and make his acknowledgments, which he would also write himself. He remained talking a little while of other things, and when he rose to go, he said with a sigh of vague reluctance, " I *should* like to see a play of Calderon," as if it had nothing to do with any wish of his that could still be fulfilled. " Upon this hint I acted," and in due time it was found in Washington, that the gentleman who had been offered the Spanish mission would as lief go to Austria, and Lowell was sent to Madrid.

STUDIES OF LOWELL

X

When we met in London, some years later, he
came almost every afternoon to my lodging, and
the story of our old - time Cambridge walks began
again in London phrases. There were not the vacant
lots and outlying fields of his native place, but we made
shift with the vast, simple parks, and we walked on the
grass as we could not have done in an American park,
and were glad to feel the earth under our feet. I said
how much it was like those earlier tramps; and that
pleased him, for he wished, whenever a thing delighted
him, to find a Cambridge quality in it.

But he was in love with everything English, and
was determined I should be so too, beginning with the
English weather, which in summer cannot be over-
praised. He carried, of course, an umbrella, but he
would not put it up in the light showers that caught us
at times, saying that the English rain never wetted you.
The thick short turf delighted him; he would scarcely
allow that the trees were the worse for foliage blighted
by a vile easterly storm in the spring of that year. The
tender air, the delicate veils that the moisture in it
cast about all objects at the least remove, the soft colors
of the flowers, the dull blue of the low sky showing
through the rifts of the dirty white clouds, the hover-
ing pall of London smoke, were all dear to him, and he
was anxious that I should not lose anything of their
charm.

He was anxious that I should not miss the value of
anything in England, and while he volunteered that the
aristocracy had the corruptions of aristocracies everywhere, he insisted upon my respectful interest in it because it was so historical. Perhaps there was a touch of
irony in this demand, but it is certain that he was very

239

happy in England. He had come of the age when a man likes smooth, warm keeping, in which he need make no struggle for his comfort; disciplined and obsequious service; society, perfectly ascertained within the larger society which we call civilization; and in an alien environment, for which he was in nowise responsible, he could have these without a pang of the self-reproach which at home makes a man unhappy amidst his luxuries, when he considers their cost to others. He had a position which forbade thought of unfairness in the conditions; he must not wake because of the slave, it was his duty to sleep. Besides, at that time Lowell needed all the rest he could get, for he had lately passed through trials such as break the strength of men, and bow them with premature age. He was living alone in his little house in Lowndes Square, and Mrs. Lowell was in the country, slowly recovering from the effects of the terrible typhus which she had barely survived in Madrid. He was yet so near the anguish of that experience that he told me he had still in his nerves the expectation of a certain agonized cry from her which used to rend them. But he said he had adjusted himself to this, and he went on to speak with a patience which was more affecting in him than in men of more phlegmatic temperament, of how we were able to adjust ourselves to all our trials and to the constant presence of pain. He said he was never free of a certain distress, which was often a sharp pang, in one of his shoulders, but his physique had established such relations with it, that though he was never unconscious of it he was able to endure it without a recognition of it as suffering.

He seemed to me, however, very well, and at his age of sixty-three, I could not see that he was less alert and vigorous than he was when I first knew him in Cambridge. He had the same brisk, light step, and though his beard was well whitened and his auburn hair had grown ashen through the red, his face had the freshness and his eyes the clearness of a young man's. I suppose the novelty of his life kept him from thinking about his years; or perhaps in contact with those great, insenescent Englishmen, he could not feel himself old. At any rate he did not once speak of age, as he used to do ten years earlier, and I, then half through my forties, was still " You young dog " to him. It was a bright and cheerful renewal of the early kindliness between us, on which indeed there had never been a shadow, except such as distance throws. He wished apparently to do everything he could to assure us of his personal interest; and we were amused to find him nervously apprehensive of any purpose, such as was far from us, to profit by him officially. He betrayed a distinct relief when he found we were not going to come upon him even for admissions to the houses of parliament, which we were to see by means of an English acquaintance. He had not perhaps found some other fellow-citizens so considerate; he dreaded the half-duties of his place, like presentations to the queen, and complained of the cheap ambitions he had to gratify in that way.

He was so eager to have me like England in every way, and seemed so fond of the English, that I thought it best to ask him whether he minded my quoting, in a paper about Lexington, which I was just then going to print in a London magazine, some humorous lines of his expressing the mounting satisfaction of an imaginary Yankee story-teller who has the old fight terminate in Lord Percy's coming

" To hammer stone for life in Concord jail."

It had occurred to me that it might possibly embarrass him to have this patriotic picture presented to a public which could not take our Fourth of July pleasure in it, and I offered to suppress it, as I did afterwards quite for literary reasons. He said, No, let it stand, and let them make the worst of it; and I fancy that much of his success with a people who are not gingerly with other people's sensibilities came from the frankness with which he trampled on their prejudice when he chose. He said he always told them, when there was question of such things, that the best society he had ever known was in Cambridge, Massachusetts. He contended that the best English was spoken there; and so it was, when he spoke it.

We were in London out of the season, and he was sorry that he could not have me meet some titles who he declared had found pleasure in my books; when we returned from Italy in the following June, he was prompt to do me this honor. I dare say he wished me to feel it to its last implication, and I did my best, but there was nothing in the evening I enjoyed so much as his coming up to Mrs. Lowell, at the close, when there was only a title or two left, and saying to her as he would have said to her at Elmwood, where she would have personally planned it, "Fanny, that was a fine dinner you gave us." Of course, this was in a tender burlesque; but it remains the supreme impression of what seemed to me a cloudlessly happy period for Lowell. His wife was quite recovered of her long suffering, and was again at the head of his house, sharing in his pleasures, and enjoying his successes for his sake; successes so great that people spoke of him seriously, as "an addition to society" in London, where one man more or less seemed like a drop in the sea. She was a woman perfectly of the New England type and tradition: almost repellantly shy at first, and almost glacially cold with new acquaintance, but afterwards very sweet and cordial. She was of a dark beauty with a regular face of the Spanish outline; Lowell was of an ideal manner towards her, and of an admiration which delicately travestied itself and which she knew how to receive with smiling irony. After her death, which occurred while he was still in England, he never spoke of her to me, though before that he used to be always bringing her name in, with a young lover-like fondness.

XI

In the hurry of the London season I did not see so much of Lowell on our second sojourn as on our first, but once when we were alone in his study there was a return to the terms of the old meetings in Cambridge. He smoked his pipe, and sat by his fire and philosophized; and but for the great London sea swirling outside and bursting through our shelter, and dashing him with notes that must be instantly answered, it was a very fair image of the past. He wanted to tell me about his coachman whom he had got at on his human side with great liking and amusement, and there was a patient gentleness in his manner with the footman who had to keep coming in upon him with those notes which was like the echo of his young faith in the equality of men. But he always distinguished between the simple unconscious equality of the ordinary American and its assumption by a foreigner. He said he did not mind such an American's coming into his house with his hat on; but if a German or Englishman did it, he wanted to knock it off. He was apt to be rather punctilious in his shows of deference towards others, and at one time he practised removing his own hat when he went into shops in Cambridge. It must have mystified the Cambridge salesmen, and I doubt if he kept it up.

With reference to the doctrine of his young poetry, the fierce and the tender humanity of his storm and stress period, I fancy a kind of baffle in Lowell, which I should not perhaps find it easy to prove. I never knew him by word or hint to renounce this doctrine, but he could not come to seventy years without having seen many high hopes fade, and known many inspired prophecies fail. When we have done our best to make the world over, we are apt to be dismayed by finding it in much the old shape. As he said of the moral government of the universe, the scale is so vast, and a little difference, a little change for the better, is scarcely perceptible to the eager consciousness of the wholesale reformer. But with whatever sense of disappointment, of doubt as to his own deeds for truer freedom and for better conditions I believe his sympathy was still with those who had some heart for hoping and striving. I am sure that though he did not agree with me in some of my own later notions for the redemption of the race, he did not like me the less but rather the more because (to my own great surprise I confess) I had now and then the courage of my convictions, both literary and social.

He was probably most at odds with me in regard to my theories of fiction, though he persisted in declaring his pleasure in my own fiction. He was in fact, by nature and tradition, thoroughly romantic, and he could not or would not suffer realism in any but a friend. He steadfastly refused even to read the Russian masters, to his immense loss, as I tried to persuade him, and even among the modern Spaniards, for whom he might have had a sort of personal kindness from his love of Cervantes, he chose one for his praise the least worthy of it, and bore me down with his heavier metal in argument when I opposed to Alarcon's factitiousness the delightful genuineness of Valdés. Ibsen, with all the Norwegians, he put far from him; he would no more know them than the Russians; the French naturalists he abhorred. I thought him all wrong, but you do not try improving your elders when they have come to three score and ten years, and I would rather have had his affection unbroken by our difference of opinion than a perfect agreement. Where he even imagined that this difference could work me harm, he was anxious to have me know that he meant me none; and he was at the trouble to write me a letter when a Boston paper had perverted its report of what he said in a public lecture to my disadvantage, and to assure me that he had not me in mind. When once he had given his liking, he could not bear that any shadow of change should seem to have come upon him. He had a most beautiful and endearing ideal of friendship; he desired to affirm it and to reaffirm it as often as occasion offered, and if occasion did not offer, he made occasion. It did not matter what you said or did that contraried him; if he thought he had essentially divined you, you were still the same: and on his part he was by no means exacting of equal demonstration, but seemed not even to wish it.

XII

After he was replaced at London by a minister more immediately representative of the Democratic administration, he came home. He made a brave show of not caring to have remained away, but in truth he had become very fond of England, where he had made so many friends, and where the distinction he had, in that comfortably padded environment, was so agreeable to him.

It would have been like him to have secretly hoped that the new President might keep him in London, but he never betrayed any ignoble disappointment, and he would not join in any blame of him. At our first meeting after he came home he spoke of the movement which had made Mr. Cleveland president, and said he supposed that if he had been here, he should have been in it. All his friends were, he added, a little helplessly; but he seemed not to dislike my saying I knew one of his friends who was not: in fact, as I have told, he never disliked a plump difference—unless he disliked the differer.

For several years he went back to England every summer, and it was not until he took up his abode at Elmwood again that he spent a whole year at home. One winter he passed at his sister's home in Boston, but mostly he lived with his daughter at Southborough. I have heard a story of his going to Elmwood soon after his return in 1885, and sitting down in his old study, where he declared with tears that the place was full of ghosts. But four or five years later it was well for family reasons that he should live there; and about the same time it happened that I had taken a house for the summer in his neighborhood. He came to see me, and to assure me, in all tacit forms of his sympathy in a sorrow for which there could be no help; but it was not possible that the old intimate relations should be resumed. The affection was there, as much on his side as on mine, I believe; but he was now an old man and I was an elderly man, and we could not, without insincerity, approach each other in the things that had drawn us together in earlier and happier years. His course was run; my own, in which he had taken such a generous pleasure, could scarcely move his jaded interest. His life, so far as it remained to him, had renewed itself in other air; the later friendships beyond seas sufficed him, and were without the pang, without the effort that must attend the knitting up of frayed ties here.

He could never have been anything but American, if he had tried, and he certainly never tried; but he certainly did not return to the outward simplicities of his life as I first knew it. There was no more round-hat-and-sack-coat business for him; he wore a frock and a high hat, and whatever else was rather like London than Cambridge; I do not know but drab gaiters sometimes added to the effect of a gentleman of the old school which he now produced upon the witness. Some fastidiousnesses showed themselves in him, which were not so surprising. He complained of the American lower class manner; the conductor and cabman would be kind to you but they would not be respectful, and he could not see the fun of this in the old way. Early in our acquaintance he rather stupified me by saying, " I like you because you don't put your hands on me," and I heard of his consenting to some sort of reception in those last years, " Yes, if they won't shake hands."

Ever since his visit to Rome in 1875 he had let his heavy mustache grow long till it dropped below the corners of his beard, which was now almost white; his face had lost the ruddy hue so characteristic of him. I fancy he was then ailing with premonitions of the disorder which a few years later proved mortal, but he still bore himself with sufficient vigor, and he walked the distance between his house and mine, though once when I missed his visit the family reported that after he came in he sat a long time with scarcely a word, as if too weary to talk. That winter, I went into Boston to live, and I saw him only at infrequent intervals, when I could go out to Elmwood. At such times I

247

found him sitting in the room which was formerly the drawing-room, but which had been joined with his study by taking away the partitions beside the heavy mass of the old colonial chimney. He told me that when he was a new-born babe, the nurse had carried him round this chimney, for luck, and now in front of the same hearth, the white old man stretched himself in an easy-chair, with his writing-pad on his knees and his books on the table at his elbow, and was willing to be entreated not to rise. I remember the sun used to come in at the eastern windows full pour, and bathe the air in its warmth.

He always hailed me gayly, and if I found him with letters newly come from England, as I sometimes did, he glowed and sparkled with fresh life. He wanted to read passages from those letters, he wanted to talk about their writers, and to make me feel their worth and charm as he did. He still dreamed of going back to England the next summer, but that was not to be. One day he received me not less gayly than usual, but with a certain excitement, and began to tell me about an odd experience he had had, not at all painful, but which had very much mystified him. He had since seen the doctor, and the doctor had assured him that there was nothing alarming in what had happened, and in recalling this assurance, he began to look at the humorous aspects of the case, and to make some jokes about it. He wished to talk of it, as men do of their maladies, and very fully, and I gave him such proof of my interest as even inviting him to talk of it would convey. In spite of the doctor's assurance, and his joyful acceptance of it, I doubt if at the bottom of his heart there was not the stir of an uneasy misgiving; but he had not for a long time shown himself so cheerful.

It was the beginning of the end. He recovered and relapsed, and recovered again; but never for long. Late in the spring I came out, and he had me stay to dinner, which was somehow as it used to be at two o'clock; and after dinner we went out on his lawn. He got a long-handled spud, and tried to grub up some dandelions which he found in his turf, but after a moment or two he threw it down, and put his hand upon his back with a groan. I did not see him again till I came out to take leave of him before going away for the summer, and then I found him sitting on the little porch in a western corner of his house, with a volume of Scott closed upon his finger. There were some other people, and our meeting was with the constraint of their presence. It was natural in nothing so much as his saying very significantly to me, as if he knew of my heresies concerning Scott, and would have me know he did not approve of them, that there was nothing he now found so much pleasure in as Scott's novels. Another friend, equally heretical, was by, but neither of us attempted to gainsay him. Lowell talked very little, but he told of having been a walk to Beaver Brook, and of having wished to jump from one stone to another in the stream, and of having had to give it up. He said, without completing the sentence, If it had come to *that* with him! Then he fell silent again; and with some vain talk of seeing him when I came back in the fall, I went away sick at heart. I was not to see him again, and I shall not look upon his like.

I am aware that I have here shown him from this point and from that in a series of sketches which perhaps collectively impart, but do not assemble his personality in one impression. He did not, indeed, make one impression upon me, but a thousand impressions, which I should seek in vain to embody in a single presentment. What I have cloudily before me is the vision of a very lofty and simple soul, perplexed, and as it were surprised and even dismayed at the complexity of the effects from motives so single in it, but escaping always to a clear expression of what was noblest and loveliest in itself at the supreme moments, in the divine exigencies. I believe neither in heroes nor in saints; but I believe in great and good men, for I have known them, and among such men Lowell was of the richest nature I have known. His nature was not always serene or pellucid; it was sometimes roiled by the currents that counter and cross in all of us; but it was without the least alloy of insincerity, and it was never darkened by the shadow of a selfish fear. His genius was an instrument that responded in affluent harmony to the power that made him a humorist and that made him a poet, and appointed him rarely to be quite either alone.

CAMBRIDGE NEIGHBORS

BEING the wholly literary spirit I was when I went to make my home in Cambridge, I do not see how I could well have been more content if I had found myself in the Elysian Fields with an agreeable eternity before me. At twenty-nine, indeed, one is practically immortal, and at that age, time had for me the effect of an eternity in which I had nothing to do but to read books and dream of writing them, in the overflow of endless hours from my work with the manuscripts, critical notices, and proofs of the *Atlantic Monthly*. As for the social environment I should have been puzzled if given my choice among the elect of all the ages, to find poets and scholars more to my mind than those still in the flesh at Cambridge in the early afternoon of the nineteenth century. They are now nearly all dead, and I can speak of them in the freedom which is death's doubtful favor to the survivor; but if they were still alive I could say little to their offence, unless their modesty was hurt with my praise.

I

One of the first and truest of our Cambridge friends was that exquisite intelligence, who, in a world where so many people are grotesquely miscalled, was most fitly named; for no man ever kept here more perfectly

251

and purely the heart of such as the kingdom of heaven is of than Francis J. Child. He was then in his prime, and I like to recall the outward image which expressed the inner man as happily as his name. He was of low stature and of an inclination which never became stoutness; but what you most saw when you saw him was his face of consummate refinement: very regular, with eyes always glassed by gold-rimmed spectacles, a straight, short, most sensitive nose, and a beautiful mouth with the sweetest smile that I ever beheld, and that was as wise and shrewd as it was sweet. In a time when every other man was more or less bearded he was clean shaven, and of a delightful freshness of coloring which his thick sunny hair, clustering upon his head in close rings, admirably set off. I believe he never became gray, and the last time I saw him, though he was broken then with years and pain, his face had still the brightness of his inextinguishable youth.

It is well known how great was Professor Child's scholarship in the branches of his Harvard work; and how especially, how uniquely, effective it was in the study of English and Scottish balladry to which he gave so many years of his life. He was a poet in his nature, and he wrought with passion as well as knowledge in the achievement of as monumental a task as any American has performed. But he might have been indefinitely less than he was in any intellectual wise, and yet been precious to those who knew him for the gentleness and the goodness which in him were protected from misconception by a final dignity as delicate and as inviolable as that of Longfellow himself.

We were still much less than a year from our life in Venice, when he came to see us in Cambridge, and in the Italian interest which then commended us to so many fine spirits among our neighbors we found ourselves at the beginning of a life-long friendship with him. I was known to him only by my letters from Venice, which afterwards became *Venetian Life,* and by a bit of devotional verse which he had asked to include in a collection he was making, but he immediately gave us the freedom of his heart, which afterwards was never withdrawn. In due time he imagined a home-school, to which our little one was asked, and she had her first lessons with his own daughter under his roof. These things drew us closer together, and he was willing to be still nearer to me in any time of trouble. At one such time when the shadow which must some time darken every door, hovered at ours, he had the strength to make me face it and try to realize, while it was still there, that it was not cruel and not evil. It passed, for that time, but the sense of his help remained; and in my own case I can testify of the potent tenderness which all who knew him must have known in him. But in bearing my witness I feel accused, almost as if he were present, by his fastidious reluctance from any recognition of his helpfulness. When this came in the form of gratitude taking credit to itself in a pose which reflected honor upon him as the architect of greatness, he was delightfully impatient of it, and he was most amusingly dramatic in reproducing the consciousness of certain ineffectual alumni who used to overwhelm him at Commencement solemnities with some such pompous acknowledgment as, " Professor Child, all that I have become, sir, I owe to your influence in my college career." He did, with delicious mockery, the old-fashioned intellectual *poseurs* among the students, who used to walk the groves of Harvard with bent head, and the left arm crossing the back, while the other lodged its hand in the breast of the high-buttoned frock-coat; and I could fancy that his classes

253

in college did not form the sunniest exposure for young folly and vanity. I know that he was intolerant of any manner of insincerity, and no flattery could take him off his guard. I have seen him meet this with a cutting phrase of rejection, and no man was more apt at snubbing the patronage that offers itself at times to all men. But mostly he wished to do people pleasure, and he seemed always to be studying how to do it; as for need, I am sure that worthy and unworthy want had alike the way to his heart.

Children were always his friends, and they repaid with adoration the affection which he divided with them and with his flowers. I recall him in no moments so characteristic as those he spent in making the little ones laugh out of their hearts at his drolling, some festive evening in his house, and those he gave to sharing with you his joy in his gardening. This, I believe, began with violets, and it went on to roses, which he grew in a splendor and profusion impossible to any but a true lover with a genuine gift for them. Like Lowell, he spent his summers in Cambridge, and in the afternoon, you could find him digging or pruning among his roses with an ardor which few caprices of the weather could interrupt. He would lift himself from their ranks, which he scarcely over-topped, as you came up the footway to his door, and peer purblindly across at you. If he knew you at once, he traversed the nodding and swaying bushes, to give you the hand free of the trowel or knife; or if you got indoors unseen by him he would come in holding towards you some exquisite blossom that weighed down the tip of its long stem with a succession of hospitable obeisances.

He graced with unaffected poetry a life of as hard study, of as hard work, and as varied achievement as any I have known or read of; and he played with gifts

254

and acquirements such as in no great measure have made reputations. He had a rare and lovely humor which could amuse itself both in English and Italian with such an airy burletta as " Il Pesceballo " (he wrote it in Metastasian Italian, and Lowell put it in libretto English); he had a critical sense as sound as it was subtle in all literature; and whatever he wrote he imbued with the charm of a style finely personal to himself. His learning in the line of his Harvard teaching included an early English scholarship unrivalled in his time, and his researches in ballad literature left no corner of it untouched. I fancy this part of his study was peculiarly pleasant to him; for he loved simple and natural things, and the beauty which he found nearest life. At least he scorned the pedantic affectations of literary superiority; and he used to quote with joyous laughter the swelling exclamation of an Italian critic who proposed to leave the summits of polite learning for a moment, with the cry, " *Scendiamo fra il popolo!*" (Let us go down among the people.)

II

Of course it was only so hard worked a man who could take thought and trouble for another. He once took thought for me at a time when it was very important to me, and when he took the trouble to secure for me an engagement to deliver that course of Lowell lectures in Boston, which I have said Lowell had the courage to go in town to hear. I do not remember whether Professor Child was equal to so much, but he would have been if it were necessary; and I rather rejoice now in the belief that he did not seek quite that martyrdom.

He had done more than enough for me, but he had

done only what he was always willing to do for others. In the form of a favor to himself he brought into my life the great happiness of intimately knowing Hjalmar Hjorth Boyesen, whom he had found one summer day among the shelves in the Harvard library, and found to be a poet and an intending novelist. I do not remember now just how this fact imparted itself to the professor, but literature is of easily cultivated confidence in youth, and possibly the revelation was spontaneous. At any rate, as a susceptible young editor, I was asked to meet my potential contributor at the professor's two o'clock dinner, and when we came to coffee in the study, Boyesen took from the pocket nearest his heart a chapter of *Gunnar,* and read it to us.

Perhaps the good professor who brought us together had plotted to have both novel and novelist make their impression at once upon the youthful sub-editor; but at any rate they did not fail of an effort. I believe it was that chapter where Gunnar and Ragnhild dance and sing a *stev* together, for I associate with that far happy time the rich mellow tones of the poet's voice in the poet's verse. These were most characteristic of him, and it is as if I might put my ear against the ethereal wall beyond which he is rapt and hear them yet.

Our meeting was on a lovely afternoon of summer, and the odor of the professor's roses stole in at the open windows, and became part of the gentle event. Boyesen walked home with me, and for a fortnight after I think we parted only to dream of the literature which we poured out upon each other in every waking moment. I had just learned to know Björnson's stories, and Boyesen told me of his poetry and of his drama, which in even measure embodied the great Norse literary movement, and filled me with the wonder and delight of that noble revolt against convention, that brave

256

return to nature and the springs of poetry in the heart and the speech of the common people. Literature was Boyesen's religion more than the Swedenborgian philosophy in which we had both been spiritually nurtured, and at every step of our mounting friendship we found ourselves on common ground in our worship of it. I was a decade his senior, but at thirty-five I was not yet so stricken in years as not to be able fully to rejoice in the ardor which fused his whole being in an incandescent poetic mass. I have known no man who loved poetry more generously and passionately; and I think he was above all things a poet. His work took the shape of scholarship, fiction, criticism, but poetry gave it all a touch of grace and beauty. Some years after this first meeting of ours I remember a pathetic moment with him, when I asked him why he had not written any verse of late, and he answered, as if still in sad astonishment at the fact, that he had found life was not all poetry. In those earlier days I believe he really thought it was!

Perhaps it really is, and certainly in the course of a life that stretched almost to half a century Boyesen learned more and more to see the poetry of the everyday world at least as the material of art. He did battle valiantly for that belief in many polemics, which I suppose gave people a sufficiently false notion of him; and he showed his faith by works in fiction which better illustrated his motive. *Gunnar* stands at the beginning of these works, and at the farthest remove from it in matter and method stands *The Mammon of Unrighteousness*. The lovely idyl won him fame and friendship, and the great novel added neither to him, though he had put the experience and the observation of his ripened life into it. Whether it is too late or too early for it to win the place in literature which it merits I do not know; but it always seemed to me the very spite of fate that it should have failed of popular effect. Yet I must own that it has so failed, and I own this without bitterness towards *Gunnar,* which embalmed the spirit of his youth as *The Mammon of Unrighteousness* embodied the thought of his manhood.

III

It was my pleasure, my privilege, to bring *Gunnar* before the public as editor of the *Atlantic Monthly,* and to second the author in many a struggle with the strange idiom he had cast the story in. The proofs went back and forth between us till the author had profited by every hint and suggestion of the editor. He was quick to profit by any hint, and he never made the same mistake twice. He lived his English as fast as he learned it; the right word became part of him; and he put away the wrong word with instant and final rejection. He had not learned American English without learning newspaper English, but if one touched a phrase of it in his work, he felt in his nerves, which are the ultimate arbiters in such matters, its difference from true American and true English. It was wonderful how apt and how elect his diction was in those days; it seemed as if his thought clothed itself in the fittest phrase without his choosing. In his poetry he had extraordinary good fortune from the first; his mind had an apparent affinity with what was most native, most racy in our speech; and I have just been looking over *Gunnar* and marvelling anew at the felicity and the beauty of his phrasing.

I do not know whether those who read his books stop much to consider how rare his achievement was in the mere means of expression. Our speech is rather more

FRANCIS J. CHILD

hospitable than most, and yet I can remember but five other writers born to different languages who have handled English with anything like his mastery. Two Italians, Ruffini, the novelist, and Gallenga, the journalist; two Germans, Carl Schurz and Carl Hillebrand, and the Dutch novelist Maarten Maartens, have some of them equalled but none of them surpassed him. Yet he was a man grown when he began to speak and to write English, though I believe he studied it somewhat in Norway before he came to America. What English he knew he learned the use of here, and in the measure of its idiomatic vigor we may be proud of it as Americans.

He had least of his native grace, I think, in his criticism; and yet as a critic he had qualities of rare temperance, acuteness, and knowledge. He had very decided convictions in literary art; one kind of thing he believed was good and all other kinds less good down to what was bad; but he was not a bigot, and he made allowances for art-in-error. His hand fell heavy only upon those heretics who not merely denied the faith but pretended that artifice was better than nature, that decoration was more than structure, that make-believe was something you could live by as you live by truth. He was not strongest, however, in damnatory criticism. His spirit was too large, too generous to dwell in that, and it rose rather to its full height in his appreciations of the great authors whom he loved, and whom he commented from the plentitude of his scholarship as well as from his delighted sense of their grandeur. Here he was almost as fine as in his poetry, and only less fine than in his more fortunate essays in fiction.

After *Gunnar* he was a long while in striking another note so true. He did not strike it again till he wrote *The Mammon of Unrighteousness,* and after that he was sometimes of a wandering and uncertain touch. There are certain stories of his which I cannot read without a painful sense of their inequality not only to his talent, but to his knowledge of human nature, and of American character. He understood our character quite as well as he understood our language, but at times he seemed not to do so. I think these were the times when he was overworked, and ought to have been resting instead of writing. In such fatigue one loses command of alien words, alien situations; and in estimating Boyesen's achievements we must never forget that he was born strange to our language and to our life. In *Gunnar* he handled the one with grace and charm; in his great novel he handled both with masterly strength. I call *The Mammon of Unrighteousness* a great novel, and I am quite willing to say that I know few novels by born Americans that surpass it in dealing with American types and conditions. It has the vast horizon of the masterpieces of fictions; its meanings are not for its characters alone, but for every reader of it; when you close the book the story is not at an end.

I have a pang in praising it, for I remember that my praise cannot please him any more. But it was a book worthy the powers which could have given us yet greater things if they had not been spent on lesser things. Boyesen could " toil terribly," but for his fame he did not always toil wisely, though he gave himself as utterly in his unwise work as in his best; it was always the best he could do. Several years after our first meeting in Cambridge, he went to live in New York, a city where money counts for more and goes for less than in any other city of the world, and he could not resist the temptation to write more and more when he should have written less and less. He never wrote anything that was not worth reading, but he wrote too much for one who was giving himself with all his conscience to his academic work in the university honored by his gifts and his attainments, and was lecturing far and near in the vacations which should have been days and weeks and months of leisure. The wonder is that even such a stock of health as his could stand the strain so long, but he had no vices, and his only excesses were in the direction of the work which he loved so well. When a man adds to his achievements every year, we are apt to forget the things he has already done; and I think it well to remind the reader that Boyesen, who died at forty-eight, had written, besides articles, reviews, and lectures unnumbered, four volumes of scholarly criticism on German and Scandinavian literature, a volume of literary and social essays, a popular history of Norway, a volume of poems, twelve volumes of fiction, and four books for boys.

Boyesen's energies were inexhaustible. He was not content to be merely a scholar, merely an author; he wished to be an active citizen, to take his part in honest politics, and to live for his day in things that most men of letters shun. His experience in them helped him to know American life better and to appreciate it more justly, both in its good and its evil; and as a matter of fact he knew us very well. His acquaintance with us had been wide and varied beyond that of most of our literary men, and touched many aspects of our civilization which remain unknown to most Americans. When he died he had been a journalist in Chicago, and a teacher in Ohio; he had been a professor in Cornell University and a literary free lance in New York; and everywhere his eyes and ears had kept themselves open. As a teacher he learned to know the more fortunate or the more ambitious of our youth, and as a lecturer his knowledge was continually extending itself among all ages and classes of Americans.

He was through and through a Norseman, but he was none the less a very American. Between Norsk and Yankee there is an affinity of spirit more intimate than the ties of race. Both have the common-sense view of life; both are unsentimental. When Boyesen told me that among the Norwegians men never kissed each other, as the Germans, and the Frenchmen, and the Italians do, I perceived that we stood upon common ground. When he explained the democratic character of society in Norway, I could well understand how he should find us a little behind his own countrymen in the practice, if not the theory of equality, though they lived under a king and we under a president. But he was proud of his American citizenship; he knew all that it meant, at its best, for humanity. He divined that the true expression of America was not civic, not social, but domestic almost, and that the people in the simplest homes, or those who remained in the tradition of a simple home life, were the true Americans as yet, whatever the future Americans might be.

When I first knew him he was chafing with the impatience of youth and ambition at what he thought his exile in the West. There was, to be sure, a difference between Urbana, Ohio, and Cambridge, Massachusetts, and he realized the difference in the extreme and perhaps beyond it. I tried to make him believe that if a man had one or two friends anywhere who loved letters and sympathized with him in his literary attempts, it was incentive enough; but of course he wished to be in the centres of literature, as we all do; and he never was content until he had set his face and his foot Eastward. It was a great step for him from the Swedenborgian school at Urbana to the young university at Ithaca; and

PROFESSOR CHILD'S HOUSE

I remember his exultation in making it. But he could not rest there, and in a few years he resigned his professorship, and came to New York, where he entered highheartedly upon the struggle with fortune which ended in his appointment in Columbia.

New York is a mart and not a capital, in literature as well as in other things, and doubtless he increasingly felt this. I know that there came a time when he no longer thought the West must be exile for a literary man; and his latest visits to its summer schools as a lecturer impressed him with the genuineness of the interest felt there in culture of all kinds. He spoke of this, with a due sense of what was pathetic as well as what was grotesque in some of its manifestations; and I think that in reconciling himself to our popular crudeness for the sake of our popular earnestness, he completed his naturalization, in the only sense in which our citizenship is worth having.

I do not wish to imply that he forgot his native land, or ceased to love it proudly and tenderly. He kept for Norway the fondness which the man sitting at his own hearth feels for the home of his boyhood. He was of good family; his people were people of substance and condition, and he could have had an easier life there than here. He could have won even wider fame, and doubtless if he had remained in Norway, he would have been one of that group of great Norwegians who have given their little land renown surpassed by that of no other in the modern republic of letters. The name of Boyesen would have been set with the names of Björnson, of Ibsen, of Kielland, and of Lie. But when once he had seen America (at the wish of his father, who had visited the United States before him), he thought only of becoming an American. When I first knew him he was full of the poetry of his mother-land; his talk was of fjords and glaciers, of firs and birches, of hulders and nixies, of housemen and gaardsmen; but he was glad to be here, and I think he never regretted that he had cast his lot with us. Always, of course, he had the deepest interest in his country and countrymen. He stood the friend of every Norwegian who came to him in want or trouble, and they came to him freely and frequently. He sympathized strongly with Norway in her quarrel with Sweden, and her wish for equality as well as autonomy; and though he did not go all lengths with the national party, he was decided in his feeling that Sweden was unjust to her sister kingdom, and strenuous for the principles of the Norwegian leaders.

But, as I have said, poetry was what his ardent spirit mainly meditated in that hour when I first knew him in Cambridge, before we had either of us grown old and sad, if not wise. He overflowed with it, and he talked as little as he dreamed of anything else in the vast half-summer we spent together. He was constantly at my house, where in an absence of my family I was living bachelor, and where we sat indoors and talked, or sauntered outdoors and talked, with our heads in a cloud of fancies, not unmixed with the mosquitoes of Cambridge: if I could have back the fancies, I would be willing to have the mosquitoes with them. He looked the poetry he lived: his eyes were the blue of sunlit fjords; his brown silken hair was thick on the crown which it later abandoned to a scholarly baldness; his soft, red lips half hid a boyish pout in the youthful beard and mustache. He was short of stature, but of a stalwart breadth of frame, and his voice was of a peculiar and endearing quality, indescribably mellow and tender when he read his verse.

I have hardly the right to dwell so long upon him here, for he was only a sojourner in Cambridge, but the memory of that early intimacy is too much for my sense of proportion. As I have hinted, our intimacy was renewed afterwards, when I too came to live in New York, where as long as he was in this *dolce lome,* he hardly let a week go by without passing a long evening with me. Our talk was still of literature and life, but more of life than of literature, and we seldom spoke of those old times. I still found him true to the ideals which had clarified themselves to both of us as the duty of unswerving fealty to the real thing in whatever we did. This we felt, as we had felt it long before, to be the sole source of beauty and of art, and we warmed ourselves at each other's hearts in our devotion to it, amidst a misunderstanding environment which we did not characterize by so mild an epithet. Boyesen, indeed, out-realisted me, in the polemics of our æsthetics, and sometimes when an unbeliever was by, I willingly left to my friend the affirmation of our faith, not without some quaking at his unsparing strenuousness in disciplining the heretic. But now that ardent and active soul is Elsewhere, and I have ceased even to expect the ring, which, making itself heard at the late hour of his coming, I knew always to be his and not another's. That mechanical expectation of those who will come no more is something terrible, but when even that ceases, we know the irreparability of our loss, and begin to realize how much of ourselves they have taken with them.

IV

It was some years before the Boyesen summer, which was the fourth or fifth of our life in Cambridge, that I made the acquaintance of a man, very much my senior, who remains one of the vividest personalities in my recollection. I speak of him in this order perhaps because of an obscure association with Boyesen through their religious faith, which was also mine. But Henry James was incommensurably more Swedenborgian than either of us: he lived and thought and felt Swedenborg with an entirety and intensity far beyond the mere assent of other men. He did not do this in any stupidly exclusive way, but in the most luminously inclusive way, with a constant reference of these vain mundane shadows to the spiritual realities from which they project. His piety, which sometimes expressed itself in terms of alarming originality and freedom, was too large for any ecclesiastical limits, and one may learn from the books which record it, how absolutely individual his interpretations of Swedenborg were. Clarifications they cannot be called, and in that other world whose substantial verity was the inspiration of his life here, the two sages may by this time have met and agreed to differ as to some points in the doctrine of the Seer. In such a case, I cannot imagine the apostle giving way; and I do not say he would be wrong to insist, but I think he might now be willing to allow that the exegetic pages which sentence by sentence were so brilliantly suggestive, had sometimes a collective opacity which the most resolute vision could not penetrate. He put into this dark wisdom the most brilliant intelligence ever brought to the service of his mystical faith; he lighted it up with flashes of the keenest wit and bathed it in the glow of a lambent humor, so that it is truly wonderful to me how it should remain so unintelligible. But I have only tried to read certain of his books, and perhaps if I had persisted in the effort I might have found them all as clear at last as the one which seems to me the clearest, and is certainly most encouragingly suggestive: I mean the one called *Society the Redeemed Form of Man.*

W. D. HOWELLS'S HOME

Concord Avenue, Cambridge

He had his whole being in his belief; it had not only liberated him from the bonds of the Calvinistic theology in which his youth was trammelled, but it had secured him against the conscious ethicism of the prevailing Unitarian doctrine which supremely worshipped Conduct; and it had colored his vocabulary to such strange effects that he spoke of *moral men* with abhorrence, as more hopelessly lost than sinners. Any one whose sphere tempted him to recognition of the foibles of others, he called the Devil; but in spite of his perception of such diabolism, he was rather fond of yielding to it, for he had a most trenchant tongue. I myself once fell under his condemnation as the Devil, by having too plainly shared his joy in his characterization of certain fellow-men; perhaps a group of Bostonians from whom he had just parted and whose reciprocal pleasure of themselves he presented in the image of " simmering in their own fat and putting a nice brown on each other."

Swedenborg himself he did not spare as a man. He thought that very likely his life had those lapses in it which some of his followers deny; and he regarded him, on the æsthetical side as essentially commonplace, and as probably chosen for his prophetic function just because of his imaginative nullity: his tremendous revelations could be the more distinctly and unmistakably inscribed upon an intelligence of that sort, which alone could render again a strictly literal report of them.

As to some other sorts of believers who thought they had a special apprehension of the truth, he had no mercy upon them if they betrayed, however innocently, any self-complacency in their possession. I went one evening to call upon him with a dear old Shaker elder, who had the misfortune to say that his people believed themselves to be living the angelic life. James fastened upon him with the suggestion that according to

267

Swedenborg the most celestial angels were unconscious of their own perfection, and that if the Shakers felt they were of angelic condition they were probably the sport of the hells. I was very glad to get my poor old friend off alive, and to find that he was not even aware of being cut asunder: I did not invite him to shake himself.

With spiritualists James had little or no sympathy; he was not so impatient of them as the Swedenborgians commonly are, and he probably acknowledged a measure of verity in the spiritistic phenomena; but he seemed rather incurious concerning them, and he must have regarded them as superfluities of naughtiness, mostly; as emanations from the hells. His powerful and penetrating intellect interested itself with all social and civil facts through his religion. He was essentially religious, but he was very consciously a citizen, with most decided opinions upon political questions. My own darkness as to anything like social reform was then so dense that I cannot now be clear as to his feeling in such matters, but I have the impression that it was far more radical than I could understand. He was of a very merciful mind regarding things often held in pitiless condemnation, but of charity, as it is commonly understood, he had misgivings. He would never have turned away from him that asketh; but he spoke with regret of some of his benefactions in the past, large gifts of money to individuals, which he now thought had done more harm than good.

I never knew him to judge men by the society scale. He was most human in his relations with others, and was in correspondence with all sorts of people seeking light and help; he answered their letters and tried to instruct them, and no one was so low or weak but he or she could reach him on his or her own level, though he had his humorous perception of their foibles and disabilities; and he had that keen sense of the grotesque which often goes with the kindliest nature. He told of his dining, early in life, next a fellow-man from Cape Cod at the Astor House, where such a man could seldom have found himself. When they were served with meat this neighbor asked if he would mind his putting his fat on James's plate: he disliked fat. James said that he considered the request, and seeing no good reason against it, consented.

He could be cruel with his tongue when he fancied insincerity or pretence, and then cruelly sorry for the hurt he gave. He was indeed tremulously sensitive, not only for himself but for others, and would offer atonement far beyond the measure of the offence he supposed himself to have given.

At all times he thought originally in words of delightful originality, which painted a fact with the greatest vividness. Of a person who had a nervous twitching of the face, and who wished to call up a friend to them, he said, "He *spasmed* to the fellow across the room, and introduced him." His written style had traits of the same bold adventurousness, but it was his speech which was most captivating. As I write of him I see him before me: his white bearded face, with a kindly intensity which at first glance seemed fierce, the mouth humorously shaping the mustache, the eyes vague behind the glasses; his sensitive hand gripping the stick on which he rested his weight to ease it from the artificial limb he wore.

V

The Goethean face and figure of Louis Agassiz were in those days to be seen in the shady walks of Cambridge to which for me they lent a Weimarish quality, in the degree that in Weimar itself a few years ago, I felt a quality of Cambridge. Agassiz, of course, was Swiss and Latin, and not Teutonic, but he was of the Continental European civilization, and was widely different from the other Cambridge men in everything but love of the place. "He is always an *Europäer,*" said Lowell one day, in distinguishing concerning him; and for any one who had tasted the flavor of the life beyond the ocean and the channel, this had its charm. Yet he was extremely fond of his adoptive compatriots, and no alien born had a truer or tenderer sense of New England character. I have an idea that no one else of his day could have got so much money for science out of the General Court of Massachusetts; and I have heard him speak with the wisest and warmest appreciation of the hard material from which he was able to extract this treasure. The legislators who voted appropriations for his Museum and his other scientific objects were not usually lawyers or professional men, with the perspectives of a liberal education, but were hard-fisted farmers, who had a grip of the State's money as if it were their own, and yet gave it with intelligent munificence. They understood that he did not want it for himself, and had no interested aim in getting it; they knew that, as he once said, he had no time to make money, and wished to use it solely for the advancement of learning; and with this understanding they were ready to help him generously. He compared their liberality with that of kings and princes, when these patronized science, with a recognition of the superior plebeian generosity. It was on the veranda of his summer house at Nahant, while he lay in the hammock, talking of this, that I heard him refer also to the offer which Napoleon III. had made him, inviting him upon certain splendid conditions to come to Paris after he had established himself

in Cambridge. He said that he had not come to America without going over every such possibility in his own mind, and deciding beforehand against it. He was a republican, by nationality and by preference, and was entirely satisfied with his position and environment in New England.

Outside of his scientific circle in Cambridge he was more friends with Longfellow than with any one else, I believe, and Longfellow told me how, after the doctors had condemned Agassiz to inaction, on account of his failing health he had broken down in his friend's study, and wept like an Europäer, and lamented, " I shall never finish my work!" Some papers which he had begun to write for the Magazine, in contravention of the Darwinian theory, or part of it, which it is known Agassiz did not accept, remained part of the work which he never finished. After his death, I wished Professor Jeffreys Wyman to write of him in the *Atlantic,* but he excused himself on account of his many labors, and then he voluntarily spoke of Agassiz's methods, which he agreed with rather than his theories, being himself thoroughly Darwinian. I think he said Agassiz was the first to imagine establishing a fact not from a single example, but from examples indefinitely repeated. If it was a question of something about robins for instance, he would have a hundred robins examined before he would receive an appearance as a fact.

Of course no preconception or prepossession of his own was suffered to bar his way to the final truth he was seeking, and he joyously renounced even a conclusion if he found it mistaken. I do not know whether Mrs. Agassiz has put into her interesting life of him, a delightful story which she told me about him. He came to her beaming one day, and demanded, " You know I have always held such and such an opinion about a

certain group of fossil fishes?" "Yes, yes!" "Well,
I have just been reading ——'s new book, and he has
shown me that there isn't the least truth in my theory";
and he burst into a laugh of unalloyed pleasure in re-
linquishing his error.

I could touch science at Cambridge only on its literary and social side, of course, and my meetings with
Agassiz were not many. I recall a dinner at his house
to Mr. Bret Harte, when the poet came on from California, and Agassiz approached him over the coffee
through their mutual scientific interest in the last
meeting of the geological "Society upon the Stanislow."
He quoted to the author some passages from the poem
recording the final proceedings of this body, which had
particularly pleased him, and I think Mr. Harte was as
much amused at finding himself thus in touch with the
savant, as Agassiz could ever have been with that delicious poem.

Agassiz lived at one end of Quincy Street, and James
almost at the other end, with an interval between them
which but poorly typified their difference of temperament. The one was all philosophical and the other all
scientific, and yet towards the close of his life, Agassiz
may be said to have led that movement towards the new
position of science in matters of mystery which is now
characteristic of it. He was ancestrally of the Swiss
"Brahminical caste," as so many of his friends in Cambridge were of the Brahminical caste of New England;
and perhaps it was the line of ancestral *pasteurs* which
at last drew him back, or on, to the affirmation of an un-
formulated faith of his own. At any rate, before most
other savants would say that they had souls of their own
he became, by opening a summer school of science with
prayer, nearly as consolatory to the unscientific who
wished to believe they had souls, as Mr. John Fiske him-

self, though Mr. Fiske, as the arch-apostle of Darwinism, had arrived at nearly the same point by such a very different road.

VI

Mr. Fiske had been our neighbor in our first Cambridge home, and when we went to live in Berkeley Street, he followed with his family and placed himself across the way in a house which I already knew as the home of Richard Henry Dana, the author of *Two Years Before the Mast*. Like nearly all the other Cambridge men of my acquaintance Dana was very much my senior, and like the rest he welcomed my literary promise as cordially as if it were performance, with no suggestion of the condescension which was said to be his attitude towards many of his fellow-men. I never saw anything of this, in fact, and I suppose he may have been a blend of those patrician qualities and democratic principles which made Lowell anomalous even to himself. He is part of the antislavery history of his time, and he gave to the oppressed his strenuous help both as a man and a politician; his gifts and learning in the law were freely at their service. He never lost his interest in those white slaves, whose brutal bondage he remembered as bound with them in his *Two Years Before the Mast,* and any luckless seaman with a case or cause might count upon his friendship as surely as the black slaves of the South. He was able to temper his indignation for their oppression with a humorous perception of what was droll in its agents and circumstances; and I wish I could recall all that he said once about sea-etiquette on merchant vessels, where the chief mate might no more speak to the captain at table without being addressed by him than a subject might put a question to his sovereign. He was amusing in his stories of the Pacific

s   273

trade in which he said it was very noble to deal in furs from the Northwest, and very ignoble to deal in hides along the Mexican and South American coasts. Every ship's master wished naturally to be in the fur-carrying trade, and in one of Dana's instances, two vessels encounter in mid-ocean, and exchange the usual parley as to their respective ports of departure and destination. The final demand comes through the trumpet, " What cargo?" and the captain so challenged yields to temptation and roars back *" Furs!"* A moment of hesitation elapses, and then the questioner pursues, " Here and there *a horn?"*

There were other distinctions, of which seafaring men of other days were keenly sensible, and Dana dramatized the meeting of a great, swelling East Indiaman, with a little Atlantic trader, which has hailed her. She shouts back through her captain's trumpet that she is from Calcutta, and laden with silks, spices, and other orient treasures, and in her turn she requires like answer from the sail which has presumed to enter into parley with her. " What cargo?" The trader confesses to a mixed cargo for Boston, and to the final question, her master replies in meek apology, *" Only from Liverpool, sir!"* and scuttles down the horizon as swiftly as possible.

Dana was not of the Cambridge men whose calling was in Cambridge. He was a lawyer in active practice, and he went every day to Boston. One was apt to meet him in those horse-cars which formerly tinkled back and forth between the two cities, and which were often so full of one's acquaintance that they had all the social elements of an afternoon tea. They were abusively overcrowded at times, of course, and one might easily see a prime literary celebrity swaying from a strap, or hanging uneasily by the hand-rail to the lower steps of

HOME OF RICHARD HENRY DANA, JR.

Berkeley Street, Cambridge

the back platform. I do not mean that I ever happened to see the author of *Two Years Before the Mast* in either fact, but in his celebrity he had every qualification for the illustration of my point. His book probably carried the American name farther and wider than any American books except those of Irving and Cooper at a day when our writers were very little known, and our literature was the only infant industry not fostered against foreign ravage, but expressly left to harden and strengthen itself as it best might in a heartless neglect even at home. The book was delightful, and I remember it from a reading of thirty years ago, as of the stuff that classics are made of. I venture no conjecture as to its present popularity, but of all books relating to the sea I think it is the best. The author when I knew him was still Richard Henry Dana, Jr., his father, the aged poet, who first established the name in the public recognition, being alive, though past literary activity. It was distinctively a literary race, and in the actual generation it has given proofs of its continued literary vitality in the romance of *Espiritú Santo* by the youngest daughter of the Dana I knew.

VII

There could be no stronger contrast to him in origin, education, and character than a man who lived at the same time in Cambridge, and who produced a book which in its final fidelity to life is not unworthy to be named with *Two Years Before the Mast*. Ralph Keeler wrote the *Vagabond Adventures* which he had lived. I have it on my heart to name him in the presence of our great literary men not only because I had an affection for him, tenderer than I then knew, but because I believe his book is worthier of more remem-

brance than it seems to enjoy. I was reading it only
the other day, and I found it delightful, and much better than I imagined when I accepted for the *Atlantic* the
several papers which it is made up of. I am not sure
but it belongs to the great literature in that fidelity to
life which I have spoken of, and which the author
brought himself to practise with such difficulty, and
under so much stress from his editor. He really wanted to *fake* it at times, but he was docile at last and did it
so honestly that it tells the history of his strange career
in much better terms than it can be given again. He
had been, as he claimed, " a cruel uncle's ward " in
his early orphanhood, and while yet almost a child he
had run away from home, to fulfil his heart's desire
of becoming a clog-dancer in a troupe of negro minstrels.
But it was first his fate to be cabin-boy and bootblack
on a lake steamboat, and meet with many squalid adventures, scarcely to be matched outside of a Spanish
picaresque novel. When he did become a dancer (and
even a *danseuse*) of the sort he aspired to be, the fruition of his hopes was so little what he imagined that
he was very willing to leave the Floating Palace on the
Mississippi in which his troupe voyaged and exhibited,
and enter the college of the Jesuit Fathers at Cape Gir-
ardeau in Missouri. They were very good to him, and in
their charge he picked up a good deal more Latin, if not
less Greek than another strolling player who also took
to literature. From college Keeler went to Europe, and
then to California, whence he wrote me that he was coming on to Boston with the manuscript of a novel which
he wished me to read for the magazine. I reported
against it to my chief, but nothing could shake Keeler's
faith in it, until he had printed it at his own cost, and
known it fail instantly and decisively. He had come to
Cambridge to see it through the press, and he remained

there four or five years, with certain brief absences. Then, during the Cuban insurrection of the early seventies, he accepted the invitation of a New York paper to go to Cuba as its correspondent.

"Don't go, Keeler," I entreated him, when he came to tell me of his intention. "They'll garrote you down there."

"Well," he said, with the air of being pleasantly interested by the coincidence, as he stood on my study hearth with his feet wide apart in a fashion he had, and gayly flirted his hand in the air, "that's what Aldrich says, and he's agreed to write my biography, on condition that I make a last dying speech when they bring me out on the plaza to do it, ' If I had taken the advice of my friend T. B. Aldrich, author of *Marjorie Daw and Other People,* I should not now be in this place.' "

He went, and he did not come back. He was not indeed garroted as his friends had promised, but he was probably assassinated on the steamer by which he sailed from Santiago, for he never arrived in Havana, and was never heard of again.

I now realize that I loved him, though I did as little to show it as men commonly do. If I am to meet somewhere else the friends who are no longer here, I should like to meet Ralph Keeler, and I would take some chances of meeting in a happy place a soul which had by no means kept itself unspotted, but which in all its consciousness of error, cheerfully trusted that "the Almighty was not going to scoop any of us." The faith worded so grotesquely could not have been more simply or humbly affirmed, and no man I think could have been more helplessly sincere. He had nothing of that false self-respect which forbids a man to own himself wrong promptly and utterly when need is; and in fact he owned to some things in his checkered past which would hardly allow him any sort of self-respect. He had always an essential gayety not to be damped by any discipline, and a docility which expressed itself in cheerful compliance. " Why do you use *bias* for *opinion?*" I demanded, in going over a proof with him. " Oh, because I'm such an ass—such a bi-ass."

He had a philosophy which he liked to impress with a vivid touch on his listener's shoulder: "Put your finger on the present moment and enjoy it. It's the only one you've got, or ever will have." This light and joyous creature could not but be a Pariah among our Brahmins, and I need not say that I never met him in any of the great Cambridge houses. I am not sure that he was a *persona grata* to every one in my own, for Keeler was framed rather for men's liking, and Mr. Aldrich and I had our subtleties as to whether his mind about women was not so Chinese as somewhat to infect his manner. Keeler was too really modest to be of any rebellious mind towards the society which ignored him, and of too sweet a cheerfulness to be greatly vexed by it. He lived on in the house of a suave old actor, who oddly made his home in Cambridge, and he continued of a harmless Bohemianism in his daily walk, which included lunches at Boston restaurants as often as he could get you to let him give them you, if you were of his acquaintance. On a Sunday he would appear coming out of the post-office usually at the hour when all cultivated Cambridge was coming for its letters, and wave a glad hand in air, and shout a blithe salutation to the friend he had marked for his companion in a morning stroll. The stroll was commonly over the flats towards Brighton (I do not know why, except perhaps that it was out of the beat of the better element) and the talk was mainly of literature, in which he was doing less than he meant

HENRY JAMES, THE ELDER

JOHN HOLMES

to do, and which he seemed never able quite to feel was not a branch of the Show Business, and might not be legitimately worked by like advertising, though he truly loved and honored it.

I suppose it was not altogether a happy life, and Keeler had his moments of amusing depression, which showed their shadows in his smiling face. He was of a slight figure and low stature, with hands and feet of almost womanish littleness. He was very blonde, and his restless eyes were blue; he wore his yellow beard in whiskers only, which he pulled nervously but perhaps did not get to droop so much as he wished.

VIII

Keeler was a native of Ohio, and there lived at Cambridge when I first came there an Indianian, more accepted by literary society, who was of real quality as a poet. Forceythe Willson, whose poem of " The Old Sergeant " Doctor Holmes used to read publicly in the closing year of the civil war, was of a Western altitude of figure, and of an extraordinary beauty of face in an oriental sort. He had large, dark eyes with clouded whites; his full, silken beard was of a flashing Persian blackness. He was excessively nervous, to such an extreme that when I first met him at Longfellow's, he could not hold himself still in his chair. I think this was an effect of shyness in him, as well as physical, for afterwards when I went to find him in his own house he was much more at ease.

He preferred to receive me in the dim, large hall after opening his door to me himself, and we sat down there and talked, I remember, of supernatural things. He was much interested in spiritualism, and he had several stories to tell of his own experience in such matters. But none was so good as one which I had at second hand from Lowell, who thought it almost the best ghost story he had ever heard. The spirit of Willson's father appeared to him, and stood before him. Willson was accustomed to apparitions, and so he said simply, "Won't you sit down, father?" The phantom put out his hand to lay hold of a chair-back as some people do in taking a seat, and his shadowy arm passed through the frame-work. "Ah!" he said, "I forgot that I was not substance."

I do not know whether "The Old Sergeant" is ever read now; it has probably passed with other great memories of the great war; and I am afraid none of Willson's other verse is remembered. But he was then a distinct literary figure, and not to be left out of the count of our poets. I did not see him again. Shortly afterwards I heard that he had left Cambridge with signs of consumption, which must have run a rapid course, for a very little later came the news of his death.

IX

The most devoted Cantabrigian, after Lowell, whom I knew, would perhaps have contended that if he had stayed with us Willson might have lived; for John Holmes affirmed a faith in the virtues of the place which ascribed almost an asceptic character to its air, and when he once listened to my own complaints of an obstinate cold, he cheered himself, if not me, with the declaration, "Well, *one* thing, Mr. Howells, Cambridge never let a man keep a cold yet!"

If he had said it was better to live in Cambridge with a cold than elsewhere without one I should have believed him; as it was, Cambridge bore him out in his assertion, though she took her own time to do it.

Lowell had talked to me of him before I met him, celebrating his peculiar humor with that affection which was not always so discriminating, and Holmes was one of the first Cambridge men I knew. I knew him first in the charming old Colonial house in which his famous brother and he were born. It was demolished long before I left Cambridge, but in memory it still stands on the ground since occupied by the Hemenway Gymnasium, and shows for me through that bulk a phantom frame of Continental buff in the shadow of elms that are shadows themselves. The *genius loci* was limping about the pleasant mansion with the rheumatism which then expressed itself to his friends in a resolute smile, but which now insists upon being an essential trait of the full-length presence to my mind: a short stout figure, helped out with a cane, and a grizzled head with features formed to win the heart rather than the eye of the beholder. In one of his own eyes there was a cast of such winning humor and geniality that it took the liking more than any beauty could have done, and the sweetest, shy laugh in the world went with this cast.

I long wished to get him to write something for the Magazine, and at last I prevailed with him to review a history of Cambridge which had come out. He did it charmingly of course, for he loved more to speak of Cambridge than anything else. He held his native town in an idolatry which was not blind, but which was none the less devoted because he was aware of her droll points and her weak points. He always celebrated these as so many virtues, and I think it was my own passion for her that first commended me to him. I was not her son, but he felt that this was my misfortune more than my fault, and he seemed more and more to forgive it. After we had got upon the terms of editor and contributor, we met

oftener than before, though I do not now remember
that I ever persuaded him to write again for me. Once
he gave me something, and then took it back, with a
self-distrust of it which I could not overcome.

When the Holmes house was taken down, he went to
live with an old domestic in a small house on the street
amusingly called Appian Way. He had certain rooms
of her, and his own table, but he would not allow that
he was ever anything but a lodger in the place, where he
continued till he died. In the process of time he came
so far to trust his experience of me, that he formed the
habit of giving me an annual supper. Some days before
this event, he would appear in my study, and with divers
delicate and tentative approaches, nearly always of the
same tenor, he would say that he should like to ask my
family to an oyster supper with him. "But you know,"
he would explain, "I haven't a house of my own to ask
you to, and I should like to give you the supper *here*."
When I had agreed to this suggestion with due gravity,
he would inquire our engagements, and then say, as if
a great load were off his mind, "Well, then, I will send
up a few oysters to-morrow," or whatever day we had
fixed on; and after a little more talk to take the strangeness out of the affair, would go his way. On the day
appointed the fish-man would come with several gallons
of oysters, which he reported Mr. Holmes had asked
him to bring, and in the evening the giver of the feast
would reappear, with a lank oil-cloth bag, sagged by
some bottles of wine. There was always a bottle of red
wine, and sometimes a bottle of champagne, and he had
taken the precaution to send some crackers beforehand,
so that the supper should be as entirely of his own giving
as possible. He was forced to let us do the cooking and
to supply the cold-slaw, and perhaps he indemnified himself for putting us to these charges and for the use of

JOHN G. PALFREY

our linen and silver, by the vast superfluity of his oysters, with which we remained inundated for days. He did not care to eat many himself, but seemed content to fancy doing us a pleasure; and I have known few greater ones in life, than in the hospitality that so oddly played the host to us at our own table.

It must have seemed incomprehensible to such a Cantabrigian that we should ever have been willing to leave Cambridge, and in fact I do not well understand it myself. But if he resented it, he never showed his resentment. As often as I happened to meet him after our defection he used me with unabated kindness, and sparkled into some gayety too ethereal for remembrance. The last time I met him was at Lowell's funeral, when I drove home with him and Curtis and Child, and in the revulsion from the stress of that saddest event, had our laugh, as people do in the presence of death, at something droll we remembered of the friend we mourned.

X

My nearest literary neighbor, when we lived in Sacramento Street, was the Rev. Dr. John G. Palfrey, the historian of New England, whose chimney-tops amid the pine-tops I could see from my study window when the leaves were off the little grove of oaks between us. He was one of the first of my acquaintances, not suffering the great disparity of our ages to count against me, but tactfully and sweetly adjusting himself to my youth in the friendly intercourse which he invited. He was a most gentle and kindly old man, with still an interest in liberal things which lasted till the infirmities of age secluded him from the world and all its interests. As is known, he had been in his prime one of the foremost of the New England antislavery men, and he had fought the good fight with a heavy heart for a brother long settled in Louisiana who sided with the South, and who after the civil war found himself disfranchised. In this temporary disability he came North to visit Doctor Palfrey upon the doctor's insistence, though at first he would have nothing to do with him, and refused even to answer his letters. " Of course," the doctor said, " I was not going to stand that from my mother's son, and I simply kept on writing." So he prevailed, but the fiery old gentleman from Louisiana was reconciled to nothing in the North but his brother, and when he came to return my visit, he quickly touched upon his cause of quarrel with us. " I can't vote," he declared, " but my coachman can, and I don't know how I'm to get the suffrage, unless my physician paints me all over with the iodine he's using for my rheumatic side."

Doctor Palfrey was most distinctly of the Brahminical caste and was long an eminent Unitarian minister, but at the time I began to know him he had long quitted the pulpit. He was so far of civic or public character as to be postmaster at Boston, when we were first neighbors, but this officiality was probably so little in keeping with his nature that it was like a return to his truer self when he ceased to hold the place, and gave his time altogether to his history. It is a work which will hardly be superseded in the interest of those who value thorough research and temperate expression. It is very just, and without endeavor for picture or drama it is to me very attractive. Much that has to be recorded of New England lacks charm, but he gave form and dignity and presence to the memories of the past, and the finer moments of that great story, he gave with the simplicity that was their best setting. It seems to me such an apology (in the old sense) as New England might

have written for herself, and in fact Doctor Palfrey
was a personification of New England in one of the best
and truest kinds. He was refined in the essential gentleness of his heart without being refined away; he kept
the faith of her Puritan tradition though he no longer
kept the Puritan faith, and his defence of the Puritan
severity with the witches and Quakers was as impartial
as it was efficient in positing the Puritans as of their
time, and rather better and not worse than other people
of the same time. He was himself a most tolerant man,
and his tolerance was never weak or fond; it stopped
well short of condoning error, which he condemned when
he preferred to leave it to its own punishment. Personally he was without any flavor of harshness; his mind
was as gentle as his manner, which was one of the gentlest I have ever known.

Of as gentle make but of more pensive temper, with
unexpected bursts of lyrical gayety, was Christopher
Pearse Cranch, the poet, whom I had known in New
York long before he came to live in Cambridge. He
could not only play and sing most amusing songs, but he
wrote very good poems and painted pictures perhaps not
so good. I always liked his Venetian pictures, for
their poetic, unsentimentalized veracity, and I printed
as well as liked many of his poems. During the time
that I knew him more than his due share of troubles
and sorrows accumulated themselves on his fine head,
which the years had whitened, and gave a droop to the
beautiful, white-bearded face. But he had the artist
soul and the poet heart, and no doubt he could take
refuge in these from the cares that shadowed his visage.
My acquaintance with him in Cambridge renewed
itself upon the very terms of its beginning in New
York. We met at Longfellow's table, where he lifted
up his voice in the Yankee folk-song, " On Springfield

Mountain there did dwell," which he gave with a perfectly killing mock-gravity.

XI

At Cambridge the best society was better, it seems to me, than even that of the neighboring capital. It would be rather hard to prove this, and I must ask the reader to take my word for it, if he wishes to believe it. The great interests in that pleasant world, which I think does not present itself to my memory in a false iridiscence, were the intellectual interests, and all other interests were lost in these to such as did not seek them too insistently.

People held themselves high; they held themselves personally aloof from people not duly assayed; their civilization was still Puritan though their belief had long ceased to be so. They had weights and measures stamped in an earlier time, a time surer of itself than ours, by which they rated the merit of all comers, and rejected such as did not bear the test. These standards were their own, and they were satisfied with them; most Americans have no standards of their own, but these are not satisfied even with other people's, and so our society is in a state of tolerant and tremulous misgiving.

Family counted in Cambridge, without doubt, as it counts in New England everywhere, but family alone did not mean position, and the want of family did not mean the want of it. Money still less than family commanded; one could be openly poor in Cambridge without open shame, or shame at all, for no one was very rich there, and no one was proud of his riches.

I do not wonder that Tourguénieff thought the conditions ideal, as Boyesen portrayed them to him; and I look back at my own life there with wonder at my good

QUINCY STREET, CAMBRIDGE

The Agassiz house in background, obscured by trees. Former location of James house in foreground

fortune. I was sensible, and I still am sensible this had its alloys. I was young and unknown and was making my way, and I had to suffer some of the penalties of these disadvantages; but I do not believe that anywhere else in this ill-contrived economy, where it is vainly imagined that the material struggle forms a high incentive and inspiration, would my penalties have been so light. On the other hand, the good that was done me I could never repay if I lived all over again for others the life that I have so long lived for myself. At times, when I had experienced from those elect spirits with whom I was associated, some act of friendship, as signal as it was delicate, I used to ask myself, how I could ever do anything unhandsome or ungenerous towards any one again; and I had a bad conscience the next time I did it.

The air of the Cambridge that I knew was sufficiently cool to be bracing, but what was of good import in me flourished in it. The life of the place had its lateral limitations; sometimes its lights failed to detect excellent things that lay beyond it; but upward it opened illimitably. I speak of it frankly because that life as I witnessed it is now almost wholly of the past. Cambridge is still the home of much that is good and fine in our literature: one realizes this if one names Colonel Thomas Wentworth Higginson, Mr. John Fiske, Mr. William James, Mr. Horace E. Scudder, not to name any others, but the first had not yet come back to live in his birthplace at the time I have been writing of, and the rest had not yet their actual prominence. One, indeed among so many absent, is still present there, whom from time to time I have hitherto named without offering him the recognition which I should have known an infringement of his preferences. But the literary Cambridge of thirty years ago could not be clearly imagined or justly estimated without taking into account the creative sympathy of a man whose contributions to our literature only partially represent what he has constantly done for the humanities. I am sure that after the easy heroes of the day are long forgot, and the noisy fames of the strenuous life shall dwindle to their essential insignificance before these of the gentle life, we shall all see in Charles Eliot Norton the eminent scholar who left the quiet of his books to become our chief citizen at the moment when he warned his countrymen of the ignominy and disaster of doing wrong.

THE END

By WILLIAM DEAN HOWELLS

LITERARY FRIENDS AND ACQUAINTANCE. Illustrated. Crown 8vo, Cloth, Ornamental, $2 50.

THEIR SILVER WEDDING JOURNEY. Two Volume Ill'd Edition, $5 00 ; Regular Edition, $1 50.

RAGGED LADY. A Novel. $1 75.

THE STORY OF A PLAY. A Novel. $1 50.

THE LANDLORD AT LION'S HEAD. A Novel. Illustrated. $1 75.

MY LITERARY PASSIONS. $1 50.

THE DAY OF THEIR WEDDING. A Story. Illustrated by T. DE THULSTRUP. $1 25.

A TRAVELER FROM ALTRURIA. A Romance. $1 50.

THE COAST OF BOHEMIA. A Novel. Illustrated. $1 50.

THE WORLD OF CHANCE. A Novel. $1 50.

ANNIE KILBURN. A Novel. $1 50.

AN IMPERATIVE DUTY. A Novel. $1 00.

AN OPEN-EYED CONSPIRACY. An Idyl of Saratoga. $1 00.

THE QUALITY OF MERCY. A Novel. $1 50.

A HAZARD OF NEW FORTUNES. A Novel. Two Volumes. $2 00.

APRIL HOPES. A Novel. $1 50.

THE SHADOW OF A DREAM. A Story. $1 00.

MODERN ITALIAN POETS. Essays and Versions. With Portraits. $2 00.

THE MOUSE-TRAP, and Other Farces. Illustrated. $1 00.

IMPRESSIONS AND EXPERIENCES. Essays. Post 8vo, Cloth, Ornamental, Uncut Edges and Gilt Top, $1 50.

STOPS OF VARIOUS QUILLS. Poems. Illustrated by HOWARD PYLE. 4to. Cloth, Ornamental, Uncut Edges and Gilt Top, $2 50. Limited Edition on Hand-made Paper, signed by Author and Artist, $15 00.

By WILLIAM DEAN HOWELLS—*Continued*.

CRITICISM AND FICTION. With Portrait. 16mo, Cloth, $1 00.

A PARTING AND A MEETING. A Story. Illustrated. Square 32mo, Cloth, $1 00.

CHRISTMAS EVERY DAY, and Other Stories. Illustrated. Post 8vo, Cloth, $1 25.

A BOY'S TOWN. Illustrated. Post 8vo, Cloth, $1 25.

In Harper's "Black and White Series":

MY YEAR IN A LOG CABIN. Illustrated. 32mo, Cloth, 50 cents.

A LITTLE SWISS SOJOURN. Illustrated. 32mo, Cloth, 50 cents.

FARCES : A LIKELY STORY—THE MOUSE-TRAP—FIVE O'CLOCK TEA—EVENING DRESS—THE UNEXPECTED GUESTS—A LETTER OF INTRODUCTION—THE ALBANY DEPOT—THE GARROTERS. Illustrated. 32mo, Cloth, 50 cents each.

Paper-Covered Editions :

A PREVIOUS ENGAGEMENT. Illustrated. 50 cents.—A TRAVELER FROM ALTRURIA. 50 cents.—THE WORLD OF CHANCE. 60 cents.—THE QUALITY OF MERCY. 75 cents.—AN IMPERATIVE DUTY. 50 cents.—ANNIE KILBURN. 75 cents.—APRIL HOPES. 75 cents.—A HAZARD OF NEW FORTUNES. Illustrated. $1 00. —THE SHADOW OF A DREAM. 50 cents.

Mr. Howells knows how to give life and actuality to his characters. He seems, indeed, to be presenting us with a series of portraits.— *Speaker*, London.

He is one of the authors whom we delight to read, and it is a great pleasure to take up a book without a suspicion or a desire to criticise, knowing that you will begin all right, go on all right, and come out all right.—*N. Y. Herald.*

HARPER & BROTHERS, PUBLISHERS

NEW YORK AND LONDON

☞ *Any of the above works will be sent by mail, postage prepaid, to any part of the United States, Canada, or Mexico, on receipt of the price.*